Creative Ideas for
Ministry with the Aged

Creative Ideas for Ministry with the Aged

Sue Pickering

CANTERBURY
PRESS

Norwich

© Sue Pickering 2014

First published in 2014 by the Canterbury Press Norwich
Editorial office
3rd Floor, Invicta House,
108–114 Golden Lane,
London EC1Y 0TG

Canterbury Press is an imprint of Hymns Ancient & Modern Ltd
(a registered charity)
13A Hellesdon Park Road, Norwich,
Norfolk, NR6 5DR, UK

www.canterburypress.co.uk

British Library Cataloguing in Publication data

A catalogue record for this book is available
from the British Library

ISBN 978 1 84825 648 4

Typeset by Regent Typesetting
Printed and bound in Great Britain by
Ashford Colour Press Ltd

This book honours
an un-named, silent woman who gave me
my first lesson on ageing nearly five decades ago,
and all those down the years
who have shaped me for ministry.

I give thanks to the Spirit of Jesus
who continues that education
and inspired this book.

Contents

3 Spiritual Conversation and Activities Around Relevant Themes   190

Foreword

This is a beautiful book. It is insightful, honest and born out of deep and challenging personal, hands-on experience.

I know this because it is my privilege as Sue's bishop to meet with her regularly to reflect on her aged care chaplaincy in a community that offers a wide range of services to the elderly from independent villas to hospital and palliative care. This is a community with all the demands of an institution seeking to create a caring and supportive environment for people who are gradually becoming more dependent and are perhaps fearful of losing their identity. Some have slipped into the confusion and uncertainty of dementia.

Sue is a still point in the midst of these very demanding community dynamics and expectations. She has this lovely ability to help people find themselves again, to know that they are loved and ultimately to feel confident to let go.

It is truly a ministry of presence. But not one she is ever over-confident or self-reliant in offering. She seems constantly delighted, almost surprised to experience God reaching out to her offering 'hand and heart to us so we can be equipped' for this ministry of presence.

So this is what she offers to those for whom she is chaplain and that is what she offers in this book.

Not merely the wisdom of a lifetime of Christian spiritual exploration, not merely the insight of an experienced and wise spiritual director, and not simply the practical experience of a working chaplain in a very demanding ministry location, but the confidence of someone who knows their need of God and knows too that God never asks what God will not resource. She experiences the faithfulness of God daily.

This book is full of practical, useable resource and insight, but you cannot fail to recognize its underlying character; it is a work that emerges out of a spiritually disciplined and centred life. It is a book that will challenge and encourage you.

I hope that when I start to have to accept my loss of independence and perhaps even identity, there is someone like Sue who can help me to see through my grief and confusion that I am profoundly loved.

Archbishop Philip Richardson
New Plymouth, New Zealand

Introduction

I can still see her, standing naked and silent in the old bath, her long grey hair plaited casually by unskilled hands, a mastectomy scar slashed across one side of her chest, her remaining breast sagging, empty. I was 16, helping out at the old people's home next door, as part of the Duke of Edinburgh Award. I had never encountered the rawness of life so graphically before, but I did what I could to wash her gently and pat the frail skin dry. She was my introduction to the vulnerability that can be part of some people's experience of ageing. It is in memory of this un-named, long dead woman that I write this book, hoping it may be of use to other people who, like me, find ministry with the aged both a challenge and a gift.

In particular this book is written for those new to aged-care ministry, i.e.:

- for clergy or lay ministers who visit aged-care facilities on a regular but infrequent (e.g. monthly) basis to conduct services or engage in pastoral conversation
- for those accompanying the dying
- for pastoral visitors in a parish or community context.

I hope the material can also be a resource for:

- chaplains in aged-care facilities who want to refresh their practice
- caregivers who may want to try some of the ideas at home
- facilitators of small groups in aged-care, church or community settings who may like to incorporate spiritual conversations in their setting.

This book is not intended to be an academic coverage of recent scholarship on ageing and spirituality, although insights from such sources inform the text. Nor is its focus on those whose disease symptoms gather under the 'dementia' umbrella, although you will find a 'word about dementia' at the start of the Pastoral Practices chapter. This book is simply a gathering of ideas shaped by my personal experience as a family member, Anglican priest and spiritual director; experience gained from pastoral visiting of older parishioners in home and hospital; chaplaincy experience at an aged-care village; and from conversations with others who have worked in ministry with the aged. Also dotted through the book are poems and snippets of stories – names disguised – to anchor what I write in the reality of ministry. My hope is that you, the reader, will find practical and useful ideas which will enable you to offer this ministry with hope, feeling encouraged to be your best self in this environment. I also hope that, by the time you have considered all that is included in this book, you will recognize that you have within you the best resource of all: your relationship with, and constant, conscious dependence on, the wisdom, creativity and grace of the Holy Spirit.

Aged-care ministry is not for the faint-hearted. Whenever we visit the elderly we are confronted by our own mortality: the slow diminution of capacity and the challenges to mobility, communication, comprehension, dignity and daily life which come to us all as we age. It can also be sad to see family dynamics at their worst as well as at their best, hard to make sense of some of the things we see and hear, hard to deal with our own reactions to grief or when illness is accompanied by disfigurement or smells that make us want to turn away.

Blessed Teresa of Calcutta, ministering to the least in those teeming streets, used to speak of meeting Christ in his 'distressing disguise', and that is what we do when we spend time with people at the end of their lives, because for many, illness, grief, loneliness, powerlessness and vulnerability are profoundly distressing and threaten to overwhelm people's body and spirit. But that is where faith comes in. If *we* have a lively faith, a working relationship with our Jesus, then this work *can* be done – but only in daily, diligent partnership with him. If those we visit *also* have a lively faith then it *can* help them to transcend their circumstances and find that deep peace which is beyond all understanding, which only God can give. That is our sacred task, with or without words, to help people connect with God in such a way as to know, at some level, that peace for themselves.

However, when we start talking with older people about matters of faith we quickly discover that the spiritual reality for many in the West today is complex and fluid. A few older people may have explored spiritual practices from other faiths; some may have practised 'new age' spirituality; others may have been involved in spiritualism and the occult; still others may have lived without much personal exposure to Christianity or felt any need to explore spiritual matters. Some, as mentioned in the previous paragraph, may have an active faith and a living connection with God which provides support and strength in the midst of their failing health. But what seems to be most common is that we will find:

- people with some early exposure to God and Church, through Sunday School for example, who have moved away from church as life changed and never went back
- others who drifted away intellectually
- others who have left – physically and emotionally – after a pivotal event or loss propelled them into the uncomfortable country of anger, doubt and grief. For many such people there remain unexpressed, unexplored and unresolved questions about the nature of God and the place of suffering.[1] Few will have had the chance to talk about such questions, to express the feelings these events or losses

---

1 See section 'Who do we think God is?' for more comments.

2

still generate, or to link their current situation with the reality of the incarnation: God with us in and through Jesus Christ.

Failing health and the narrowing of one's world that can come with ageing may provide a catalyst for people to reflect on the 'big questions' of life, death, suffering and what might come next. If we are prepared to sit and listen to their stories as they talk about some of these challenging areas, we may find:

- clues to God's real but unrecognized presence in the life we are listening to
- that not attending church does not necessarily equate with lack of belief in God
- that many elders still pray – predominantly for their families
- a surprising number have had a spiritual experience which they have never shared before
- some people want to 'put things right' before they die
- many have someone in their history whom they remember praying with them or for them
- most people will be able to recollect some example of being loved or of giving love – this experience can provide a bridge to a deeper understanding of God's love for them.

For those who have already recognized they are on a spiritual journey and have a working relationship with God, many of the spiritual practices they need will be in place. They may even have recognized that as they age they are called to let go – and let go – and let go, e.g. they reluctantly let go of their bodies' strength and flexibility and they accept that, even without the spectre of dementia, most people will experience some degree of memory loss as they age. However, unlike this inevitable physical or mental wear and tear, their *spiritual life* can continue to develop, *if* they are willing to do the hard work which spiritual growth requires at this stage of life.

Those people who have not been conscious of their spiritual nature and have paid little or no attention to the development of their inner life or connection with a 'higher power' will need encouragement and support if they want to begin to explore such matters as faith, forgiveness or transcendence. Some, of course, have neither the desire nor the capacity for such exploration.

In our ministry with the aged, the spiritual focus we bring is what makes our contribution to elders' welfare unique and, I suggest, touches the core of an individual's well-being in a way that is largely ignored by the medical model of care which still dominates much of Western medical practice and assessment. Gradually those of us in ordained ministry are reclaiming our primary purpose – the cure (care) of souls – a purpose that, after the Second World War, seemed to sink and all but disappear beneath the weight of society's ambivalence about the role of clergy. From the 1960s onwards, many ministers trained in pastoral counselling in a bid to find for themselves a role which people could understand and value. The ability to offer pastoral counselling was, and still is, a worthwhile addition to a minister's skill-set, but it is not the core focus of Christian ministry. Whether in a parish or community group, in their own homes or in residential care settings, our core work is to *care for people's souls* and to help them know that they are profoundly, persistently loved by the God who created them and will welcome them home.

The home visit context

We might think that making a pastoral visit at someone's home is more straight-forward than an encounter in a residential care setting or hospital. After all, there should be fewer interruptions, and we both have a particular focus – perhaps the sharing of home communion, a prayer before an operation, or a post-bereavement visit. But it will become clear from the list below that a particular set of potential challenges accompanies us as we minister with those who still try to maintain their independence, frequently with substantial support from community agencies or a family member who has taken on the caregiver role, often at great emotional and perhaps personal cost. These challenges include:

- the loneliness of the person whom we are visiting and their longing for us to stay when we have limited time
- the question of whether or not we accept their hospitality or gift
- the awkward wondering about a person's competence to remain in their own home
- the ethical dilemma if we suspect family neglect, even elder abuse
- the emotional impact when the person we are visiting becomes unwell or dies
- the vexed issue of boundaries – knowing what we can and cannot do
- grappling with our own helplessness
- our own capacity to help them deepen their God-connection.

Working with the elderly may trigger unresolved issues or unexpected emotions emerging out of our own experience, particularly the relationships with our own parent/s and our experience of their health/dying/death. Many of our reactions can be worked through if we have good pastoral or clinical supervision, i.e. someone trained to help us reflect on our pastoral practice and its inevitable impact on our life and well-being. Without such supervision we risk blurring the boundaries of our pastoral relationships and taking over roles that are not ours: protective son or daughter, counsellor or therapist, health-care provider, aged concern advocate, even financial adviser.

One role that definitely *is* ours is the role of spiritual companion – lay or ordained, we can do our utmost to help the person build his or her confidence in God. If you feel unprepared for this central task of ministry, ask the Holy Spirit to guide you in building your capacity to accompany another's spiritual journey competently. Options include reflecting on how you have been helped on your own spiritual jour-ney, working with a spiritual director or mentor, or accessing books or courses being offered through local church networks to help you gain skills and confidence in helping others explore who God is for themselves.[2]

The care home context

A care home can be an intimidating context for ministry: lack of privacy, lounges full of people with varying degrees of age-related health issues, interruptions for hairdressing appointments and tea trolleys, fire alarm practices, televisions in every lounge, and often over-extended staff with little time – and in some cases little motivation – to gather interested residents for a service. If you are fortunate enough to be visiting or working in a church-based home then there are likely to be regular forms of worship such as fortnightly Communion and weekly Sunday afternoon services, and chaplaincy may be provided on a regular basis (voluntary or paid) apart from those service times. If you are working in or visiting a care home that is part of a national or international company, check their promotional material. They may well indicate that they 'meet the spiritual needs of their residents'. What this really means in practice will vary, so it pays to ask for some indication of how these needs are being met.

So how do we go about establishing or strengthening a care home ministry?

- **Research the ethos of the care home** you are visiting (church/corporate/council funded etc.).
- **Establish a prayer team** for this ministry – meet for prayer regularly and before any service.
- **Be regular and reliable in your visiting** – your ministry begins with your simple presence.
- **Imagine yourself with Jesus** in the care home and pray as you are led.
- **Find out what religious services are already being held and contact details of any other ministers who visit the home regularly.**
- **Build relationships** with key staff in the care home environment. It is worth making an appointment to talk with the clinical or nursing care manager (responsible for the health of residents) and/or the activity co-ordinators/diversional therapists (responsible for implementing a balanced and stimulating programme for residents).This latter role may include ensuring that church services are held on a regular basis and putting out a monthly programme on which all events are scheduled. Getting your service details included on such a programme should not be too difficult.
- **Find out how information is circulated** – most homes will have a staff communication book which is a diary in which people write information about hospital appointments, doctors' visits, key events, etc. If there is one, see if you can put

2 You may like to read my *Spiritual Direction – a practical introduction*, Canterbury Press, 2008, which provides comprehensive material to deepen your capacity to accompany others on their spiritual journey.

in your service details or visiting times and maybe even a list of those residents whom you know would appreciate being able to attend.

- **Make a determined effort to get to know the residents.** In a larger care home this can be difficult if you are visiting only once a month, but it is certainly worth trying to learn their names. The activities co-ordinator may be able to provide you with a list of the denomination of residents so that you can begin to build up a picture of those residents for whom religious observance is a continuation of a lifetime practice, and those for whom it is a welcome diversion on a boring Sunday afternoon! If they cannot provide such a list, then ask the care manager for the information, or the freedom to access that information yourself if privacy issues are not problematic. If all else fails, see if there is a list of residents and their rooms near reception for the use of visitors, or check to see if people's walking-frames have a label with their name.

- **Offer short services on special occasions** e.g. Carols at Christmas, Easter, Remembrance Day or All Souls, or in response to any grave national or international event so people at the home can be part of a reaching out to their community, country or beyond their shores.

- **Offer room blessings** when a resident has died, once their personal effects have been removed and before a new resident comes in to occupy that room (see under 'Pastoral Practices').

- **Offer to do a workshop** with staff about spirituality, spiritual care of the elderly, and about grief, death and dying and what you can offer in terms of support.

- **Be as supportive as you can to the staff.** It would be a bonus to have a staff member or two present at the services we offer, but the reality is that many caregivers are already stretched. Increased documentation, staffing restrictions which mean fewer nurses/carers on the floor, strict protocols for medication rounds, the increasing frailty of those in care, the sheer physicality of individual caregiving, lessen their chance of direct involvement. As you regularly come to visit and get to know the residents, you will build up some relationships with staff too, and may be called upon to support them in their own family or personal crises.

- **Once you feel that your presence is accepted**, there will be no issues about being able to walk into the residents' lounge before a service, say 'Hi' to everyone, and turn off the television!

With faithful regular visiting, compassionate listening and sharing of our pastoral skills, we may be able to *advocate* for residents or for staff, offering ideas and input to enhance the quality of care, and building people's awareness of the value of attending to the spirit, as well as the body and the mind.

One thing I learned very early in aged-care ministry was 'Do not assume anything!' We all have preconceptions – dare I say 'prejudices' – about population groups and their characteristics, but experience rapidly told me, for example, that:

- not all elderly people are deaf
- visual impairment can be hard to detect
- people with dementia can certainly enjoy participating in services and spiritual reminiscence
- people in their nineties can still ask sticky theological questions and expect (and deserve) considered responses.

Importantly, we dare not assume *anything* about a person's relationship with God until we have spent time with them and heard their story. Bringing a soul home is the work of the Spirit of God: how that happens is up to the individual and Christ. *Our task*, in partnership with God's Spirit, is to be as Christ to them: compassionate, loving, respectful of the individual's position and free will, always seeking to heal and bring to wholeness, one step at a time, beginning with where each person finds herself, not bullying or frightening people into the kingdom. As we build trust and model God's love and acceptance and welcome, others are drawn to this love, even as their lives near their end.

On visiting our neighbour in a rest home

'I want to go home ...'
What can be said in reply when there is no going back?
The silence drips between our careful words
touching the worn woman
trapped by age and diminishing strength,
by balance betrayed,
wrenched from home
and all familiar sights and smells and food and bed
and freedom to choose the shape of her day.

A bright orchid is offered – a touch of beauty in the barren room,
a reminder of life outside brought near,
a reference point to what has been,
but clearly is no more.

Who was the orchid for?
The one now dozing in self-defence ...
or we who lean in the doorway, ready to run?

Before going any further, take a few moments to re-read this poem and picture yourself, *first* as the woman newly come to a strange environment with little around her to speak to her of personal identity and home, and *then* as the uneasy visitor, noting the feelings and thoughts running through your mind as you 'lean in the doorway, ready to run'.

The sacrament of the present moment

Like many of you with your own families, I spent time reading to my son as part of our bed-time routine when he was small. Snuggled up under the blankets, smelling of soap and smiles, he would listen deeply, intent on every word, captivated by pictures and sounds. He would lean against me and I against him, and for that moment in time we were fully present to the shared joy of books and language and of each other.

Ministry with the aged – with anyone – depends on our capacity to be *present* to the other, no matter how difficult that might be. And it *is* difficult – we've all found our minds wandering as we've half-listened to someone while preoccupied with our own thoughts – or we've seen someone else's focus drift as we've been trying to tell them something important. We are diminished when someone fails to attend to us; we diminish others when we fail to attend to them.

🕯 Reflect for a moment on your experience of being 'present' or 'absent' to others, or they to you.

It is no coincidence that scripture uses the particular phrase 'Here I am' when people are being called into a special relationship with God or are asked to undertake a critical task:

- 'Here I am,' said Abraham as God began his testing (Genesis 22).

- 'Here I am,' said Moses, drawn to the mysterious burning bush and God's directive to free the Hebrew people from slavery in Egypt (Exodus 3).

- 'Here I am,' said Samuel, initially, mistakenly, responding to the priest Eli because he did not yet recognize the voice of God (1 Samuel 3).

- 'Here I am,' said Mary, after the angel Gabriel's visitation with news of God's favour and her call to bring the Christ child into the world (Luke 1).

- 'Here I am, Lord,' said Ananias, able, because of his deep relationship with God, to express his fear, before going to the infamous Saul/Paul to bring him healing and baptism (Acts 9).

'Here I am,' they say, confirming they are paying attention with their whole being. *In the present moment* God meets them and draws them into both response and commitment. A titanic journey into deeper trust in God awaits each one, but it begins *at a particular moment*.

What is it about being in the present moment that is so critical to any ministry? If you think about it, the present moment is all any of us really has. This is poignantly accentuated in aged-care ministry when memory may be diminishing, comprehension may come and go, death waits in the shadows, and we face the unpredictable reality of the person in front of us with whatever their mind can access and their body express *at that particular moment*. And that might be their anxiety, pain and regrets, their hopes, achievements and thankfulness, and their God story – whether sturdy enough to support them now, or threadbare from neglect yet capable of being re-woven into a cloth of grace.

The present moment becomes a sacrament (an 'outward and visible sign' of the work of the Spirit) when we surrender it – and ourselves – to God, with the radical openness that goes with our own 'Here I am' response. This means being open to the Spirit's wisdom when we come alongside any individual, letting go of preconceptions about how things might unfold, and putting aside our need to 'fix things' or 'get things right'. This means facing our fear and anxiety about the context, or about talking to someone whose world seems so very different from ours.

If we approach each encounter empty of ego-need as far as we are able and open to the Spirit's guidance, we welcome God into the 'Right Now'. God's Spirit can flow through us, and we can be uncluttered channels of God's grace to another, even in the simplest of ways, as I discovered years ago:

> *My early memories of care home contexts were of passive old people marooned in a lounge which was filled with high volume television chatter and smelt of urine. When I was about to start aged-care chaplaincy, I visited the care home to see someone I knew there, taking with me some home-grown sweet-peas. When my friend had enjoyed them, I noticed a resident nearby watching what I was doing, so I offered her the flowers too. I looked at her walking-frame and there was her name – so I called her by name and introduced myself. Our eyes and smiles made the connection. It was natural and easy after that to walk around that entire lounge of some dozen people, some dozing but easily woken, others blind but able to smell the familiar sweet, peppery fragrance, and others for whom memories were triggered and sweet-pea stories of their own emerged.*

Without having to plan or make anything happen, God had enabled me to find a way into what I'd thought a rather intimidating context. I could see that what mattered was being present to each person, trusting God to open up opportunities for engagement with people as I made myself available to listen. 'Weep with those who weep, knit with those who knit' seemed to be the message – turn up and be with them. '*Be*' with them. And that's the simplicity and the challenge of any aged-care ministry – to *be* with people who are totally in the present moment in such a way that it becomes grace-filled.

We do not engage in this ministry alone. All day long God offers hand and heart to us *so we can be equipped* for our ministry of presence. But the sad reality is that often we are caught in the web of busy-ness and self-reliance and forget to acknowledge God in what we are doing (Proverbs 3.5–6). The prophet Isaiah captures God's longing:

I was ready to be sought out by those who did not ask,
to be found by those who did not seek me.
I said, 'Here I am, here I am,' to a nation that did not call on my name.
I held out my hands all day long to a rebellious people,
who walk in a way that is not good. (Isaiah 65.1–2b)

Can you feel the yearning heart of our God

- who longs for us to recognize God's presence and provision in the midst of our pastoral task
- who wants us to delight in the creation and in each other
- who wants us to walk in faith, not in fear
- who provides us with a work to do and equipping for the task?

'Here I am,' says God – can you see me? Reflect for a moment on your recent experience of noticing God's presence. Talk to God about your experience or about your desire to be more aware.

This is the other dimension to the sacrament of the present moment, *God's self-revelation*, moments that come to us as a gift in the midst of sadness or grief or change. Think for example of the post-resurrection appearances of Jesus – to Mary, mysteriously in the mist of mourning; to his own frightened disciples, numbed by his death and meeting behind locked doors; to dejected fishermen in need of a catch and hope (John 20, 21); to those on the grief-weary road to Emmaus (Luke 24). In every instance there was uncertainty, lack of recognition until *one moment* when they realized his presence.

And that can happen to us. One Easter I had been reading of Joseph taking Jesus' body down from the cross. I was conscious of the awkward and determined dignity of the task, the cold seeping through the still body. Later that day I was contacted because a resident had died:

I spent time with the resident's family as they recounted the story of his dying, and, when they were ready, we commended him to God. But then something un-expected happened – I was asked to help wash his body and change the bed linen. What I had been reading that very morning suddenly took on a new immediacy as I held the heavy head, tried to move unresponsive limbs and looked upon the truth of death.

It was as if Jesus were saying: 'Here I am beneath your hands as you wash my body after death ...'

Being surrendered to the Spirit in the present moment with each individual is a sacra-mental act which blesses them, and blesses us. Nowhere is this focus on the present moment more relevant than when we interact with those with dementia. Turn to Pastoral Practices, 'A word about dementia' for further comment and suggestions.

You are the hands and voice of Jesus

You may have come across the often-told story about a man trapped on a rooftop in a flood. This condensed version has a slightly modified ending:

> A man prays to God to save him as the flood water rises. Various rescuers appear and are turned away by the man who says he is waiting for God to intervene. Inevitably the waters keep rising: the man is washed off the roof and drowns. When he gets to heaven, Jesus asks him, 'Why didn't you take the help I provided?' 'What help?' the man answers. Jesus sighs.

We may smile at the man's inability to recognize God at work in the world through people and circumstances, but many of us are just as blind when it comes to seeing the people around us as agents of God's love, purpose and provision. Somehow, like the man on the roof who spurned skilled rescuers in motor-boats and helicopters, we keep looking for an extraordinary revelation of the power of God working outside the laws of nature, instead of recognizing the God who comes alongside us in ways that seem ordinary but bear God's imprint and perfect timing. Although we are immersed in God as a fish is immersed in the sea, so often we behave as if we are marooned far inland, cut off from the freedom and flourishing of our natural environment – God – who is only ever a prayer away.

Teresa of Ávila (or perhaps you know her as Teresa of Jesus) was a sixteenth-century Carmelite nun whose depth of prayer and strength of character enabled her to be a reforming influence among religious orders in Europe. Teresa wrote extensively on the spiritual life and took seriously the reality of the incarnated Christ. Her belief that *we are* the body of Christ, quite literally, is widely quoted:

> Christ has no body now but yours,
> No hands, no feet on earth but yours,
> Yours are the eyes with which he looks
> Compassion on this world,
> Yours are the feet with which he walks to do good,
> Yours are the hands, with which he blesses all the world.

Those we meet in any ministry context may not have fully taken on board this *first expression* of the incarnation, this beautiful truth that *God reaches them through other people* and every act of care and encouragement or even gentle challenge may be seen as a gesture of divine love. Sadly, a surprising number of people find it hard to believe that God could care for them in this way, because they carry within them a sense of being unlovable, of being unimportant. Low self-esteem and shame, perhaps arising from abuse, reduce a person's expectation that others – including God – could see them as worthy of time and compassion. This sense of being worthless can be compounded by a move into residential care with its associated losses, disruption of routines and changes in contact with significant people. It is further exacerbated by physical or mental decline and the fear of being 'no use to anyone'.

One of the challenges of aged-care ministry is to be a faithful bringer of the truth of God's care for the individual. That means living out Teresa's words, conscious that we 'hold the Christ light' for others,[3] trusting that God can and will work through us, if we invite the Spirit into each encounter. Whenever we visit an older person we come to them, not with a social worker's perspective, nor an old friend's shared history, nor a family member's excruciating mix of duty and love, hope and anxiety. We come to assure them that they still matter to God, we come to re-present Jesus, to listen with his ears, to speak with his words, and to warm the person's heart with his deep compassion and joy.

Lay or ordained, we are there to be the good news of Christ, not to brow-beat people or force them to believe, but so to live the story of grace, of redemption, of God's abiding, steadfast presence in the midst of life's ups and downs, that when the opportunity arises we can gently speak of what we know – that in Christ we have a friend and brother who is 'one of us, yet from the heart of God'.[4] And so we turn up week by week, month by month, building relationships over time, calling people by name, making eye contact, gently touching a hand or shoulder, assuring them of God's unconditional love by deeds as well as words, and by being *fully present* to each person when we are with them, even if time is limited.

As we do this, we help people discover a ***second expression*** of the incarnation of Christ – that *they* are part of God's work in the world. Many people are accustomed to thinking of God revealing God-self in the beauty of the natural world, through holy scripture, through people with ministry roles, through music and the arts, perhaps through answers to prayer, or through God-incidences that are woven through ordinary life circumstances. But it seems hard for people to accept that *they too can be bearers of God's care to others.* They hesitate to see themselves as having both the responsibility and the joy of reaching out to other people in concern and friendship as the Spirit leads. For people who have come to a stage in their lives when they are more 'acted upon' than 'acting', it can take a while to grasp that, in God's economy, they continue to have a purpose and a place – right to that time of transition when they exchange this life for the next.

A consequence of this double-blindness – not seeing themselves as worthy of God's care, nor as part of God's mission – is a state of un-consciousness: not physical sleep or coma, but a lack of awareness of the presence of God in the whole of life and a failure to respond to the Spirit who encourages little acts of service that may be life-changing to the recipients. So as we build relationships with the elderly we invite them to begin to notice the God-moments, to see themselves as bearers of the Christ-light to those around them. We encourage those who can to smile at each

---

3 See 'The Servant Song' which includes the lines, 'I will hold the Christ-light for you, in the night-time of your fear.'

4 The Church of the Province of New Zealand, *A New Zealand Prayer Book*, Collins, London, 1989, p. 467.

other, to be kind, to refrain from gossip, to pray for those at their dinner table or in the room next door, to pray for the staff, especially for those whom they find difficult – and to give positive feedback or compliments when they are due. This does not mean that we are trying to create a 'Pollyanna' environment where there is no space for sadness, frustration or other raw and real emotions, but rather to champion another perspective that says 'I am still a person who can reach out to others' instead of being overwhelmed by the struggles and challenges of ageing. It can be an amazing awakening to sense that 'even I' can be an agent of grace, a bringer of light into someone else's apparently dreary day.

The *third expression* of the incarnation of Christ is to do with the mystery of humankind being made *in the image of God*. Whether we think about it or not, we bear within us the divine likeness – overlaid perhaps with the troubles of the world, smudged with sin, tarnished by trauma, but resolutely shining in our innermost being, waiting for us to acknowledge this truth and begin to give space for the Spirit of God to help our spirit – this God-image within – to gleam and grow into the glory which is our birthright as children of God. So, whenever we engage with another human being we are encountering someone who bears the image of God. No matter how wrinkled, how affected by disease or dementia, how upsetting the appearance, if we look with the eyes of Christ, we can see before us a person whom God loves, a unique expression of the divine Spirit. Jesus is very clear that whenever we feed, welcome, clothe, tend, or visit anyone in need, we are ministering to him: 'Truly I tell you, just as you did it to one of the least of these who are members of my family, you did it to me' (Matthew 25.40).

The more closely we work with people offering support and care to them, and to the Christ whose image they bear, the more we come to know that while we may be the hands and voice of Jesus to them, *they* may also bring the words and love of Christ to us. An old lady may catch hold of our hand and ask, 'And how are you, my dear?' She has the time to listen, and care to give. Do we smile and make a conventional, 'Fine, thanks' reply, determined to keep a 'professional distance' between the helper and the helped? Or do we stop and share a little of ourselves with her, so we become more real to each other as we allow ourself to be cared for, to *receive*, for just a few precious moments?

Aged-care ministry is not a matter of our always being the ones who are 'doing the ministering'. Those of us who minister are blessed by those among whom we work. We can be as Christ to each other.

Who do we think God is?

You may have watched a popular television series which traces the ancestry of well-known people. In *Who Do You Think You Are?* the participants' view of their life is often changed as genealogical research helps clarify their sense of identity. The programme provides the featured famous with the chance to update their understanding of what has shaped them and come to terms with who they may now see themselves to be.

Our early way of understanding God is often informed by our experience of people who are 'as God' to us (parents, teachers – people with power), and is further shaped by an eclectic mix of church participation and teaching (or lack of it), media representations of God (from traditional paintings and literature to controversial film-making, songs or sculpture), metaphors from scripture and nature (lamb, bread of life, rock etc.), and the impact of our own experiences whether they be positive or full of loss, abuse or struggle.

As we age, it becomes increasingly important to *update* how we see God, to be able to answer for ourselves the question Jesus posed of his disciples, 'Who do you say that I am?' (Mark 8.29–30).

Take a few minutes to think about *your* answer, *your* way of seeing God at the present moment.

The way in which we see God changes over time, and benefits from updating. Traditional ways of seeing God shape much of our God-picture, and it helps to have a good grasp of the way God is portrayed in scripture. This includes, of course, images that speak of God in terms of:

- protection: God as shield, Psalm 18.2; God as rock, Psalm 18.31; God as shepherd, Luke 15.4–7
- wisdom: Proverbs 8 and 9
- aspects of the natural world: God as fire, Hebrews 12.29; light, John 8.12; vine, John 15
- relationships: God as lover, Song of Solomon; husband, Isaiah 54.5; potter, Jeremiah 18.

For some people feminine images of God are especially helpful, for example:

- woman in labour, Isaiah 42.14
- midwife, Psalm 22.9–10
- mother, Psalm 131, Isaiah 66.13
- mother eagle, Deuteronomy 32.10–12
- nursing mother, Isaiah 49.15–16
- mother hen, Matthew 23.37.

A chameleon changes its colours to adapt to its environment, but it remains true to its nature as a chameleon. God comes in varied ways to individuals in their unique circumstances but God remains God. In our own lives, and in those around us, *unconventional* images of God can emerge at moments of need, usually to empha- size a particularly relevant attribute of God. For example, I have come across people who have described God as being like a:

- fire-fighter – strong and courageous, able to extinguish the 'flames' of anxiety and doubt
- companion dog – faithful and constantly present
- quilter – patching together the bits of our lives and making of them something beautiful
- parent – waiting at the bus station for their child to come home
- lead rider on a tandem bicycle
- mountain guide.

For each person the particular way of seeing God conveyed exactly what was most appropriate for the person at that time. An image from their own contemporary context carried meaning for them and helped them sense the presence of God right then and there in their circumstances, in a way that the more traditional images were not able to do at that point. It kept them *connected* to God.

However, it is always prudent to take a moment to 'test' any unconventional image of God, by asking the person what this way of seeing God tells them about God's character and their personal situation. As we listen to what they say, we can be asking ourselves, does this way of seeing/experiencing God point towards the God revealed in the two 'books' of the Word and Creation? Does it reinforce what we know of God's character? How does it help draw the person closer to the Way, the Truth and the Life we see revealed in Jesus?

🕯 Take a moment to identify any unconventional images of God in your own spiritual life.

When asked about their faith history, many older people will tell you, usually apolo- getically, that they have not attended church for a long time. For many it seems as if God and Church are one and the same thing. They are not used to talking God- language and we can struggle at times to find a way into their spiritual reality.[5] But when we ask respectfully about their beliefs, several common ways of seeing God emerge:

- Some still carry the remnants of an all-powerful God-figure who inhabited their childhood days and nights with a mixture of threats of punishment and a confus- ing assurance that prayers would be answered when many seemed to go unheard.

---

5 For more on this, see the section on 'spiritual conversation'.

Such an image of God may not provide the kind of hopefulness or comfort that those approaching the end of their lives might look for.

- Others may have turned away from God as the pain of personal or global events has raised such difficult questions as 'Where was God when ...?' or 'If God is good, why is there suffering?' The 'all-powerful protector God' seems no match for the dire reality some people have encountered. That image of God has let them down and they may have had nowhere to go with their anger and confusion. Often with little access to wise spiritual guidance, these people, instead of being able to use the challenge of these events as a catalyst for grappling with and updating their image of God, have seen these questions – and their sense of God – sink and disappear beneath the weight of grief, doubt, ongoing work and family responsibilities.

'Bertha' said that music was more important to her than prayer: music gave her peace and freedom. She came from a very religious household, and during the Second World War, she had prayed every day for the safe return of her beloved older brother. He never returned. This experience of 'unanswered prayer' shaped the rest of her life and she has never re-visited her image of the God whom she felt let her down.

- Still others, confronted by these very common questions, have found a way of doing the hard work of exploring the nature of God and God's action in the world (theodicy). With or without competent spiritual support they have found a deep personal faith, leaning on God as each challenge has arisen, and coming to know unequivocally that they are loved, supported, guided and precious in God's sight.

If we are to stand with integrity alongside others who are just beginning to explore these major questions, even as they approach life's end, we need to have done our own hard work in response to the life events which have challenged us.

- Can we declare with the psalmist, '(God) alone is my rock and my salvation, my fortress, I shall never be shaken' (Psalm 62.2)?
- Can we sing to God with Jean Valjean in *Les Misérables*, 'In my need, you have always been there'?
- Can we say with disciple Thomas, and mean it, 'My Lord and my God' (John 20.28)?

If we are to be loving ministers of God who is Love, we need to know that Love for ourselves, that Love which draws people with its depth, compassion, winsomeness, acceptance and strength. For when we have experienced that Love, we are no longer bound by doctrinal emphases on how to achieve salvation; instead we know in our innermost being that Love will meet the person at the point of their deepest need and bring healing and hopefulness, and the mystery of mercy.

🕯 Do you know God as Love – not just in your mind, but in your heart?

Our answer to this pivotal question will shape the way we minister, for better or for worse. We may have cringed when we have seen well-meaning ministers approach older people, urgently, with not-so-subtle efforts to 'save their souls', trying to worry them into the kingdom with talk of 'hell', or luring them with promises of reconnection with loved ones, conditional on their 'joining the church'.

A totally different approach emerges from our re-presentation of the humanity of Jesus as well as his divinity. For people in palliative care particularly, the fact of Jesus' awareness of his own impending death (Luke 8.21–22; John 8.21–28; 12.27–36), his imagining of what the horrible reality might be like (Luke 18.32–33), and his struggle to come to terms with what lay ahead as recounted in the Gethsemane story (Matthew 26.36–46), make sense. For them to be introduced or re-connected to God through this narrative helps them see the truth of Emmanuel – God with us.

If we do encounter people who seem to have turned away from God at some point, it can be really useful to ask them: 'Who was the God you turned away from when ... happened? or 'What was that God like – the one you no longer believe in? Chances are they will not yet have encountered a God who is present in our lives, in our struggles and pain, for in Jesus we have a God who does not stay remote from the suffering of the world, but chose to experience it himself, to be alongside us in solidarity, even to the point of death on a cross. In Jesus, we have a God who knows what it is like to be a human being facing death, dealing with pain, leaving loved ones behind, but also transcending uncertainty and claiming – through faith – an eternal God-connection – for beyond death lies resurrection life in all its mystery and wonder and potential.

It is part of the joy and challenge of ministry with the aged to help people update their way of seeing God. However God chooses to reveal God-self, the foundational character of God is *always* present: holy, compassionate, merciful, wise and kind; always wanting the best for us, drawing us towards healing and connecting us with our innermost truth, our network of family and friends, our community, our world – and of course, our God.

What constitutes 'spiritual conversation'?

The word 'spirituality' comes from the Latin word *spirare* 'to breathe' and refers to what is *at our core*, often as unnoticed as our breathing (re*spira*tion), but vital to our well-being. 'Spiritual conversation' can mean different things to different people depending on how we define 'spirituality' and the context in which the conversation takes place. When, for example, we are visiting or working in a care home or hospital context, the environment is naturally influenced by a medical model of care, which, in an effort to be inclusive and avoid offence, primarily refers to 'spirituality' in concepts related to psychological well-being,[6] e.g.

Spirituality is the aspect of humanity that refers to the way individuals seek and express meaning and purpose, and the way they experience their connectedness to the moment, to self, to others, to nature and to the significant or sacred.[7]

Spiritual conversations conducted by health professionals are often shaped around taking a brief spiritual history[8] or assessing a person's spiritual needs in general terms as they relate to medical care. When spiritual distress is identified, i.e. where there is conflict between people's beliefs and their current experience, or where there is a loss of meaning or sense of connection, referral may be made to the person's minister, spiritual adviser or the facility chaplain if there is one.

While 'spirituality' used to be subsumed in the term 'religion', in recent decades the word has taken on a life of its own in the Western context (Europe, Britain, the USA and Australasia). Now, when we are talking with the elderly and their families, we cannot assume we speak a common language around which to base a spiritual conversation, as might have been true even 30 years ago. While some people in the general population still express their spirituality through religious beliefs and practices, for others 'spirituality' has become disconnected from its roots in the great faith traditions of the world and has attached itself instead to a range of values and actions which might come from humanist, psychological, esoteric, indigenous, Eastern or pagan origins. Attractive though a self-selected 'accountable to no one' spirituality, divorced from religious belief and practice, may be, it can lack a *unifying* narrative with relational depth and altruistic outcomes. From the Christian viewpoint, this means that the 'I–Thou' of classic Christian engagement with the personal, loving mystery of God may be missing; the gospel imperative to serve others may be replaced by serving self.

---

6 See Harold G. Koenig, *Spirituality in Patient Care*, 2nd edn, Templeton Foundation Press, Philadelphia, 2007, pp. 39–40.

7 In C. Puchalski and B. R. Ferrell, *Making Health Care Whole: Integrating Spirituality into Patient Care*, Templeton Press, West Conshohocken, PA: 2010.

8 See, e.g., American Family Physician website: http://www.aafp.org/afp/2001/0101/p81. html for a comprehensive article.

Before going far in any spiritual conversation, then, we need to try to establish something of the person's spiritual position. If, for example, someone says, 'I'm spiritual, but not religious', we have an opening to ask what he or she means by 'spiritual'. Answers will generally focus around 'not going to church but still believing in "something"', 'believing there is more to life than science can explain', 'wanting to care for the planet', 'being in touch with nature', 'meditating', etc. – perhaps with some passing reference to historic religious attendance (e.g. Sunday school) or a memorable spiritual experience. There is no evidence of adherence to a coherent set of beliefs and practices in the context of a community of faith. For such people, spiritual practices might mean marking the rhythms of nature, wearing crystals, practising mindfulness, or fasting. It might mean holding rituals associated with special events such as planting a tree where a baby's placenta is buried. Spirituality might be expressed through being committed to simple living, social justice work or care of the environment. According to Brian McLaren:

> Whatever the specifics, spiritual people have – or at least wish they had – some set of moves, rhythms, habits or practices, things that … keep them from sleep-walking or going on auto-pilot, so they live with greater sensitivity to the sacred aliveness and meaning that surround them.[9]

The late Gerald May, psychiatrist and spiritual director, gave us a way of taking spiritual conversation deeper when he wrote with deceptive simplicity, 'Spirituality is the dynamic process of love in our lives.'[10] If we come into this world as a 'fresh expression' of the image of God and spend our time here learning to love, it makes sense to see spirituality as love overcoming personal isolation, deepening our relationships with others and the divine, and expanding our capacity for service.

For Christians, whose unifying narrative is the story of the life, death and resurrection of Jesus Christ, God is acknowledged as that love to which May refers, 'Love' with a capital 'L'. Spiritual conversation then becomes a shared discovery of how God / Love is working in the lives of those we visit.

For those who have no religious affiliation, May's definition enables conversations to focus on the person's experience of the giving and receiving of Love and naturally extends to their experience of suffering. We work on the 1 John 4.13–21[11] principle summed up in the Taizé chant 'Ubi caritas et amor, deus ibi est' ('Where true love and charity abide, God is dwelling there'). As we listen to the stories about family relationships, loss, fulfilment, generosity, disappointment or betrayal, we note the themes that connect with the stories of Jesus.

9 Brian McLaren, *Naked Spirituality*, Hodder & Stoughton: London, 2011, p. 19.

10 Gerald May, *Care of Mind, Care of Spirit*, Harper Collins: New York, 1982, p. xvi.

11 1 John 4.13–21: 'God is love, and those who abide in love abide in God and God in them' (16b). For more on this principle, see the section on 'Pastoral Practices'.

There will come a time when we can naturally introduce more of God into pastoral conversations by specifically asking some God-questions around key aspects of the life we're listening to. We can choose any question from any section as a starting point and, depending on the response, ask another:

Love:	Where have you felt most loved? When have you felt most alone?
Losses:	Which of your loved ones have died during your lifetime?
	What helped you cope when ... died? Who was there for you then?
	What was your sense of God's presence/absence in that difficult time?
Church:	Are you part of a faith community / do you go to church now / in the past?
	What made you stop going to church?
Prayer:	Has prayer been part of your life in the past? How about now?
	How hard is it for you to pray when you are in pain?
	Who has prayed for you? Who prays for you now?
	What would you like us to pray for?
Experience:	Have you ever had a spiritual experience of 'something greater than yourself' whether you call it God or not?[12]
God-connection:	When have you felt close to God? When have you felt far away from God?
Image of God:	What do you think God is like?
	What way of seeing God helps you / frightens you?

How comfortable do you feel asking 'God-questions' like these in a pastoral context?

When we have earned the right to speak of Jesus,[13] we can introduce him quite naturally, as this little piece of dialogue from a pastoral visit shows:

When you told me about your husband leaving you for another woman, I thought of the time when Jesus was betrayed by Judas – you've probably heard the story: Judas was one of Jesus' trusted companions but, for 30 pieces of silver, he agreed to reveal Jesus' whereabouts, so Jesus could be arrested and sent to trial. What was it like for you when your husband betrayed your trust?

---

12 This classic question is linked to decades of research into religious experience. See the Alister Hardy Research Centre (now based at Lampeter) for further information and examples: www.trinitysaintdavid.ac.uk/en/lrc/librariesandcentres (accessed 6.2.14) or books by Paul Hawker, *Soul Survivor* and *Secret Affairs of the Soul* (details in 'Further Reading').

13 By demonstrating pastoral sensitivity, for example showing respect, being focused, actively listening, etc.

What we are doing in an exchange like this is:

- letting the woman know that we have *heard* her story
- introducing Jesus without expecting anything of her
- helping her glimpse Jesus in a way she may never have encountered before: someone who knows what it's like to be human, to be betrayed by someone he trusted. He stands alongside her in solidarity: he is Emmanuel. God with her, with us.

Spiritual conversations help people reflect on their life and address *spiritual needs*, deep longings which, if fulfilled, enable people to live true to their uniqueness as beings made in the image of God.[14] A list of spiritual needs, initial questions and scripture for personal or group reflection follows.

> You may like to set up a small group and explore one 'spiritual need' at a time, using the suggested question to get the discussion started. By approaching spiritual needs through scripture stories, especially the Gospels, we create a context in which talking about Jesus is natural and group members' personal stories and experiences are more likely to emerge.

The spiritual needs, in no particular order:

1 **A need for meaning and purpose** as 'productivity' declines, earlier life-roles recede, and the familiar patterns of health, social life, housing, mobility and communication are deconstructed.
   'What gives your life meaning now?'
   Jesus left behind and found in the temple: Luke 2.41–51.
2 **A need for significant relationships** as old connections disappear, peers die and the distance that can so often separate family members compromises contact.
   'Who is important to you at this stage of your life?'
   Jesus, Martha, Mary and Lazarus: John 11.1–6.
3 **A need to grieve loss upon loss**, some new and raw, others hitherto unspoken or historical.
   'How do you grieve when you lose someone you love?'
   Jesus wept: John 11.17–37.

---

14 Nursing researchers Judith Shelly and Sharon Fish, *Spiritual Care: The Nurse's Role*, 3rd edn, IVP, Downers Grove, Illinois, 1988, identified the need for forgiveness, the need for relationship, and the need to find meaning and purpose in one's life. Other researchers have added to this list as more understanding is reached about the pivotal place of spiritual well-being at all stages of our lives, e.g. Elizabeth MacKinlay, *Spiritual Growth and Care in the Fourth Age of Life*, Jessica Kingsley Publishers, London, 2006; and Harold G. Koenig, *Spirituality in Patient Care*, 2nd edn, Templeton Foundation Press, Philadelphia, 2007.

4 **A need for reconciliation and forgiveness,** for putting things right, for reconnecting with estranged family or friends, for coming to terms with one's own failures and weakness.
   'How does forgiveness figure in your life?'
   Jesus restores Simon Peter: John 21.9–17.

5 **A need to be treated with respect and kindness,** an honouring of personal uniqueness.
   'How are you treated by those around you?'
   Jesus calls the children: Luke 18.15–17.

6 **A need to allow oneself to be cared for,** to face growing dependency with grace.
   'How hard is it for you to let someone help you?'
   Jesus and the anointing at Bethany: Mark 14.3–9.

7 **A need to prepare for death,** to express feelings and move towards a place of inner peace.
   'What have you already done to prepare for your death?' 'What might you want to do?'
   The infant Jesus in Simeon's arms: Luke 2.25–33; Jesus at the last supper – the foot-washing: John 13.3–15.

8 **A need to strengthen inner resources,** e.g. prayer, reflection, engagement with arts and music.
   'How are you strengthened in your inner self?' 'What gives you joy?'
   Jesus praying: Luke 6.12.

9 **A need to review one's image of God,** being prepared to face doubt and disappointment so a new way of seeing God may emerge from the rubble of broken expectations and trauma.
   'How would you describe the God you believe/don't believe in now?'
   Jesus as shepherd: John 10.1–16; Jesus as 'mother hen'.

10 **A need to make sense of/transcend suffering,** to find a way of integrating emotional or physical pain into a metaphor or theme that can link their personal narrative with a bigger story.
   'What helps you cope with pain and suffering?'
   Jesus in the garden of Gethsemane: Matthew 26.36–46.

11 **A need to let go of control** and, for the faithful, to trust oneself to the grace and mercy of God.
   'What are you letting go of as you age?'
   Jesus on the cross – the ultimate letting go: Luke 23.39–46.

12 **A need for hope** – in the midst of grief and loss, in the face of death, there can still be hope, whether that is through, for example, a strengthening faith and belief in the teachings of Christ, or the assurance of physical comfort and companioned dying.
   'What do you hope for as you get closer to the end of your life?'
   Jesus shepherd in life and in death: Psalm 23; Nothing can separate us from God: Romans 8.38–39.

🕯 In order to familiarize yourself with these spiritual needs, take some time to look through the above list, and note the extent to which those relevant to you are – or are not – being met in *your own* life.

🕯 How do these spiritual needs relate to *one* older person with whom you have a pastoral relationship?

Health professionals are often required to talk about spiritual needs in language that omits reference to God or Jesus or faith or prayer. However, *we* are ministers of the gospel, modelling God's care by our faithful visiting and support. Informed by the Spirit of Jesus, our spiritual conversations deliberately open up the place of prayer, the stories of scripture, and the signs of grace, as our loving God reaches out to the person with whom we are engaged.

In a multicultural society we will of course respect the faith positions of others, but, where we are working with someone whose cultural/religious background is Christian and who is open to the possibility of exploring or revisiting God-ideas or spiritual experience, we risk losing the chance to engage in a constructive spiritual conversation if we are too cautious or concerned about giving offence. It is a fine line, because we know that, if we get it wrong, we risk putting people off altogether. So how do we strike the balance? How do we 'speak of what we know'?

The Queen's Christmas Message in 2013 provided an example of respectful engagement with a diverse Commonwealth community without diluting or omitting references to the key to her own long reign and daily duty: the Christian faith. After reminding us all of the value of reflection and family, she concluded her message by saying:

> For Christians, as for all people of faith, reflection, meditation and prayer help us to renew ourselves in God's love, as we strive daily to become better people. The Christmas message shows us that this love is for everyone. There is no one beyond its reach.

Here, we see sensitivity spiced with boldness, and a willingness to 'own' the distinctiveness of the Christian hope and teachings. As we attend to the promptings of the Spirit we too will be given the words we need and the love and courage to speak them.

Self-care for the minister or caregiver

In any ministry we run the risk of experiencing 'compassion fatigue' or 'burnout'. Because ministry is our vocation, we naturally want to give our time, skills and energy to those whom we serve. But unstinting giving comes at a cost. Yes, we may receive love and appreciation from those we meet and their families, but, nice though that may be, it is not sufficient to keep our inner resources from being poured out until they, and we, are spent and we step down – and out.

Take a few minutes to read and pray with the parable of the wise and foolish bridesmaids/virgins (Matthew 25.1–13), noticing your feelings and thoughts. With which group of women do you naturally identify? Why?

This parable raises several issues relevant to self-care for those of us in ministry:

- **The risk of being a 'rescuer'.** When I've prayed with this parable, I've recognized that, because it's in my nature and upbringing to 'be prepared', I would probably be one of the 'wise' women! However, I also recognized that I would find it very difficult to turn down someone's request for help and would therefore have shared my 'oil' and risked running out myself. And this has happened. On a couple of occasions, I've had to take time out from ministry because I was exhausted. This meant some soul-searching and inner work on my 'need to be needed'. Early childhood patterns and emotionally needy adults in my life had set me up to try to make things better for anyone and everyone, and this, of course, could not be sustained. It certainly affected me and, though I didn't realize it at the time, meant that I often got in God's way. I needed to learn about inviting God to be at the centre of anything I was going to undertake; I needed to learn about not doing things for people they could actually do for themselves, about involving others, about having the humility to ask for practical assistance and prayer support, and organizing some time off on a regular basis. I had to accept I was not 'superwoman' or 'perfect' and did not need to be for God to love me. I hasten to say that this is still a 'work in progress'!
- **If our 'lamps' run out we have to bear the consequences.** My sense is that often people leave ministry because they have not found the balance between giving and receiving and can see no way of being a pastor or preacher unless they give it *every*thing – but then this leads to mistakes and not being able to give *any*thing. Poor decision-making, spiritual, emotional and physical exhaustion are the consequences of not keeping our lamps topped up and render us incapable of ministering to anyone.
- **Wisdom is associated with being able to say 'No' sometimes.** For many in ministry the hardest thing is to say 'No' when someone asks us to help. I don't think that we have to say 'Yes' to every ministry request, nor are we expected to run ourselves into the ground. We are to live a full life of service, but doing the things *God* gives us to do, rather than the things we – or others – think we *should* be

doing. The old words from the Book of Common Prayer put it clearly: 'O heavenly Father, so (to) assist us with thy grace, that we may continue in that holy fellowship, and do all such good works *as thou hast prepared for us to walk in*; through Jesus Christ our Lord, to whom, with thee and the Holy Ghost, be all honour and glory, world without end. Amen.'

It is natural to want to agree to every opportunity for ministry immediately, much harder to stand back and seek time for discernment before giving our answer. Having a good knowledge of other available resources, being wary of requests that stroke our egos, knowing our own limits of energy and time, accepting that as we age things take longer, all help us to say 'No' when faced with something that would overload us and ultimately let others down. If, after reflection and prayer, we say 'Yes', we are more likely to be able to follow through, less likely to have to pull out nearer the time and make life difficult for everyone relying on us.

'Balance' is the word that comes frequently to mind!

Driving to work I often see a large wood pigeon (kereru, with a body the size of an average chicken). Often they sit on a narrow branch or power line, with only the occasional twitch of the tail or slight shift of weight to remind me that, while balance might look effortless, it takes alertness and a series of mini-adjustments to maintain stability.

You may have picked up a common theme running through the paragraphs above – prayer and discernment. What will help us to keep our balance is to deepen our prayer life. Ways of doing this include:

- spending time in contemplative (listening) prayer, letting our minds quieten, resting in God, developing the capacity to *listen* to the Spirit instead of talking all the time
- praying with the scriptures
- taking our spiritual life and need for spiritual nourishment seriously
- working with a spiritual director
- meditative walking or running or swimming or gardening
- connecting with creation
- engaging in the arts to relax and refresh us
- sharing conversation with people who are there *for us*
- writing or expressing our inner thoughts and reactions regularly
- reflecting at the end of the day on what has been life-giving or draining
- taking an annual week in *silent* retreat.

It is hard to be disciplined in our own interest, but it is, in the long run, in the interests of those we serve. For many in ministry, personal prayer is the very thing that is squeezed out by all the other demands on our time. Scripture regards taking time aside with God as mandatory, not optional. 'Be still and know that I am God,' writes David (Psalm 46.10); Elijah discovers God in the 'still small voice' (1 Kings 19). Jesus is usually up well before dawn for prayer and resourcing from his Father (Mark 1.35; Luke 5.16). So, if you already find yourself overwhelmed by the demands on your life and wonder if you will be able to sustain your commitment to ministry made with such joy and confidence perhaps years ago, then the reality is that you won't be able to – unless – unless you make prayer your priority, prayer that includes not only petition and intercession, but also the prayer of silence when we still our interior chatter, let our soul settle into the welcoming arms of God and allow the Holy Spirit to work directly with our spirit, bringing us ever closer to the Source of all wisdom and compassion – our God. After all,

Unless the LORD builds the house, those who build it labour in vain.
Unless the LORD guards the city, the guard keeps watch in vain.
It is in vain that you rise up early and go late to rest,
eating the bread of anxious toil;
for he gives sleep to his beloved.[15] (Psalm 127.1–2)

How can we even contemplate serving others, unless we have ourselves been immersed in the love of God? For God alone can provide what we need for ministry, whatever the context. With Jesus we stroll along corridors, sit by deathbeds, laugh or cry with residents and their families, and, where we can, support staff in their often under-resourced, sacrificial work. And when we visit the isolated elderly at home, we have the chance – by our focused listening and compassionate presence – to model the value of each person to God, to be an agent of God's grace, and to speak of the resurrection hope that is God's gift. But we can do this only if we are ourselves grounded in God.

---

15 Or 'for he provides for his beloved during sleep'.

I

Reconnecting with Old Treasures

Matthew 6.19–21 speaks of storing up for ourselves indestructible 'treasures in heaven' which enable us to live joyfully in the Spirit in this life as we prepare for the next. In our Western cultural tradition 'treasure' has become almost exclusively associated with monetary wealth: gold and silver, investments and property, precious gems and artefacts. But for many indigenous people, and certainly for Maori in New Zealand, *taonga*[1] often refers to something very different – forests and waterways, stories and *waiata* (songs), people and *whakapapa* (family genealogy) and mountains. It is this broader sense of treasure which we can tap into when we are in conversation with the elderly, for everyone, whether in residential care or their own home, will have some treasures from their own cultural, relational and geographical context:

- memories of special stories or songs, poems or paintings
- a bedtime ritual or precious time shared with a loved one
- words spoken at state funerals or weddings or public events
- places which carry sacred meaning or connection
- ways of being with family or friends at particular times of the year
- ways of celebrating holidays or holy days or the seasons.

Take a few minutes to look at the list above and jot down your own 'treasures' – things that have nurtured you over the years, things that bring you comfort, things that help you connect with others, with your community and with God.

Making the most of the familiar

I visited my elderly aunt a few months before she died. Her distressed daughter and I sat with her, listening as her mind meandered among the generations in a disordered sequence of memories and sentences, the muddle lightened by the occasional spark of her old humour. Before I left, I reached for her hands and said, 'Let's say the Lord's prayer together.' And so we did, and it came from her lips without hesitation or error, a clear, strong memory of her faith and her identity in Christ. Her daughter

---

1 *Taonga* – Maori for 'treasure'/'something of great spiritual and cultural value'.

looked at me and smiled – we were both reassured that beneath the confusion her mother was 'still there', and her spirit could be soothed by the familiar prayer which had always been part of her life.

The 'treasures' and familiar aspects of people's lives can provide a rich resource for spiritual conversation and, when we combine them with poetry, images, sacred texts and music, can enhance the relevance of liturgy and people's access to the sacred. These treasures may be part of a group's religious heritage, but can also stem from a shared natural environment, from culturally recognized music, literature or art, or be linked to a particular event of relevance to a local community. The familiar may include common landmarks or architectural features, everyday food items or recipes, modes of transport and communication, common birds and trees or flowers, items from the kitchen cupboard, shed or allotment. Two examples follow.

Where I live in Taranaki, the landscape is dominated by the volcanic cone, named Mt Egmont/Taranaki. Speaking about this *'taonga'*, this mountain, with groups of elderly folk who come to a community-based day programme, I nearly always find someone who climbed Mt Taranaki in their younger days, others for whom the mountain shaped their farming life, others still who love the different faces of the mountain as he[2] interacts with clouds and sun. If I were using this familiar landmark to spark a spiritual conversation or inspire a service, I'd include such resources as:

- Psalm 121, 'I lift up my eyes to the hills – from where will my help come?' (NRSV).
- 'Climb every mountain' (*The Sound of Music*).
- Christina Rossetti's poem 'Uphill'. Beginning 'Does the road wind uphill all the way?' it speaks of struggle towards the end of life's journey and inclusive hospitality and welcome.
- The concept of God's presence and perceived absence[3] – sometimes our mountain is clothed in cloud for days on end, and visitors could be forgiven for thinking we were talking about something that didn't exist. Sometimes our experience of God can be like that – God may seem hidden as we undergo trials, suffer grief or pain, or choose a life-path that takes us further away from God with each step. But sooner or later, if we turn back towards God, the cloud *will* clear, God will be visible again through grace and the action of the Holy Spirit.

A second example is based on a song, familiar to many who lived through the years of the Second World War – 'The White Cliffs of Dover'. Its lyrics speak of hope, and new life – ultimately pointing us to the greater freedom and fulfilment of the kingdom of God. Resources which gather naturally around this theme:

---

2 In Maori legend Mt Taranaki fought Mt Tongariro over the lovely Mt Pihanga and lost, retreating to the west!

3 When considering the perceived absence of God *in the life of an individual*, it is worth taking into account two additional factors – the person's mental state, as depression can veil awareness of God's presence, and where the person is on her spiritual journey, for sometimes God's perceived absence deepens a person's longing for God.

28

- Scriptures, for example, 'Guide me in your truth and teach me, for you are God my Saviour, and my hope is in you all day long' (Psalm 25.5, NIV).

  'May the God of hope fill you with all joy and peace as you trust in him, so that you may overflow with hope by the power of the Holy Spirit' (Romans 15.13, NIV).

  'Even youths will faint and be weary and the young will fall exhausted; but those who hope in the LORD shall renew their strength, they shall mount up with wings like eagles, they shall run and not be weary, they shall walk and not faint' (Isaiah 40.30–1, NIV)

- If you want to consider a very modern song of hope in God, look at Aaron Schust's 'My Hope is In You', available in several music video variations on YouTube.

- Stories of the difference people have made working for peace and for justice, for example William Wilberforce (slavery), Rosa Parks and Martin Luther King (racial equality), contemporary heroine Malala Yousafzai who faced death because of her dedication to the education of girls, even New Zealand's young Sam Johnson who motivated thousands to form a 'student volunteer army' after the Christchurch earthquakes, bringing comfort and practical help. And there are stories closer to home – some of your residents may have achieved change for the good of their community or been devoted caregivers who care for those with special needs. Some may still make a daily difference to others' quality of life by their presence.

- The concept of Christian hope – we can speak of the presence of Christ in the midst of life's trials *now* as well as the future hope of the fulfilment of the coming of Christ and the 'new heaven and the new earth'. While many elders may have been brought up to think of the consolation of God as something that happens after we die, an understanding of the promise of Jesus never to leave or forsake us means that we have access, via the Holy Spirit, to God's wisdom, peace and joy *in this life*, in our circumstances, no matter what life may bring.

The Sacred Space services (see in Appendix 1, 'Short Services of the Word') give examples of how 'ordinary' starting points such as a season of the year (spring), a natural element (rocks), a beloved painting ('The Light of the World'), or a familiar poem ('I said to the man who stood at the gate of the year'), can be springboards for a service of the Word that relates well to the people you serve.

Another source of delight for older people is to hear the *stories* behind familiar hymns, for example:

- In 'Amazing Grace', John Newton touches the mystery of conversion and the wonder of knowing himself forgiven from sins too awful for us to imagine, committed during his time as a slave-ship captain. In New Zealand, a country without an established church and set up constitutionally to be secular, this was the hymn chosen to be at the heart of memorial services for those lost in the

Christchurch earthquakes and the Pike River mining disaster. 'Amazing Grace' reaches the hearts of people across the spectrum of spirituality. Why? Because it tells the story of the redemptive hope to be found in Christ – something for which, recognized or not, we all long.

- The story behind 'Now thank we all our God' reveals amazing courage and Christian conviction. It was written about 1636 by Lutheran Martin Rinkart, who ministered to villagers in Eilenburg, Saxony, at the beginning of the Thirty Years War. Refugees brought overcrowding and deadly pestilence. Rinkart buried over 4,000 people in one year and was widowed himself, yet wrote this hymn as a grace for his children. It is a reminder to us to seek out the small mercies in the midst of any hardship.

Making the most of the new

New ways of being 'Church' have been emerging over the past two decades. Some of the freshness and flexibility found in such ventures can be incorporated into care home or parish contexts too.

Perhaps you've heard of the 24/7 prayer movement gaining momentum across the world. If you haven't then go to www.youtube.com/playlist?list=PL5E975 62D8476D910 (accessed 7.1.14) where you'll find five short video clip resources to help you get a sense of what might be possible. Such a prayer room, suitably adapted, could be set up in part of a care home or church hall even for an afternoon. Certainly it might not be available to quite the same extent as a well-staffed central city site, but with a little prayer and a keen couple of people, who knows what the Spirit might do?

There is no reason why older people cannot be introduced to praying in different ways, for example praying with scripture using their imagination or the *lectio divina* process,[4] or walking a short prayer path with 'stations' where they can stop, rest and reflect. Offering such an experience before or during Holy Week can help deepen the Easter experience for many.

There is no reason why new technology cannot be used to enhance worship or prayer. Increasing numbers of older people use email, Skype, Facebook and other social media to keep in touch with their wider family, so we don't need to assume that the elderly are going to be wary of technology if we use it during services of the Word or Communion. When I have introduced a YouTube version of old hymns or a new song the congregation have not heard before, I have rarely had a complaint – quite the opposite in fact, as the fresh perspective can bring new life to the old.

One Christmas, for example, I used a video clip of a flashmob in a large New York department store (http://www.youtube.com/watch?v=ohagajJvzhU; accessed 7.1.14). The 'mob' were young members of an operatic school and they sang the

---

4 For further details, see the section 'Praying with scripture'.

'Hallelujah Chorus' in a large food hall – to the delight of those who witnessed the scene at the time, and those who witnessed it as part of our Christmas service.

For this reason, in the material for services that follows, I have in some cases suggested using YouTube clips for music or songs that are well outside the body of hymns older people may have grown up with. The benefits of using such clips include being able to select a suitable version of a song/hymn/chant etc. and, often, to have the lyrics printed on the screen as the song is being sung – a distinct advantage for older people. The energy and loud volume of some young congregational singing gives a glimpse of a new way of being 'Church', and may give faithful old souls some sense of hope that the story of Jesus continues to be told and received with joy by a younger generation.

If you want to introduce short, easy-to-remember chants, then consider using material from the Taizé community, Margaret Rizza, Bernadette Farrell and others who have helped de-mystify Latin chants in particular. A variety of musicians and artists, for example Secret Garden, Libera, Keith Duke, Sons of Korah (singing the psalms) have written contemporary music which can touch the hearts and minds of the elderly. Appropriate music from an unfamiliar source such as an African singing group (the University of Johannesburg Choir or Ladysmith Black Mambazo) can touch people deeply and enhance worship. For these technological inclusions to work you will need to have access to:

- someone with whom you can discuss music choices from a wide range of available material
- a portable data projector, laptop or tablet computer or
- the songs etc. on a memory stick and the technical knowledge to play it through an existing TV
- a wide range of music – if you can access iTunes so much the better, but if not then many versions of the hymns or songs you might want to use will be found on YouTube, and there are of course apps which allow these to be downloaded.

Communion services for groups

When I was new to care-home ministry, I had been used to leading church services that proceeded in a relatively predictable and orderly fashion. I soon learned:

Do not expect the services in care homes to be like those in church!

Yes, people will be coming to worship God, to be encouraged in their faith, to be reassured of God's care for them, and to find some solace or comfort, but services will rarely start right on time, people may have to leave partway through or arrive late, occasionally someone may become distressed or call out loudly, papers will be dropped on the floor, walking-frames will have to be relocated, and hearing aids and microphones adjusted.

For those of us used to ministering in a church setting, such inevitable 'dis-organization' and the length of time taken before we can begin a service can make us impatient and tense. Clearly this is another example of the need both for prayer beforehand and having others to share this service with you, if at all possible. A team of three or four is ideal – leader, pianist/musician, helper with the distribution of Communion, and if possible a general support person in case someone wants a service sheet or help finding the right page, or to assist late arrivals or respond if someone collapses. (Find where the emergency call-bell is in the space you are using, it should be clearly indicated.)

For a half-hour service, allow at least an hour and a half – half an hour beforehand to help gather up the people and set up the space slowly, and half an hour afterwards to meet people individually, tidy up and to begin to build a connection with staff as you help them return the residents to other lounges, to a meal or back to their rooms. Although this appears a big time commitment for a short service, the benefits in terms of relationship establishment and deepening cannot be overestimated.

It may be disconcerting to have a member of the care-home congregation nodding off during the service, but again, we cannot assume that they are unaware of what is going on. Those who seem asleep may still be taking in what is happening or being sung or said. If we believe that the spirit of a person is open to the Spirit of God and that 'nothing' can prevent the love of God reaching a receptive soul, then it follows that we just do what we can in love for Christ and leave God to do the rest in and with the individuals, whether or not we seem to have their attention.

'Annie' roused herself from sleep partway through a Communion service and fixed me with the most beautiful smile – as if she'd visited heaven in her dreaming. I haven't a clue what she 'understood' of what we were doing, but I know that she looked at peace and her smile warmed me and those around her. When she received the bread and wine a little later, she took them reverently, as if for the very first time. Perhaps there was some grace in her forgetfulness as the Eucharist came to her afresh.

When preparing a service for the elderly, it helps if services are, in terms of **content**:

- short – 30 to 45 minutes is ideal – both in terms of concentration and continence!
- child-like in the best sense – uncomplicated, inclusive, interesting and, where appropriate, fun
- a balance between the familiar and the fresh when choosing readings, music, etc.
- gently creative – doing things a little differently and making room for the open-ended
- meeting some of the spiritual needs listed earlier
- attempting to include something that will connect with those who have vision or hearing impairment – i.e., something to smell or touch, taste or imagine
- providing something that people can take away and use later as an aid to memory.

In terms of **resources** a few practical considerations can make a big difference:

- Communion service sheets – use a large font (e.g. 16pt Garamond) with people's responses in **bold;** a short service need take no more than two sides of an A4 sheet, printed on light card.
- If you don't have hymn books or folders available, then type up the old[5] hymns (getting lyrics from the internet saves time) and for longer services (for example at Easter or Christmas) photocopy using a booklet format and A3 paper so people have something to take away for later reflection.
- Gather a range of items to use as a worship focus if you are taking the service in a lounge rather than in a chapel. **Using a trolley as a portable altar** means you can have a couple of candles, a cross, some flowers, an A3 picture perhaps, or other objects and coloured cloths which can help convey the focus of a particular service. It is also a very practical way of ensuring that you can locate the altar in the best possible place – for visibility, hearing, effects of light/shadow and proximity to those you are serving.
- Music – details of music for most of the services in this book will be found before or after the service text. If you do not have a competent pianist in your team, then consider investing in some good-quality CD compilations of favourite hymns (if the venue has a CD/DVD player), or, if you are able, download music and bring a laptop or tablet with a good speaker system to the venue. Check that the words of the CD or downloaded hymns you are playing are the same as the words you put in your service sheet. Chants provide a gentle repeated melody, are easy to sing and settle in one's mind, and are ideal to play while you are getting organized or waiting for people to arrive.
- Particular objects – enough for one for every person present – if you are doing a special service: sprigs of rosemary for Remembrance Day, palm crosses for Palm Sunday.

Distributing communion is a wonderful opportunity to minister to each resident personally:

- A smile, their name said warmly, an *unhurried* giving of the bread or wine, lets them know that they are important and valued.
- Provide your own real bread but check with staff if there is anyone who is unable to swallow bread or liquid.
- To help prevent cross-infection, have hand sanitizer close by when distributing the bread. Those with later stage dementia may need to be shown how to put the bread to their mouth, or you may need to do it for them.

---

5 Old hymns are those which are out of copyright – if unsure, check with your local diocesan office or with the music publishers, e.g. Canterbury Press, publishers of Hymns A&M. It is important that copyright is not infringed.

- Use disposable small cups for distribution of Communion to very frail residents and to those who prefer not to use a shared cup – if you have enough helpers, then you can offer both the small cups and a chalice, or leave the chalice as the symbolic 'cup of blessing' on the altar table.
- Use a non-alcoholic wine or grape juice for the individual cups, use port or similar in the chalice.
- Have tissues and paper towels with you if needed for shaky hands.
- Look for clues as to whether residents are visually impaired so you can guide their hands if necessary – often people are reluctant to 'own' this disability and it can be some time before you notice.

To help you shape your own Communion services to suit your particular context, there follows:

- A service outline of a generic Communion service, but aspects can be omitted or added for special occasions.
- A copiable service sheet for a complete Communion service using a flexible structure into which you can insert special prayers/talk/activity/music, etc.
- Resources for Communion services, including options for Advent, Christmas, Lent, Easter, Pentecost and Ordinary Time, etc.
- An alternative Communion service from a contemplative stance with some silence and symbols to touch and share – suitable for a smaller group setting or an option for use at home. With this contemplative service, the song 'Be still and know that I am God' is used as an anchor, i.e. the first verse at the start, first and second verses in the middle and all three verses at the end.

MAKE SURE THAT YOU SPEAK SLOWLY, USE PAUSES AND HONOUR
SILENCE IN ALL SERVICES YOU LEAD WITH OLDER PEOPLE.

BASIC ELEMENTS OF A COMMUNION SERVICE

WELCOME
Introduce yourself, your team; talk about any aspects of the service which may be special or different.

OPENING SONG/HYMN
Warming up, gathering community, beginning to get a sense of the needs and well-being of those present.

PRAYER OF CONFESSION AND ASSURANCE OF GOD'S GRACE AND FORGIVENESS
People are invited to bring their regrets before God; a short silence (30 seconds) is followed by a simple form of confession, and an unequivocal assurance of forgiveness, pronounced by a priest or, if not available or required in your context, using words from scripture, e.g. Psalm 86.4–5; Matthew 11.28–30; 1 Corinthians 13.4–7; Ephesians 4.31–32. If a priest is not present, you may prefer to replace 'your' with 'our', e.g. 'May **you** know that **your** sins are forgiven ...' becomes 'May **we** know that **our** sins are forgiven ...'.

PRAYERS FOR OTHERS AND FOR OURSELVES
Reaching out to others, connecting with the global environment, joining our prayers with those of others around the world, as well as praying for our families, fellow residents, staff and ourselves.

THE LORD'S PRAYER
The old version (using 'trespasses') seems to be the more easily remembered for most people, but a modern version is included in the second sample Communion service as an option.

GOSPEL
A short Gospel passage either from the Lectionary, or to suit a particular message/time of year/event.

BRIEF WORDS AND/OR ACTIVITY

Short talk – five minutes – and/or activity if you have people there to help you manage this. This may be placed at any suitable part of the service, depending on what you are focusing on, and is designed to encourage personal engagement with the service content. For those with dementia, simply enabling them to engage slowly with the materials in the Activity section might be helpful without a lot of talking.

ANOTHER SONG/HYMN OR REFLECTIVE MUSIC/CHANT OR PSALM
(if time allows)

A quieter song/chant/psalm gives an opportunity to listen to some beautiful sacred music or gives them an example of honest communication between the psalmist and God.

HOLY COMMUNION

An abbreviated form of Great Thanksgiving, followed by a leisurely distribution of the blessed elements; if no priest is available or required in your context, then use the words of scripture: Matthew 26.26–28.

PRAYER AFTER COMMUNION

A short prayer which you pray on everyone's behalf, full of thankfulness for the grace of God.

CLOSING HYMN OR SONG

Designed to highlight the central theme and remind those present of God's love for them and all people.

BLESSING

HOLY COMMUNION: THE SUPPER OF THE LORD

WELCOME
You are welcome to this service today – a service in which we will pray, sing, be assured of God's kindness, hear the good news of the Gospel, share the Lord's Supper, and listen to God's word, lit up for each one of us by the Holy Spirit. Be in no doubt of God's love for you right here, right now, as you bring yourself and your needs to Jesus, friend and Saviour to us all.

OPENING SONG

CONFESSION (said together)
God of grace and mercy, we bring to you those things which we regret –
things spoken or not spoken, done or not done,
things which have stopped us from sharing your love in the world,
things which have hampered the building of your kingdom of justice and joy.
In the silence, hear our sorrow and bring us healing,
hear our desire to be your people in this place,
to recognize your presence in our lives,
and to be bearers of your love and grace to others. AMEN.

Silence.

Know that your sins are forgiven;
be strengthened by the grace of God.
May the love of God warm your heart.
May the mercy of God console your spirit.
May the peace of God fill you with joy. AMEN.

PRAYERS FOR OTHERS AND FOR OURSELVES

THE LORD'S PRAYER
Our Father, which art in heaven,
hallowed be thy name,
thy kingdom come; thy will be done
on earth as it is in heaven.
Give us this day our daily bread
and forgive us our trespasses,

as we forgive those who trespass against us.
And lead us not into temptation,
but deliver us from evil.
For thine is the kingdom, the power and the glory.
For ever and ever. AMEN.

GOSPEL READING

BRIEF TALK OR ACTIVITY

CHANT AND/OR PSALM

HOLY COMMUNION

Jesus gathered with his friends in an upper room, knowing that he would soon be going to his death. He wanted to make his farewell to them, and in doing so, he gave us a way of connecting with him and with all Christians through the ages, for all time.

Now we come to share in this blessed sacrament, in which we are spiritually united with our Lord and Saviour, with our Lover and Friend. As we eat this bread and drink this wine, we are once again brought close to God and strengthened for the future.

The Lord is here.	**God's spirit is with us.**
Lift up your hearts.	**We lift them to the Lord.**
Let us give thanks to the Lord our God.	**It is right to offer thanks and praise.**

The night before he died, our Lord Jesus Christ took bread;
when he had given thanks to you, O God, he broke it,
gave it to his disciples, and said:
'Take, eat, this is my body which is given for you;
do this to remember me.'

After supper, he took the cup;
when he had given you thanks, he gave it to them, and said:
'Drink this, all of you, for this is my blood of the new covenant,
which is shed for you, and for many, for the forgiveness of sins;
do this as often as you drink it, to remember me.' (NZPB, p. 733, slightly adapted)

The sacrament will be brought to you where you are sitting.

PRAYER AFTER COMMUNION
Loving and generous God, we are full of thanksgiving
for this gift of grace made possible by the death and resurrection
of your Son, Jesus Christ.

Help us to share the good news of what you are doing in our lives each day.

Help us to be kind to each other, to pray for those whom your Spirit brings to mind,
and to remember that you are only ever a prayer away.

May we go from this place blessed so we may be a blessing to others.
In Christ's name we pray.
AMEN.

CLOSING MUSIC

SENDING OUT WITH A BLESSING

ADVENT: THE SEASON OF WAITING

TALK

Many of us have enjoyed the popular TV series *Waiting for God* set in an aged-care village. The comic approach of the programme hides the reality that people in residential care can simply be thought of as waiting for death to come, hence they don't need a lot of attention or resourcing now!

Instead, let's encourage those of us in our last years to live our life purposefully, doing the work that comes with the final chapters of one's life – passing on items once held dear, putting things right through reconciliation or forgiveness, getting one's affairs in order, even planning one's funeral. In other words, actively engaging with life *now*, rather than opting out of life prematurely because death is inevitable. Waiting then becomes a period not of passivity but of preparation.

And so we come to the season of Advent, the start of the Church's year, a period of reflective waiting and preparation for the coming of Jesus, Emmanuel, God with us. We spend time in these weeks before Christmas preparing as best we can for the birth of Jesus, not simply in a stable, but in our hearts and minds in a new way. For once again Jesus brings with him the fragrance of heaven, the light of Love, glimpses of hope.

The season of Advent invites us then to do some 'spiritual preparation': we invite God to be with us as we prepare for the new life we shall come to know beyond the valley of the shadow of death, when we are at last with God. And we invite God into our habits now, our current struggles with people, our own weaknesses, our secrets, our hopes and fears, our pain and our pleasure. We ask for God's forgiveness and give thanks for who we are in Christ – a beloved son or daughter of God, no matter what.

ACTIVITY

Ask those present what sort of things they have waited for or seen others wait for in their lifetime. Give a couple of examples: an email or letter, a new baby, medical test results, bureaucratic red tape to be sorted out, keeping vigil with a loved one at a deathbed. On a whiteboard or large piece of paper, write their answers and then talk about what it was like waiting – this may elicit a range of feelings, from 'excited', to 'anxious', to 'desperate' to 'confused' or 'joyful anticipation'. Ask questions such as:

'What helped you to manage the waiting time?'
'Who was there for you, with you, in this time of uncertainty?'
'Where might God have been as you waited?'
'Where is God now?'

If it doesn't emerge from the group, introduce the concept of God being with them through the Spirit of Jesus, whenever they have to wait, and in anything they are waiting for. Ask the question, 'How might you recognize God's companionship?'

Brainstorm answers, for example in the 'still, small voice' which comes to their mind in times of quiet receptivity to God, in the helpful unfolding of circumstances, in the timely phone call or visit from someone who cares, through scripture or song lyric, in a bird nesting and caring for its young, in the rhythm of dawn and sunset.

OPENING HYMN
'O come, O come Emmanuel'.

CHANT
'Wait for the Lord', Taizé, *Songs of Taizé, Vol. 2 My Soul is at Rest*, Kingsway, KMCD841, 1995, track 4.

CLOSING HYMN
'Come thou long expected Jesus'.

GOSPEL READING
John 5.2–9 – the healing of the waiting man at the Pools of Bethesda.

PSALM
Psalm 40.1–2 – 'I waited patiently for the Lord; he inclined to me and heard my cry ...'

VISUAL/TANGIBLE AIDS
Some seedlings almost ready to flower/fruit.
A piece of unfinished knitting which visually impaired can feel.
An empty letterbox.

CHRISTMAS: GOD WITH US

TALK

Some people think of God as being like a watchmaker who made the intricate mechanism we know as the earth, its humanity and living creatures, and then withdrew – a 'hands-off' kind of God who doesn't get embroiled in the daily dust of life but keeps a distant 'watch', unmoved by pain or disasters, untouched by joy.

At Christmas time we are brought face to face with a very different image of God – we are introduced to a God who risks becoming flesh, and, even before his birth, is under threat from forces bent on destroying his goodness. This God is Emmanuel, God with us; his name is Jesus, 'one of us, yet from the heart of God' (NZPB, p. 467).

Gifted to us through the womb of Mary, raised by human parents, feeling what we feel, knowing the rough and tumble of family life, experiencing the oppressive rule of Rome, this Jesus understands what it is like to be human, not in a theoretical way or as a distant observer, but as an *insider* who knows from personal exposure to temptation, grief, pain, frustration, betrayal and suffering, what human beings face. Jesus knows too our capacity for compassion, for creativity, for laughter and music-making, for warmth and friendship, for joy. This Jesus enabled God to enter human life, to live it and redeem it from within, by freeing the Spirit of God to inhabit every willing human heart.

Two thousand years ago, some people had the privilege of seeing and walking with God in human form, with Jesus the Christ. Now we are invited to recognize Jesus in each other, through the presence of his Spirit engaging with our own spirit to help us connect deeply with others and express the fullness of life which is God's hope for us from our conception.

ACTIVITY I

Find a large picture of the nativity (A3 or even A2) and have enough small copies (A4 or A5) to give to each person to take away. For the benefit of any who are visually impaired, describe the nativity scene in detail, emphasizing the key familiar features: poor surroundings; the trinity of Mary, Jesus and Joseph – the love between and within each one; the visiting shepherds; the travellers from a distant land bringing gifts fit for a king but pointing to the grief ahead.

Encourage those present to imagine the scene as well as they can and allow a minute for them to settle. Then give them an invitation to '*put yourself in the picture and ponder what it's like to be there*'.

Emphasize that they don't have to strive to make something appear in their mind, but to be open to the possibility that God might choose to communicate with them through their imagination now or at a future time. Allow enough time for this to unfold and, if numbers are small and you know them well, see if anyone will share with you what happened or didn't happen. Encourage them to return to the imagined scene any time they want as Christmas approaches.

ACTIVITY 2

Choose a children's Christmas story book that is visually appealing and carries a new perspective of the age-old story. This may come from a different cultural perspective, e.g. *A Kiwi Christmas* by Joy Cowley (Pleroma: Otane, Hawkes Bay, NZ, 2013). If you have time and access to a data projector at your service venue, scan the pictures and insert into a PowerPoint document so you can read the text and show the pictures to your residents at the same time. Finish the story by making it relevant to the twenty-first century and where you are. For example, in *A Kiwi Christmas*, a central theme is 'light' – the angel Gabriel appears as a fantail bathed in light, the moment of incarnation occurs when Mary feels that God's light has come within, and finds 'a home in her heart'. We can ask those present, 'Where do you find light in your life today?'

If you cannot find a suitable story, then discuss where such a birth might take place in this day and age and who might be the first ones to visit the infant Christ – see if they can imagine what it might have been like for these new parents, starting family life for example in a cellar in a dodgy pub, or sheltering in a cave on the moors, visited by travellers, or the President of the United States!

OPENING SONG

'Lord Jesus Christ, you have come to us'; favourite carols.

CHANT

'Christus lux mundi' – Taizé.

GOSPEL READING

Luke 2.1–20.

PSALM

Psalm 23.1–4.

VISUAL AIDS

As listed for each activity.

LENT: PENITENCE

TALK

(Place this talk BEFORE the Confession and Absolution because of its penitential focus; amend text start to suit yourself)

I can remember my grandmother doing the washing – and many of you may have done what she did: washing the family laundry in an old copper, using a blue-bag for whiteness and then, working by hand, pushing the clothes through the wringer into rinsing water and then through the wringer again. It was a lot of hard work, but the results were worth the effort! *(Invite feedback to see if others have had that experience.)* How times have changed – now we use powder whiteners and spray-on stain removers before we put our clothes into an automatic washing machine, add an appropriate detergent, and push a few buttons.

If only we could as easily wash away old hurts and guilt, old stains on our character, the dullness and fading colours which can be part of life as we age. If only we could rinse and wring out the failures and sins of our past and see them become whiter than snow.

The good news that Jesus brings is that he can do this for us if we will allow him. Just as the laundry workers in your care home take responsibility for making sure your clothes are washed and dried and ironed and returned to you, so Jesus is prepared to receive your 'dirty linen' and, with your co-operation, bring you forgiveness for all the ways you have fallen short: things like holding grudges, deliberately putting others down, gossiping, judging others. Jesus longs to heal and restore you to well-being of mind and spirit, so you may know the deep inner peace which God can give you.

Isaiah 1.18 reads, 'Though your sins are like scarlet, they shall be like snow.' So – if there is anything you regret, any sin unforgiven, any burden that you carry, in a few moments of silence bring these before God, trusting God's forgiveness and the promise of a fresh start, a clean heart.

ACTIVITY

(If you choose this option, make sure you have the time to work with anyone who needs one-to-one conversation after the service, or at least arrange a follow-up visit. Place the whiteboard where everyone can see it – leave it blank for now.)

As we go through life we all do things we wish we hadn't done, or we leave undone some things we wish we had done. Some of these acts or omissions will have been minor, known only to us, others will have affected other people, changing how we relate to them and what we think of ourselves.

One of the amazing gifts of God is the gift of forgiveness, available to any of us if we seek it.

(Write on the whiteboard some generic sins, e.g. stole from my employer; told a lie; cut ties with my daughter; treated my wife/husband/partner badly; let a friend down, etc. – choose things that are realistic for the group you're with.)

The first step is to face up to what you have done, 'confess it' – that is, tell God the truth about it, no matter how embarrassed or ashamed you might feel. If you are not able to do this in the context of this service today, then there is another, more private way to seek God's forgiveness:

- Imagine having your own little whiteboard in your room: when you are by yourself and have asked God to help you, imagine writing on the whiteboard those things which burden you.
- Talk to God about each one, express your remorse and ask for God's forgiveness.*
- Then, when you are ready, imagine wiping each act or omission from the board, saying, 'God forgives me, may I forgive myself.'

(*Then, as you are talking about the 'wiping off of each act or omission', begin to wipe off each 'sin' with the dry cloth – slowly and deliberately – and when they are all wiped off, announce that God has forgiven these sins for all time.)

If you look closely at this whiteboard now, you will see that there is *no trace* of what has been erased. God 'doesn't keep score of the sins of others' (*The Message*, 1 Corinthians 13). God's forgiveness is complete, freeing you to live in peace, reconciled to yourself and others. God's invitation is for us all to 'take hold of this forgiveness and live our lives in the Spirit of Jesus' (NZPB, p. 460). In this time of Lenten preparation may God walk with you and work with you to free you from any burdens of guilt or self-condemnation. So, when Easter comes, you may, with Christ, know the truth of resurrection life.

MUSIC
'Psalm 32 Forgiven' (Sons of Korah, *Redemption Songs*, Wordsong: Australia, 2000, track 6 or 8).
'Just as I am, without one plea …'.

GOSPEL READING
Matthew 9.2–8: Jesus heals a paralytic.

PSALM
Psalm 51.1–2, 6–7, 10–12, 15–17.

VISUAL AIDS
Washing powder/stain remover/a picture of old-fashioned copper and wringer.
Large (A2 or A1) whiteboard, markers and eraser cloth.

WEDNESDAY OF HOLY WEEK: EUCHARIST

WELCOME

OPENING COLLECT
Jesus the anointed,
teach us to honour those who need our help,
and we shall give without condescension,
and receive with humility. AMEN. (NZPB, p. 584)

HYMN
'My song is love unknown'.

CONFESSION

Lord, have mercy.	Kyrie eleison.
Christ, have mercy.	*Christe eleison.*
Lord, have mercy.	Kyrie eleison.

Confident of the breadth of God's forgiveness and the depth of God's love, we bring to God our regrets and failures, our weakness and our wilfulness.

Silence.

Know that God hears and forgives.
Be at peace.

INTERCESSION
We bring to God all those for whom our hearts ache, all those who are unwell in body, mind or spirit.

Silence.

We bring to God our own needs for this day,
and the needs of those around us.

Lord, we know that you hear us.
We know that you hear us always.

THE LORD'S PRAYER
Our Father, which art in heaven,
hallowed be thy name,
thy kingdom come; thy will be done
on earth as it is in heaven.
Give us this day our daily bread
and forgive us our trespasses,
as we forgive those who trespass against us.
And lead us not into temptation,
but deliver us from evil.
For thine is the kingdom, the power and the glory.
For ever and ever. AMEN.

'Anointing of Jesus' from Augustine's 'La Cité de Dieu',
c. 1475–80, illustration attributed to Le Maitre François.

GOSPEL READING
Matthew 26.1–13.

When Jesus had finished saying all these things, he said to his disciples, 'As you know, the Passover is two days away – and the Son of Man will be handed over to be crucified.' Then the chief priests and the elders of the people assembled in the palace of the high priest, whose name was Caiaphas, and they plotted to arrest Jesus in some sly way and kill him. 'But not during the Feast,' they said, 'or there may be a riot among the people.'

While Jesus was in Bethany in the home of a man known as Simon the Leper, a woman came to him with an alabaster jar of very expensive perfume, which she poured on his head as he was reclining at the table.

When the disciples saw this, they were indignant. 'Why this waste?' they asked. 'This perfume could have been sold at a high price and the money given to the poor.' Aware of this, Jesus said to them, 'Why are you bothering this woman? She has done a beautiful thing to me. The poor you will always have with you, but you will not always have me. When she poured this perfume on my body, she did it to prepare me for burial. I tell you the truth, wherever this gospel is preached throughout the world, what she has done will also be told, in memory of her.'

THE GREAT THANKSGIVING
(Adapted from New Zealand Prayer Book, pp. 420–3)

The Lord is here.	**God's Spirit is with us.**
Lift up your hearts.	**We lift them to the Lord.**
Let us give thanks to God.	**It is right to offer thanks and praise.**

On the night before Jesus died, he took bread. When he had given you thanks, holy Father, he broke it, gave it to his disciples and said: 'Take, eat, this is my body which is given for you; do this to remember me.'

After supper he took the cup; when he had given you thanks, he gave it to them and said: 'Drink this, all of you, for this is my blood of the new covenant which is shed for you and for many for the forgiveness of sins; do this as often as you drink it, to remember me.'

Send your Holy Spirit, that these gifts of bread and wine which we receive may be to us the body and blood of Christ, and that we, filled with the Spirit's grace and power, may be renewed for the service of your kingdom.

We break this bread to share in the body of Christ.
We who are many are one body, for we all share the one bread.

* * *

Lamb of God, you take away the sin of the world, have mercy on us.
Lamb of God, you take away the sin of the world, have mercy on us.
Lamb of God, you take away the sin of the world, grant us your peace.

The Communion will be brought to you where you are sitting.

Jesus, receive our love and worship.
Show us how to give you what we have,
for nothing is too big or small for us to offer,
or for you to use. AMEN. (NZPB, p. 584)

CLOSING HYMN
'When I survey the wondrous cross'

BLESSING
May you find in the cross a sure ground for faith, a firm support for hope, and the
assurance of sins forgiven. And the blessing of God Almighty, Father, Son and Holy
Spirit, be with you and those whom you love, now and always. AMEN.
(NZPB, p. 536)

*If you wish, the Chaplain/Minister will anoint each of you on the forehead as you
leave this service.*

Small mercies
(Matthew 26.1–13)

It might have embarrassed another man,
this public demonstration of devotion,
this flagrant waste of resources
but
he looked through and beyond the gesture,
glimpsing the grace in the tenderness
offered to ease
the terrifying truth of what lay ahead.

He ignored the criticism flying around his head,
the mutterings and the misunderstandings.
With a deep surprising joy,
he embraced her gift of care,
love lavished on one who was about to die.

He carried the fragrance with him
all the way to the cross,
like a love song singing in his soul.

EASTER: RESURRECTION

TALK/ACTIVITY

'Flowering the cross' is not an original idea – I first encountered it at St Mary's New Plymouth, New Zealand, and have adapted the activity slightly for use in a care-home context where it has been received well over the years. It is an activity done *after* the Gospel reading and short talk.

Here is what you will need:

- an altar set up with five small tea-light candles, chalice and paten, etc.
- a cross-shaped holder filled with dampened 'oasis', covered with netting to keep the flowers in place (approx. dimensions 30″ high × 18–20″ across)
- 30–40 individual flowers with stems strong enough to be pushed into the 'oasis' e.g. chrysanthemums, leucodendrons, camellias, rosemary, roses (de-thorned), small hydrangeas, etc.
- a large flat basket to hold the flowers; clippers for trimming stems
- a trolley with a towel on which the cross can be laid. Push this trolley around between the rows of seats so everyone can put a flower into the cross – you may need to assist some with visual impairment or arthritic hands, but most people will want to manage themselves. Play music while this is happening and move without haste.

(Before reading this Gospel you may want to summarize John 20.1–10 to set the scene for those listening.)

GOSPEL READING

John 20.11–18: Mary Magdalene goes to the tomb.

TALK TEXT

Imagine this Gospel scene as well as you can:

- the early morning mist as darkness begins to lift
- the grieving woman determined to find out what has happened to the body of her dear friend
- the unexpected vision of angels who ask Mary why she is weeping

- the confusion as a stranger whom she thinks is the gardener asks the very same question
- the shock, surprise, delight and joy as Jesus calls her by name – Mary.

Just think of what it must have been like to find her dear one alive, not shrouded in a tomb as she had expected; take a moment to allow yourself to feel a little of what Mary felt at that moment of recognition.

Jesus called Mary by name, *and calls each one of us by name today.*
But sometimes we are too preoccupied or sad or tired or in pain to hear him.
Open your heart to him and *listen* as he calls your own name – tenderly, lovingly.
Listen for his call now in a few moments of stillness … *(if possible allow a full two minutes for people to settle and listen and then gently invite them to be present in this room at this time once more).*

Do not worry about what you did or did not hear. If you are open to God, Jesus' voice will come, perhaps not how you expect it to, but it will come when you listen deeply, with your heart full of hope and your mind open to mystery. Jesus' voice will come to remind you that:

- *Love* is stronger than death so you need not fear the future.
- Jesus brings us *freedom* so we may live true to the image of God in which we are made, so we may be fully ourselves and be a gift to those around us.
- Even in old age we can continue to grow more like Christ because his Spirit continues to increase in us love, joy, peace, patience, kindness, goodness, gentleness, faithfulness and self-control (Galatians 5.22).

OPENING HYMN
'Jesus Christ is risen today' (*The Hymns Album*, Huddersfield Choral Society, 2006, track 4).

MUSIC
Instrumental Easter hymns or other reflective music.

CLOSING HYMN
'This joyful Eastertide' (*The Hymns Album*, details above, track 18).

ACTIVITY RESOURCES
As listed at the beginning of this page.

PENTECOST: THE GIFT OF THE SPIRIT

(Note there are two readings: Acts 1.1–5; 2.1–4 and John 14.15–29. Read these as part of the Talk or Activity.)

TALK
(Before you do this talk, check out what fire safety measures there are in the room you take the service in, and amend the list accordingly if some are located elsewhere.)

In a care home there are lots of safety features to protect you, especially from fire. Looking around this room we can see smoke detectors and a sprinkler system, a red fire alarm box; not far way is a hose reel and special doors designed to keep smoke and fire from spreading. From time to time you may have practice fire drills and the staff are expected to know what to do to ensure your safety.

Some of you may have 'fire' stories to share ... *(allow some time for this if they or one of your team wants to talk).*

So in our culture, at this particular time in history, fire is seen mainly as something to be careful with, to *contain* and *control* lest it get out of hand and cause loss of life or damage to property.

(Read the Acts passages.)

In the Acts passages we've just heard, there was a totally different response to the coming of 'tongues of fire' – this fire was welcomed and brought joy, not fear; this fire brought awe, not panic; this fire was a visible sign of the Holy Spirit descending on each of the people gathered there. As they listened to the good news of God's love for everyone, the Spirit of Jesus came upon them, just as he had promised a few days earlier.

This Spirit cannot be contained or controlled but spills out into the world, inspiring people everywhere, helping us to pray, to be vessels of grace, to be co-creators with God, to use our time and resources wisely, to build up the community here in this place, so we may reveal God's glory through the sparkle that remains in our eyes – no matter what age we are.

(Read the John 14.15–29 passage about the coming of the Paraclete.)

This Spirit is within you, to encourage, to guide and comfort, to bring to mind familiar words of scripture, to prompt you to act for someone else's good as well as for your own. This Spirit is the 'still, small voice' of God the Father coming to you in the quietness of your hearts as you pray. It is the voice of lover to beloved, your God to you. Listen and know you are deeply loved by God, now and for ever.

*(For this activity, begin by reading the John 14.15–29 passage.
Give everyone a large match – but no matchboxes!)*

Have a close look at what you are holding – something that has the potential to make fire but cannot do it alone. What else is needed before a flame will appear? Something to strike the match against – something that is strong and will not itself be destroyed in the process. This symbolizes the person and work of the Holy Spirit: we cannot grow in grace by ourselves, we need the Paraclete, the strong Helper, the Spirit of Jesus sent to be alongside our spirit, always present to help and guide us.

(Now read the Acts passages: Acts 1.1–5; 2.1–4.)

The apostles were empowered to go out and proclaim the gospel. Instead of the frightened few after the crucifixion, they became courageous, vocal, wise and determined – all through the power of the Holy Spirit. With the Holy Spirit's help we too can shine for God, we can burn away old habits and hurts, we can light the way to Jesus for others, we can deal with our health issues, we can even face our dying, trusting that God will be there with us all the way to rest and heaven.

(At the end of the talk or activity give each person a 'Holy Spirit flame' – see below – to hang on their walker, or beside their bed or to use as a bookmark.)

MUSIC
'Come, Holy Ghost, our souls inspire.'
'Veni sancte spiritus' (*Chants*, Margaret Rizza, Kevin Mayhew: Suffolk, 2002, track 3).
'This little light of mine' (Harry Dixon Loes, c. 1920 – a children's gospel song).

READINGS
Acts 1.1–5; 2.1–4 and John 14.15–29.

MATERIALS
For each person, make a flame-shaped bookmark out of light cardboard, with a hole in the top and a loop of ribbon tied through it. Print on each bookmark the text of John 14.26–27 in big, bold type.

ORDINARY TIME: BUILDING GRATITUDE

TALK

There's a Joni Mitchell song, 'Big Yellow Taxi', that goes like this *(sing it if you like!)*:

'Don't it always seem to go.
That you don't know what you've got till it's gone.
They paved paradise.
And put up a parking lot.'

We've seen a lot of change in our lives – some of it good and some of it not so good. Sometimes we don't realize the importance of *everyday* things like power and water until a storm system or an earthquake shatters our complacency and brings us to our knees *(use local relevant examples instead)*. We don't take time to appreciate key relationships – maybe we've never told those closest to us that we love them – and now some are unwell, some are overseas, perhaps some are estranged: how sad. Perhaps we haven't appreciated our health; maybe we've not realized how amazing our bodies are until muscles refuse to work, backs don't bend, lungs are struggling and our heart's getting tired of pumping, day after day, year after year. It's really easy to take the everyday things around us for granted. It's easy to take our own neighbourhood, our bodies, families and friendships for granted. It's easy to take God for granted too. God's there in the background and some day we might spend more time getting to know God through reading scripture, appreciating creation, reflecting, praying … maybe tomorrow … or the next day …

An antidote to undervaluing the everyday blessing around us, is to cultivate a habit of *thanksgiving*. This simply means pausing at the start of the day to thank God for life, breath, food, shelter, anything specific for which we are grateful, and then doing the same at the end of the day as part of an evening practice of reflection, giving thanks for the grace we've experienced during the past 12 hours. This might include everyday things like a neighbour visiting for a chat, a walk to the local shops, hearing the children coming home from school, smelling flowers brought by a friend.

Thanksgiving helps put us in right relationship with God; it connects us with God and helps us draw on God's strength. Jesus knew this. When he paused to thank his Father before raising Lazarus from the dead, he was acknowledging the source of the power soon to be revealed, and showing those present the virtues of trust, humility and gratitude. Giving thanks brings a blessing on us and blesses God too.

ACTIVITY

One of the most ordinary activities we get involved in is eating a meal – many of us eat with other residents here; some of us find that hard because we have been used to having our meals in private.

(Introduce the activity by saying:)

How many different people contribute to our mealtimes (e.g. baker, farmer, driver, food pack designer, etc.). Many, many people for whom we can give thanks – they have all used their God-given gifts to bring us food.

As I lay out this table setting for two, think about who you'd like to ask for a meal …

(Prime your team so one or more of them can give their opinion if the group is slow to respond. Then invite them to imagine Jesus coming to sit with them for a meal … what might they talk about?)

How might you feel? What question/s would you like to ask? etc.

(This might lead to the question of saying 'Grace' before the main meal of the day. Check if there's a care-home policy regarding this practice. Whatever their policy, individuals would still be free to say a Grace of their own to themselves before meals if they wanted to and can remember! Give them a card with a Grace in large print for them to use if they wish.)

MUSIC
'For health and strength and daily food, we give thee thanks, O Lord' (traditional). 'Give thanks with a grateful heart' – choose a YouTube clip with text, e.g. http://www.youtube.com/watch?v=Bk_7wUR2Wdg (accessed 2.2.14).

READINGS
John 11.38–44; Ephesians 5.19–20.

MATERIALS
A meal setting for two (plates, cutlery, glasses, napkins, salt and pepper, etc.); copies of an A6 card with this simple Grace in large print for older people to use:

Gracious God, you are welcome at this table with us.
All we have comes from your generous heart and we are thankful.
May this food nourish our bodies.
May your Spirit nourish our souls. AMEN.

HOLY COMMUNION: A CONTEMPLATIVE CELEBRATION

We gather while reflective instrumental music is playing.
We allow ourselves to slow down and settle as we prepare for the service.

Leader: The candle is lit as a reminder of the presence among us of Christ, our Light.
We sing: Be still and know that I am God (×3).

We allow the concerns of our minds to be held in the love of God.

CONFESSION

Leader: We take a piece of sandpaper from the basket and take time to remember our own 'roughness', our hardness of heart, and anything we have done to spoil our relationship with God, with others and with ourselves. We pray that our 'rough edges' might be smoothed, that we might be shaped into the people God knows we can be: our truest, kindest selves.

After a minute of silence, we place the sandpaper in the basket that is brought around to us, and we are given a small dab of moisturizing cream ...

Leader: As you rub this delicate cream into your hands,
may you be reminded of God's gentle, tender action in your lives.
Receive God's healing, forgiving love, softening your hearts
and bringing you peace.

PSALM

1   God is our refuge and strength, a very present help in trouble.
2   **Therefore we will not fear, though the earth should change,**
though the mountains shake in the heart of the sea;
3   though its waters roar and foam,
though the mountains tremble with its tumult ...
4   **There is a river whose streams make glad the city of God,**
the holy habitation of the Most High.
5   God is in the midst of the city; it shall not be moved;
God will help it when the morning dawns ...

10 'Be still, and know that I am God!
    I am exalted among the nations.
    I am exalted in the earth.'
11 The Lord of hosts is with us; the God of Jacob is our refuge.
    (Psalm 46, selected verses)

We sing together: **Be still and know that I am God (×3).
I am the Lord that healeth thee (×3).**

THE GOSPEL *is read, and then we spend 5–10 minutes in silent reflection.*

Leader:	We place before God the prayers of our hearts
(lifts up a Bible)	for men and women of faith and goodwill wherever they may be;
(lifts up an atlas)	for God's justice and peace to flow through the world;
(a picture)	for those who share this home with us;
	for those whom we love *(a sprig of rosemary is given to each person)*;
	for ourselves in our ageing.

Leader: We gather our prayers in the prayer which Jesus taught us:
**Our Father, which art in heaven,
hallowed be thy name,
thy kingdom come; thy will be done
on earth as it is in heaven.
Give us this day our daily bread
and forgive us our trespasses,
as we forgive those who trespass against us.
And lead us not into temptation,
but deliver us from evil.
For thine is the kingdom, the power and the glory.
For ever and ever. AMEN.**

We share Christ's peace as we greet our neighbour with a smile.

EUCHARIST
This celebration is done in silence with the focus on the actions following the order given.

Jesus took the bread and wine.
Jesus gave thanks.
Jesus broke the bread.
Jesus offered the cup.

(The sacrament is taken to each person where they are sitting.)

A short time of silence is kept as we give thanks to God for this gift of the body and blood of Christ.

We sing together: Be still and know that I am God (×3).
I am the Lord that healeth thee (×3).
In thee, O God, I put my trust (×3).

We link hands and say together:

The grace of our Lord Jesus Christ, and the Love of God,
and the Fellowship of the Holy Spirit, be with us all,
now and always. AMEN.

Short services of the Word

The purpose of a service of the Word is to honour God, to build community, to strengthen and to comfort, and to enable those present to *participate* in worship as far as they are able. In these non-Eucharistic services we have the chance to order the liturgy according to our context and bring to the foreground those scriptures and music which illuminate a particular theme. Each service will be made up of some or all of the following elements, adapted to suit your context.

Gathering

The aim is to create a space into which people may come and feel safe, held in love, and reminded of the core of the Christian hope – the life and death and resurrection of Jesus, and the steadfast love of the Lord which never fails. Include in the 'gathering' a warm welcome, a focus verse of scripture and perhaps a brief introduction to the theme of the day.

Music

To sing and to listen to – familiar hymns always have a place but you may want to consider:

- contemporary worship songs
- a specially chosen popular song with lyrics which speak to the older person's situation
- Taizé chants (with a translation if needed) provide a way of introducing new music with few words and repetition of a simple melody – a helpful combination for older people
- a variation of something familiar, e.g. 'Nunc dimittis' from Rachmaninoff's *Vespers*
- YouTube videos (with lyrics)
- singing something yourself or with your team just for them as a gift – something beautiful as part of their worship of God.

Prayers

In this format people are offered simple personal prayers using 'I' language – addressing God directly with respect and honesty. Also included are some gems from the Church's tradition. Often it is appropriate to include some form of corporate confession, followed by an assurance of God's forgiving love and mercy.

Readings

Scripture – Gospel or a Psalm with responses, poetry or a topical passage from an autobiography, novel or spiritual writing which links with the theme.

Silence and reflection

Elderly minds appreciate an unhurried opportunity to mull things over. Allow between two and five minutes.

Short talk and/or activity

Place this wherever it fits most appropriately – it doesn't always have to be in the same place. Two or three ideas are given for each theme so you can use the same service several times with a different focus.

Thanksgiving

Including a prayer of thanksgiving builds an 'attitude of gratitude' which can be a boost to those who are wondering where God might be in their everyday lives. Naming the ways in which people have been blessed by simple things such as the sunshine, a good meal, a friend's visit, the smile from a table-mate, the touch of a child, can help people build their capacity to see God at work in the 'ordinary' comings and goings of the day.

Encouragement

Many of us lack encouragement in our lives. For the elderly this drought can be devastating as they experience increasing diminishment of function and future. Honouring their courage, determination, sense of humour and their extraordinary lives strengthens their spirit and soul. Choose your own words of encouragement relevant to the people you are with or a verse or two from scripture or something emerging from the liturgy, talk or activity section.

Blessing

Along with a traditional Triune blessing in the name of Father, Son and Holy Spirit, or Creator, Redeemer and Giver of Life, we can ask God to bless their bodies in their weakness, their minds, even if memory is muddled, and their spirits that they may go from strength to strength in the knowledge of Jesus Christ.

Two types of services of the Word follow: Evening Prayer and Sacred Space.

Evening Prayer

There are already many resources for services such as Evensong (e.g. Book of Common Prayer, New Zealand Prayer Book, Iona Community, Northumbrian Office, as well as a volume in the *Creative Ideas* series from Canterbury Press), but what follows are short services crafted specially for older folk whose nights may be less than restful. Sleep is often interrupted by attending to bodily needs or by the noises of the night, and for many, night-time means time to think, and sometimes time to worry and fret.

These services are designed to address this reality, with prayers reflecting the aged person's perspective, interspersed with familiar older prayers. Psalms are included, both as an opportunity for participation and as an example of honest communication between the psalmist and God. Using the psalms opens up a vocabulary of emotion and lament as well as praise, and may encourage some folk to feel more comfortable in shaping their prayers to God in a more personal way.

Each of the themes considers both the 'light' and 'shadow' of an aspect of night-time so we can acknowledge the 'both/and' of much of human experience and give respect to the struggles that can demand our attention as we become less active.

For each theme, there is a page for you as leader – with details of music used, ideas for short talks or guidelines for an activity. There is also a double-sided larger-font service sheet for participants to keep. Although some elderly who attend your services will be vision-impaired, they may still appreciate having something to take away so family or friends can read it with them later.

The 'light' and 'shadow' of each theme is listed below.

Darkness … and fear.

Dreaming … and nightmares.

Rest … and restlessness.

Comfort … and pain.

Bedtime … and isolation.

Lullabies … and punitive silence.

Stories … and absence of caring.

Leader's Resource Sheet: Darkness

MUSIC
'Within our darkest night' (Taizé), *O Lord Hear My Prayer* (Kingsway, KMCD736, track 5) or 'Veni, lumen cordium' (Come, light of (our) hearts): Margaret Rizza, *Chants1* (Kevin Mayhew, 1490102, track 10, vocal version) or Rizza's *Icons* (Kevin Mayhew, 490109, track 4, instrumental version); 'You'll Never Walk Alone', Katherine Jenkins, *Second Nature* (Universal: EU, 2004, 986903–3, track 15).

HYMN
'Lead, kindly light' – a familiar hymn; you may want to use a YouTube version from cathedral choirs, individual singers (e.g. Aled Jones), with or without onscreen lyrics or 'Brother, sister, let me serve you' (the Servant Song, available in many versions) which contains the line 'I will hold the Christ-light for you, in the night-time of your fear'.

There are several short talks to choose from with this theme:

1 **Nicodemus coming to Jesus by night**: Nicodemus was a Pharisee, one of a group of scholarly laypeople who, in considering how contemporary issues might be addressed, sought to affirm the *spirit* of the Torah (what Christians know as the first five books of the Old Testament) interpreted by reason, rather than being tightly bound by the *letter* of the Mosaic law, as were the priestly group, the Sadducees. Nicodemus was open to wondering, to questioning, but was also wary of the influence of the conservative Sadducees who had the dominant voice in temple politics, hence his coming to Jesus under the cover of darkness.

   In spite of Nicodemus' years of study and faithful religious practice, he needed Jesus to help him grow in understanding; he needed help to shift his perspective from a very literal view of a physical re-birth to spiritual re-birth through baptismal waters and the coming of the Holy Spirit.

   No matter how long or how short a time we have been followers of Christ, we need his Spirit to help us grow in faith and deal with weakness, suffering, ageing and temptations. Nicodemus had the courage to approach Jesus and to ask questions, to be honest about what he did and didn't understand and to be open to what Jesus had to say.

   Can we be as honest? Can we, in the night-time when it's quiet, speak to Jesus of our questions or doubts, and of our faith no matter how fledgling it might be? Can we let him know our longing for a sense of God's love so that the promise contained in John 3.16 might become our lived reality?

2 Give the *background* to the writing of 'Lead, kindly light', i.e. John Newman's personal circumstances and spiritual distress, *or* the story of the hymn's use in

times of mortal danger, for example bringing comfort to trapped miners in the Welsh mining disaster of 1909 *or* its association with the *Titanic* (sung during the last service taken by the chaplain before the ship fatally struck an iceberg) *or* Queen Victoria's request to have it read as she was dying. An internet search will quickly reveal a range of information to use about these situations.

3 **Fear and anxiety.** Because of our personality, genetic predisposition or experience, some of us are plagued by anxiety. If we are Christians, this anxiety can be accompanied by guilt and questioning, 'Surely if I am a Christian, I shouldn't be anxious or afraid?' The reality is that, even if we are following Christ, we can still have worrying feelings and troubling thoughts. However, we are not left without help; as Christians we know that:

- the sooner we stop pretending all is well when it's not
- the sooner we *name* the fears which are destroying our peace
- the sooner we turn in prayer to our Lord and tell him our truth, then
- the sooner we will know the burden lifted and the fear diminished, allowing that peace which transcends our circumstances to seep gently into our mind and spirit.

Evening Prayer: Darkness

As night-time nears, we remember that Jesus spent hours at night praying to God the Father, listening with all his soul, seeking grace for tomorrow. May we approach night-time knowing that we are not alone; may we have the courage to tell our truth to the God who loves us, hears our needs, and whose Spirit equips us for the day to come.

MUSIC
'Within our darkest night, you kindle a flame that never dies away' (Taizé).

PRAYER
Sometimes, O God, I find the night-times difficult.
Old memories rise – some of them comforting, others not so.
I fret over family, think of old friends departed,
I worry about what is to come.
Help me, dear Jesus: by your Spirit
you were with me when I was young,
you are with me now in this moment,
you will be with me for ever.
In you is my peace. AMEN.

Leader: Where can I go from your spirit?
           Or where can I flee from your presence?
All: If I say, 'Surely the darkness shall cover me,
           and the light around me become night',
           even the darkness is not dark to you;
           the night is as bright as the day,
           for darkness is as light to you. (Psalm 139.7, 11–12)

GOSPEL
The story of Nicodemus who came to Jesus by night. (John 3.1–16)

REFLECTION
If I came to Jesus by night, what would I want to say to him?
What would he say to me at this moment of my life?

HYMN

1 Lead, kindly light, amidst th'encircling gloom,
   lead Thou me on!
   The night is dark, and I am far from home,
   lead Thou me on!
   Keep Thou my feet; I do not ask to see
   the distant scene; one step enough for me.

2 I was not ever thus, nor prayed that Thou
   should'st lead me on;
   I loved to choose and see my path; but now
   lead Thou me on!
   I loved the garish day, and, spite of fears,
   pride ruled my will. Remember not past years!

3 So long Thy power hath blest me, sure it still
   will lead me on.
   O'er moor and fen, o'er crag and torrent, till
   the night is gone,
   and with the morn those angel faces smile,
   which I have loved long since, and lost awhile! (Cardinal J. H. Newman)

THANKSGIVING
As I think back over this day, it's hard to
remember what has happened or who I've seen …
**But I am thankful for this moment, for life,
for breath, for people who are kind and caring.
So I can say with David, the writer of the psalms:
'I give thanks to you, O Lord my God,
with my whole heart,
and I will glorify your name for ever.
For great is your steadfast love towards me:
for you have delivered my soul
from the depths of Sheol.'** (Psalm 86.12–13)

Leader: Words of encouragement.

Together: The Lord's Prayer.

66

CLOSING PRAYER

Lighten our darkness,
we beseech thee, O Lord;
and by thy great mercy
defend us from all perils
and dangers of this night;
for the love of thy only Son,
our Saviour, Jesus Christ. (Book of Common Prayer)

BLESSING

May the light of Christ bathe your being in peace and rest,
this night and all your nights. AMEN.

Leader's Resource Sheet: Dreaming

If you want to know more about dreamwork and its usefulness in our spiritual lives, you may want to obtain a copy of the following comprehensive classic resource: *Dreams and Spiritual Growth: A Christian Approach to Dreamwork: With More Than 35 Dreamwork Techniques*, by Louis M. Savary, Strephon Kaplan-Williams, Paulist Press, 1984.

In terms of dreaming and the elderly, it is recognized that the older we get, the less REM (rapid eye movement) sleep we experience and the less we dream; it is also important to note that medication may significantly affect brain chemistry, sleep and dreaming.

If you encounter anyone who is having recurrent distressing dreams that are like replays of a disturbing event, then it would be wise to alert the care-home clinical manager so that, if the person wishes, some professional help can be arranged. Even decades later, it is possible for elderly survivors of war or other violence to be troubled by dreams which replay events as if they were yesterday. This is a symptom of post-traumatic stress, and with the right help, healing is possible.

MUSIC
'Glory to thee my God this night' (Hymns A&M).
'Sleepsong', Secret Garden, *Earthsongs* (Universal: Norway, 2005, 9870339, track 6. For lyrics see http://www.secretgarden.no/earthsongs_presentation/sg_earthsongs.html (accessed 19.2.14)).

If you wanted to attend to the hard parts of life and the dreams that have *not* been realized – perhaps in Lent when we are faced with the pain of the dream of Jesus apparently failing in Gethsemane and the cross – you may want to consider a contemporary song, e.g. Susan Boyle's rendition of 'I dreamed a dream' (*Les Misérables*). In her story we glimpse a 'resurrection': her ability was recognized, and help has been provided for her to live her life with less stress than her fame initially caused.

READING
Martin Luther King's speech is readily available, e.g. http://www.americanrhetoric.com/speeches/mlkihaveadream.htm (accessed 29.11.13).

1 There is a strong scriptural theme of God meeting, reassuring, guiding and warning people through visions/dreams of the night. To focus this talk, pay close attention to our Gospel and the pivotal dreams protecting the coming Christ-child.

   God is very active here: meeting Joseph while he is wondering how to 'put Mary aside' having found she is pregnant; warning the wise men not to alert Herod to the whereabouts of the new-born king; urging Joseph to take evasive action and leave at once for Egypt with his wife and son.

   There may follow a discussion if anyone present, including you and your team, is able to or wants to talk about their own experience of being helped or warned by a timely dream.

2 If you want to shift the focus to the other meaning of 'dream', i.e. 'hope for the future', then consider the 'I have a dream' speech which Martin Luther King delivered on the steps of the Lincoln Memorial in August 1963, a key moment in the history of the American Civil Rights Movement. King, though flawed like the Old Testament David, was an outstanding example of one person influencing the direction of an entire nation and paying the ultimate price for his inspired rhetoric against racism and his moving vision of a new America. Other examples of dreaming for a better community can be shared.

3 What is your dream for the world of your grandchildren and great-grandchildren? Take the microphone round if you can to elicit responses or, if you have enough helpers, give each resident a piece of cloud-shaped paper and a pen and ask them to write a few words they'd be willing for you to read aloud about their dream for those who will come after them, for example peace, job security, knowing Jesus, an unspoilt natural environment, curing cancer, food for everyone, fewer natural disasters. Gather the 'dreams' and slowly read them aloud; if you have an altar, put them reverently before the cross and pray together for their fulfilment in God's perfect way and in God's perfect time. (At the end of the service, return the papers to the residents if you can or take them home and dispose of them confidentially.)

Evening Prayer: Dreaming

Then afterward I will pour out my spirit on all flesh; your sons and
your daughters shall prophesy, your old men shall dream dreams.
(Joel 2.28)

HYMN
1   Glory to thee, my God, this night,
    for all the blessings of the light:
    keep me, O keep me, King of kings,
    beneath thine own almighty wings.

2   Forgive me, Lord, for thy dear Son,
    the ill that I this day have done;
    that with the world, myself, and thee,
    I, ere I sleep, at peace may be.

3   Teach me to live, that I may dread
    the grave as little as my bed;
    teach me to die, that so I may
    rise glorious at the awful day.

4   O may my soul on thee repose,
    and with sweet sleep mine eyelids close;
    sleep that shall me more vigorous make
    to serve my God when I awake.

PRAYER
Thank you, O God, that you are Lord
of our waking and sleeping,
our day-dreams and our night-dreams.
If we are woken by confusing images,
help us bring our uncertainty or distress to you,
and let your Spirit soothe our soul.
If we see old friends and long-gone family
in our night visions, let us be thankful
for this reminder of those we've loved so well.
Let us remember that our life does not end
at death, but continues in Christ. AMEN.

Leader:	O Lord, you have searched me and known me.

All:	**You know when I sit down and when I rise up;**
	you discern my thoughts from far away.
	You search out my path and my lying down,
	and are acquainted with all my ways.
	Even before a word is on my tongue,
	O Lord, you know it completely. (Psalm 139.1–4)

GOSPEL
Significant dreams surrounding the coming of the Christ-child (Matthew 1.18–25; 2.7–14).

REFLECTION
What night-time dreams or day-dreams have shaped my life?

Dreams help us process the events of the day and are needed for our health, even if we don't always remember them. Sometimes, however, dreams can become frightening. These 'nightmares' can alarm us, but mostly they are simply trying to help us notice something in our emotional lives or relationships which needs attention. If you are troubled by a repetitive or scary dream, talk to someone you trust so you can discover your unique interpretation of what the symbols in the dream might be 'saying' about your current circumstances. God still visits and helps us through our dreams.

HYMN (*continued*)
5 When in the night I sleepless lie,
   my soul with heavenly thoughts supply;
   let no ill dreams disturb my rest,
   no powers of darkness me molest.

6 Praise God, from whom all blessings flow;
   praise him, all creatures here below;
   praise him above, ye heavenly host:
   praise Father, Son, and Holy Ghost.

READING
A portion of 'I have a dream' speech by Martin Luther King.

THANKSGIVING
Lord God, we are thankful for all those whose dreams
have helped shape the world for the better.
Thank you for the people we know
who have worked for their community
and improved the lives of those around them,
sometimes at great personal cost.
Jesus dreamed of bringing into being
his kingdom of justice and peace,
his kingdom of mercy and equality.
Thank you for his dream and the way he uses
ordinary people like us to help bring his dream to life. AMEN.

Leader: Words of encouragement.

THE LORD'S PRAYER

LULLABY
'Sleepsong' (Secret Garden).

Leader: I will both lie down and sleep in peace;
Response: for you alone, O LORD, make me lie down in safety. (Psalm 4.8)

BLESSING
May God be with us in our waking and in our dreaming, now and for ever. AMEN.

Leader's Resource Sheet: Rest

Although care homes are called 'rest' homes in some contexts, this does not mean that residents have ample time to rest and reflect. You (and your team if you have one) may also lead very full lives. So it may be difficult for you – and for the residents – to find and protect quality 'rest' where the body is quiet and the mind is alert enough for long enough to be receptive to the movement of the Spirit, so attention can be given to the inner life. Without this time the important 'work' of adjustment, letting go and resolution cannot take place, so there is an invitation here for you and those you serve to reclaim some 'sabbath' time.

MUSIC

Opening chant, 'Come be with me', Keith Duke, *Sacred Dance* (Kevin Mayhew, Suffolk, 2005, 1490179, track 4).

The closing chant references the saying from St Augustine, '... you have made us for yourself (O God), and our heart is restless until it rests in you' (St Augustine, *Confessions* 1, 1, 1: PL 32, 659–661): 'Restless is the heart', Bernadette Farrell, http://www.youtube.com/watch?v=Ox96BWfIyg4 or on her CD *Restless is the Heart* (OCP, Portland, Oregon, 2000, 10827, track 5).

You may want to slot a more upbeat music video into the service somewhere, e.g.: http://www.youtube.com/watch?v=CSp-3kvKQZs – Psalm 62 song by Aaron Keyes with lyrics, 'Praise Song' (My soul finds rest in God alone) or http://www.youtube.com/watch?v=yNqmpQPp-ns&list=RD3xVbVfdKDz8 – traditional African, 'Ukuthula' (Peace in this world of sin the blood of Jesus brings).

Note the quote from Pascal's *Pensées* (Penguin Classics edition, 2003, p. 148) is Pascal's original base for what many of us have come to know as 'Within our hearts is a God-shaped vacuum'. See http://theconstructivecurmudgeon.blogspot.co.nz/2006/05/incorrect-pascal-quotes.html for the full context (accessed 13.3.14).

TALK

1 Jesus was like a modern celebrity followed everywhere by paparazzi. Wherever he went, news got out and people followed him or met him along the way, desperate for healing, for a sight of the man whose reputation as a worker of miracles and champion of the marginalized preceded him. Those who kept him company, his disciples, experienced the pressure, though they were not the centre of attention, and Jesus knew they needed to rest and gather strength.

　　Jesus offers that same invitation to you and to me, to 'come aside and rest', to be still long enough to care for our bodies, to listen to our thoughts and to the 'still, small voice' of the Holy Spirit who longs to bring insight, healing and peace.

How might we set aside time to 'rest' with Jesus? It's hard when we are in pain, or anxious about ourselves or someone in our family – but that is where we begin. We bring to Jesus, or to God the Father, what is happening *now* – we share it with him as with a close friend who cares for us deeply. We ask the Holy Spirit to help us to notice God in the everyday – in the unhurried, gentle touch of a caregiver, in the scrawled crayon picture from a great-grandchild, in the sound of birdsong or the warmth of sun on skin … in the small mercies of life. *(You may like to have available copies of a little handout on 'Simple Prayer' which you will find in the section on 'Pastoral Practices: Praying'.)*

2 If there has been a recent death at the care village you may want to talk about the Christian hope of life after death. A common prayer and response for the deceased is that they may 'rest in peace **and rise in glory**'. Tom Wright, former Bishop of Durham, writes of the Christian dead as being in 'a state of restful happiness … held firmly within the conscious love of God and the conscious presence of Jesus Christ' while they await a bodily resurrection into a new, incorruptible form (*Surprised by Hope*, SPCK, London, 2007, pp. 183–4; for the discussion about resurrection, see pp. 171–6). Equipped for the purposes of God in the new heaven and the new earth, they will re-present the glory of God, the fullness of eternal life.

3 For a lighter approach, you may want to have large pictures available of resting animals – there are plenty on the internet of cats, dogs, lions, etc. 'lounging' around. These may elicit stories of residents' own pets and furry friends from the past and be a good reminder that God loves all of creation – even when they spend 23 hours out of 24 asleep!

Evening Prayer: Rest

Come to me, all you that are weary and carrying heavy burdens,
and I will give you rest. Take my yoke upon you and learn from me ...
(Matthew 11.28–29a)

Leader: Hear the word of God to you, as you come to worship:
'I will be your God throughout your lifetime
until your hair is white with age.
I made you, and I will care for you.
I will carry you along and save you.'
(Isaiah 46.4, New Living translation)

MUSIC
'Come, be with me ...' (*Sacred Dance*, Kevin Duke).

PRAYER
God my comforter,
when it comes time for bed,
sometimes sleep eludes me.
When I am tossing and turning,
help me to trust you with my life,
help me lean against you
and know I am held safe in your love.
Let my swirling thoughts settle;
fill my mind with the fragrance
of your friendship.
May the Spirit of Jesus teach me to rest.
AMEN.

Leader: For God alone my soul waits in silence:
from him comes my salvation.
All: **He alone is my rock and my salvation,
my fortress; I shall never be shaken ...**

Leader: On God rests my deliverance and my honour;
my mighty rock, my refuge is in God.
All: **Trust in him at all times, O people;
pour out your heart before him;
God is a refuge for us.** (Psalm 62.1–2, 7–8)

GOSPEL
Jesus encourages his disciples to rest. (Mark 6.30–32)

REFLECTION
Our days can be full of routines with little space for resting body, mind and spirit. Imagine going with Jesus in a boat to a quiet part of Lake Galilee.

What do you need? Pour out your heart to Jesus ...

We may live in fortunate circumstances, well cared for and with reasonable health, or we may be struggling with ageing, with deteriorating mobility and faculties, feeling far away from those we love. Whatever our personal circumstances, whatever we, or others, do to help us make the most of the life we have, we may *still feel restless*, as if there is some gaping emptiness, some primal yearning within us. And there is – as Blaise Pascal wrote in *Pensées*: '... this infinite abyss can be filled only with an infinite and immutable object; in other words by God himself'. God alone can resolve our inner restlessness. Only when we recognize there is but one answer to our turmoil and begin to turn towards God, towards Jesus, will our souls begin to open up to the peace of God which passes all understanding.

THANKSGIVING
Creator God,
you formed us to be in relationship with you.

All: **Thank you for reminding us that we are made for you;**
                         that inside each one of us,
                         inside me,
                         there is a special place where my spirit dwells,
                         and in that space, your Spirit meets mine:
                         filling any emptiness with your love,
                         dissolving any tension with your joy,
                         calming any restlessness with your peace,
                         warming, teaching,
                         consoling, enlivening,
                         companioning me – now and for all time. AMEN.

Leader: Let us bless the Lord.
                         Thanks be to God.

Leader: Words of encouragement.

All: The Lord's Prayer.

CLOSING PRAYER
Be present, merciful God,
and protect us through the silent hours of this night,
that we, who are wearied
by the changes and chances of this fleeting world,
may rest upon your eternal changelessness.
Through Jesus Christ our Lord.
AMEN. (NZPB, p. 128, BCP Compline)

MUSIC
'Restless is the heart until it finds its rest in you' (Bernadette Farrell).

Leader's Resource Sheet: Comfort

MUSIC

'You are always there for me', *Earthsongs,* Secret Garden (Universal Music AS, Norway, 2005, 9870339, track 4, vocals Russell Watson). Before playing this song, read the lyrics aloud from http://www.secretgarden.no/earthsongs_presentation/sg_earthsongs.html (accessed 19.2.14).

'Love divine, all loves excelling', Charles Wesley (Hymns A&M).

For a contemporary music video, see, e.g., http://vimeo.com/14375358. Matthew Smith, 'Lord Jesus, comfort me', *Watch the Rising Day* (2010, Detuned Radio Records).

Early in Handel's *Messiah* a tenor sings God's words to Jerusalem: 'Comfort me, comfort O my people.' You may want to use this as an alternative to one of the other pieces.

TALK/ACTIVITY

1   When we are in pain or struggling with health issues, it is all too easy to become very self-focused. How do we become free from the prison of preoccupation with our body's deterioration or pain?

   First, we deal with the thought that 'the pain is not serious enough to talk to God about'. Pain is pain. If it affects our well-being, then God wants to share it with us, so bring that pain or discomfort to God. We can ask God to help us accept available pain relief on a *regular* basis, and to be with us in the pain, so we may begin to transcend the suffering we are experiencing. It can be a slow and difficult transition, but as we open ourselves to God's comfort, we are strengthened inwardly. We may even find ourselves offering comfort to others – giving God the chance to work through us, even in old age.

   (You may already have noticed in ministry that an issue you work through yourself with God's grace and compassion may crop up in pastoral work very soon after! If you want to, share a story – names suitably disguised, of course – to illustrate this movement.)

   There is a kingdom principle here: God blesses us because God is compassionate and, as we are released from inward-facing focus on our own physical or emotional pain, as we are touched by God's grace, we are, in turn, encouraged to be there for others, sharing the compassion we have already received from God. 'Love makes the world go round' and this is how it happens – we share the love God gives us with others.

2 The story of the man spectacularly delivered from forces that were not of God ends with an invitation from Jesus to engage in what we might term today 'friendship evangelism' – a simple sharing of what Jesus had done for him. Rather than getting diverted to discuss the fate of the unsuspecting pigs, use the story to introduce the concept of *testimony* – sharing our story of God's presence and action in our lives.

Invite anyone present to share such a story of their own – this may take time but if someone is able to speak a little about a particular faith experience when they knew they were helped by God in some way, others may well be encouraged, and it helps to demonstrate a way of sharing the Good News – simply speaking about our experience without being 'pushy'.

If no one is able to do this, then you or some of your team could have ready a brief story of God at work in your lives – your call to ministry perhaps, answered prayer or 'God-incidences'.

3 Have a number of items associated with 'comfort', for example a child's dummy or teddy bear, a hot-water bottle, a family photo, a woollen scarf, a quilted bedcover, chocolate, restful music, etc. You may want to tell a story related to one of the items to start the ball rolling and then lead into a discussion of things that bring us comfort, or what we put our trust in.

This may raise the question of superstition – people clutching a rabbit's paw, or a favourite piece of clothing, or a four-leaf clover to give them comfort when facing a testing situation. Some sports-people, for example, follow a particular routine or wear special clothing or jewellery to give them good 'luck'.

Of course we know that our comfort resides not in 'luck' but in our relationship with Jesus, our faith in God, our trust that no matter what comes our way, God does not leave us to face it alone. Have available items which Christians use – not because they have faith in the objects themselves but in what they represent. These objects help them feel connected to God in the midst of everyday life with all its uncertainty, e.g. a Bible, a calendar with scripture verses, sacred music, a rosary or a holding cross (see Pastoral Practices: 'Using a holding cross').

Evening Prayer: Comfort

Blessed be the God and Father of our Lord Jesus Christ, the Father of mercies and the God of all consolation, who consoles us in all our affliction, so that we may be able to console those who are in any affliction with the consolation with which we ourselves are consoled by God.
(2 Corinthians 1.3–4)

MUSIC
'You are always there for me' (*Earthsong*, Secret Garden).

Leader: God is always there for us. Only ever a prayer away.

PRAYER
Comfort used to come through simple things, O God –
as I stroked my comfy cat,
as I held my lover's hand,
as a friend wiped away my tears,
and brought me cake and tea.
But now, O Lord,
I need a different sort of comfort,
something to soothe my elderly soul
which is tired and sometimes sad.
Hear my weary voice.
Touch me today with your gentleness
and hold me to your heart. AMEN.

GOSPEL
A redeemed man shares his story of Jesus' impact on his life (Mark 5.18–20).

REFLECTION
When have you been comforted or helped?
When have you comforted or helped someone else?

Leader: The righteous flourish like the palm tree,
           and grow like a cedar in Lebanon.

All: They are planted in the house of the LORD;
           they flourish in the courts of our God.
           In old age they still produce fruit;
           they are always green and full of sap,
           showing that the LORD is upright;
           he is my rock, and there is no
           unrighteousness in him. (Psalm 92.12–14)

HYMN
Love divine, all loves excelling,
joy of heaven to earth come down,
fix in us thy humble dwelling,
all thy faithful mercies crown.
Jesus, thou art all compassion,
pure, unbounded love thou art;
visit us with thy salvation,
enter every trembling heart.

Come, almighty to deliver,
let us all thy grace receive;
suddenly return, and never,
never more thy temple leave.
Thee we would be always blessing,
serve thee as thy hosts above;
pray, and praise thee, without ceasing,
glory in thy perfect love.

Finish then thy new creation:
pure and spotless let us be;
let us see thy great salvation,
perfectly restored in thee;
changed from glory into glory,
till in heaven we take our place,
till we cast our crowns before thee,
lost in wonder, love and praise. (Charles Wesley)

THANKSGIVING
We are full of gratitude, O God,
for your gifts of comfort,
coming to us in surprising ways:
a child's smile, a gentle voice,
a strong uplifting hand, a wise word,
an understanding glance.
We thank you, O God,
that we can be givers of comfort too.
Help us to bring your kindness to our families and friends,
and to those around us, here where we live.
AMEN.

Leader: Words of encouragement.

Together: The Lord's Prayer.

CLOSING
Watch thou, dear Lord, with those who wake,
or watch, or weep tonight,
and give thine angels charge over those who sleep.
Tend thy sick ones, Lord Christ;
rest thy weary ones; bless thy dying ones;
soothe thy suffering ones; pity thine afflicted ones;
shield thy joyous ones; and all for thy love's sake.
AMEN. (Prayer of St Augustine of Hippo)

BLESSING
The blessing of God who comforts us as Father, Son and Holy Spirit, be with you
and those you love, now and for ever. AMEN.

Leader's Resource Sheet: Bedtime

MUSIC

'Spirit of God', *God Beyond all Names*, Bernadette Farrell, OCP (Portland, Oregon, 1991, CD number 9411, track 2).
'Nocturne', *Songs from a Secret Garden*, Secret Garden (Polygram: Norway, 1995, track 1).

HYMN

'I heard the voice of Jesus say', H. Bonar (Hymns A&M).

POETRY

'Christopher Robin is saying his prayers', A. A. Milne.

TALK/ACTIVITY

1 The Gospel passage lends itself to an imaginative approach, so during the Reflection time, after you have read the whole passage, gently take the people back to the key relational moment – the encounter between Jesus and the man lying on his bed. Allow a good two or three minutes for them to begin to get in touch with the scene. Let them know that they do not have to try to make anything happen – some people form pictures easily in their minds, others get a felt impression without visual detail. The main invitation is to engage with the Jesus/human being encounter in their imagination. Even if 'nothing happens' during the Reflection or service itself, something may well have been started which the Spirit will build on in God's good time. Encourage them to return to this Gospel passage again in their own time and way. (If you are a bit uncertain about how to do this, turn to the section 'Praying with scripture'.)

2 Share with those present either your memories of bedtime routine or what you used to do with your children to help them prepare for bed. You may like to have with you a teddy bear or soft toy, and A. A. Milne poetry to aid memory and conversation.

   Ask those present to share something of their bedtime routines as children (very old memories are sometimes surprisingly accessible). If no one is able to do it, then name the elements listed below and see how many of those present relate to the particular activity and what it felt like:

   • a warm bath
   • a story

- a cuddle and bedtime kiss
- prayers
- light dimmed and curtains drawn
- door left ajar or shut.

It's possible that some present may not have happy memories of bedtime, so it's important to acknowledge that reality and to talk about their routines or lack of cherishing with them if they wish to do so. They can choose a different bedtime routine now, something that will be gentler and calming before sleep.

Although some of these elements will not be the same in a care home, residents can still adapt the above pattern to their own situation, e.g.:

- a hot supper drink
- reading or listening to something that brings peace and comfort
- looking at photos of family or friends
- thinking back over the day with thanksgiving
- intentionally remembering living loved ones in prayer, as well as
- praying for one's own needs.

They should also be able to state their preference in terms of lights on or off, doors open, ajar or shut, curtains open or closed and heating setting.

Evening Prayer: Bedtime

I will both lie down and sleep in peace;
for you alone, O Lᴏʀᴅ, make me lie down in safety.
(Psalm 4.8)

Leader: We have had thousands of bedtimes in our lifetime and we have slept in lots of beds: alone, with others, in times good and bad. Now our bedtime routines are supervised by someone else and we sleep on special mattresses to keep our old bones from aching.
Jesus had nowhere to lay his head as he walked the paths of Galilee, taught the people and healed the sick. *Then* he spent night hours in prayer; *now*, through his Spirit, he companions us – night *and* day.

MUSIC
'Spirit of God, rest on your people, waken your song deep in our hearts' (Bernadette Farrell).

Leader: I lift up my eyes to the hills –
from where will my help come?

All: **My help comes from the Lᴏʀᴅ,**
who has made heaven and earth.
He will not let your foot be moved;
he who keeps you will not slumber.
He who keeps Israel
will neither slumber nor sleep.

Leader: The Lᴏʀᴅ is your keeper;
The Lᴏʀᴅ is your shade at your right hand.
The sun shall not strike you by day,
nor the moon by night.

All: **The Lᴏʀᴅ will keep you from all evil;**
he will keep your life.
The Lᴏʀᴅ will keep your going out
and your coming in
from this time on
and for evermore. (Psalm 121)

GOSPEL
A man takes up his bed and walks. (Luke 5.17–25)

REFLECTION
Put yourself in the picture as if you were the man lying on the bed.
Jesus is beside you, eyes full of compassion, his voice full of hope.

HYMN
I heard the voice of Jesus say,
'Come unto me and rest;
lay down, thou weary one, lay down
thy head upon my breast.'
I came to Jesus as I was,
weary and worn and sad;
I found in him a resting-place,
and he has made me glad.

I heard the voice of Jesus say,
'Behold, I freely give
the living water, thirsty one;
stoop down and drink and live.'
I came to Jesus and I drank
of that life-giving stream;
my thirst was quenched, my soul revived,
and now I live in him.

I heard the voice of Jesus say,
'I am this dark world's Light;
look unto me, thy morn shall rise,
and all the day be bright.'
I looked to Jesus and I found
in him my Star, my Sun;
and in that Light of life I'll walk,
till travelling days are done. (H. Bonar)

Leader: Words of encouragement.

MUSIC
'Nocturne' (Secret Garden).

THE LORD'S PRAYER

THANKSGIVING
We bring to you, O God, hearts full of praise.
We cannot begin to tell
what life would be like without you.
Thank you for your healing presence,
for the way you uphold and enable us
through the Spirit of Jesus.
We give you thanks for this day
and for each other. AMEN.

BLESSING
May God who is your strong support, insightful friend, and quickening energy, meet
you in the darkest night and bring you joy and peace.
And the blessing of God, Father, Son and Holy Spirit, be with you now and always.
AMEN.

Leader's Resource Sheet: Lullabies

MUSIC

You may already have a favourite lullaby to share, but if not then here are some options:

- Charlotte Church CD, *Voice of an Angel* (Sony, 1998, tracks 11 & 12).
- 'Summertime', the lullaby from *Porgy and Bess* (Gershwin).
- The lullaby from the opera *Hansel and Gretel* by Engelbert Humperdinck (nineteenth-century composer), available e.g. on Libera CD, *Visions* (EMI, 2005, track 6), text as follows:

When at night I go to sleep, fourteen angels watch do keep;
Two my head are guarding, two my feet are guiding;
Two are on my right hand, two are on my left hand,
Two who warmly cover, two who o'er me hover,
Two to whom 'tis given, to guide my steps to heaven.

- *A Christmas Lullaby*, Jane Lindner (sheet music available on website, accessed 8.12.13): http://www.sheetmusicplus.com/title/a-christmas-lullaby-sheet-music/ 3864476?ac=1.

TALK/ACTIVITY

1 Conversation around lullabies which the group may remember – the circumstances and the melody. It can be a lovely surprise to hear someone sing when usually they may say very little or seem remote. If there is a composer/competent musician in your team then you may want to write a lullaby and put it to music – perhaps designed for older people, e.g. my lullaby below:

2   Again the Gospel passage lends itself to imaginative reflection – this time the participants are encouraged to put themselves in the place of the shepherds who, with out-of-this-world music echoing in their ears, make the journey to see the infant Jesus. Again, after you have read the Gospel passage, focus on the *relational* element: the meeting between an individual shepherd (each person there with you) and the baby Jesus, giving them time to get a sense of what that meeting might be like, what the baby does, what they do, etc.

   If you have time to invite a few of them to talk about their imaginative reflection – even in just a few words – this helps to reinforce their experience. However, it's also important that there are no 'oughts' or 'shoulds' about this process; the blessing of it is in the opening up of themselves to the grace of God through their imaginative engagement with scripture.

3   If you want to emphasize God's knowledge of us throughout our lives, even before we were born, refer to Jeremiah 1.4–8. This passage gives a clear indication of God's desire for each of us to fulfil the potential which is already part of our earliest existence within the love of God. Each of us is an individual and bears the image of God into the world in a unique way. Although we may not have been gifted with the ability or responsibility of a prophet, nevertheless we all have talents to use for the building up of the kingdom of God.

   As the people in your congregation in the care home are nearing the end of their lives, it is appropriate to emphasize that God looks with compassion on our efforts, rejoices with us when we are fully alive in Christ, and understands and forgives our failures when we bring them to God.

Evening Prayer: Lullabies

And she gave birth to her firstborn son and wrapped him in bands of cloth,
and laid him in a manger, because there was no room for them in the inn.
(Luke 2.7)

Leader: Our focus verse tells us of the new mother Mary, and the dedicated
Joseph watching over their brand-new baby. It wouldn't be a surprise
if Mary sang to their little boy as mums – and dads – have sung to their
infants around the world for millennia. Perhaps your mum or dad did the
same for you – and you for your children and grandchildren – and so the
custom of singing lullabies, psalms or scripture to settle our precious ones
into restful sleep continues.

PRAYER
God, you are the same yesterday, today and for ever;
faithful and loving, kind and forgiving,
you were with us in our earliest life
and remain with us now.
Some of us were much wanted –
lullabies and laughter supported our sleep.
Some of us went to bed hungry or hurt,
with worry our only companion.
As we come to you today, O Jesus,
whatever our early history may be,
help us heal from any pain from our past:
sing us a lullaby that will bring us your peace. AMEN.

HYMN
Away in a manger, no crib for a bed,
the little Lord Jesus laid down his sweet head;
the stars in the bright sky looked down where he lay,
the little Lord Jesus, asleep on the hay.

The cattle are lowing, the Baby awakes,
but little Lord Jesus, no crying he makes;
I love Thee, Lord Jesus! look down from the sky,
and stay by my cradle till morning is nigh.

Be near me, Lord Jesus, I ask Thee to stay
close by me for ever, and love me, I pray;
bless all the dear children in Thy tender care,
and fit us for heaven, to live with Thee there.

GOSPEL
The shepherds, serenaded by angels, visit the Christ-child (Luke 2.8–20).

REFLECTION
Imagine yourself going to visit the Christ-child. What song would you sing for him?

Leader: It was you who formed my inward parts;
          you knit me together in my mother's womb.

All: **I praise you for I am fearfully and wonderfully made.**
          Wonderful are your works;
          that I know very well.
          My frame was not hidden from you,
          when I was being made in secret,
          intricately woven in the depths of the earth.
          Your eyes beheld my unformed substance.
          In your book were written
          all the days that were formed for me,
          when none of them existed. (Psalm 139.13–16)

WORD OF ENCOURAGEMENT
The LORD your God is in your midst, a warrior who gives victory;
he will rejoice over you with gladness, he will renew you in his love;
he will exult over you with loud singing. (Zephaniah 3.17)

THE LORD'S PRAYER

THANKSGIVING
We thank you, O God, for singing and song,
and for love: longed for, and given.
We thank you for your gift of life,
received so many decades ago,
still treasured on good days and even on bad.

Though our hearing may be dulled,
may we remember the songs which have
brought us closer to you and
to our deep fulfilment in Christ,
songs which speak of your steadfast love and care,
in Jesus' name we pray. AMEN.

MUSIC
A lullaby.

BLESSING
May the song your soul longs to sing
break through the worries of your day
into the life that you live.
May the baby born in a stable
so many years ago,
be born again in your heart.
May you and Jesus sing together
this night and all your nights.
And the blessing of God who is Composer, Singer and Song,
fill your heart with joy, now and evermore. AMEN.

Leader's Resource Sheet: Stories

MUSIC
'Here am I, Lord', *Sacred Weave* (Kevin Mayhew, 2003, track 4).
You may like to use a YouTube version of 'Tell me the old, old story', e.g. http://www.youtube.com/watch?v=vXmqCgCEWEo (accessed 10.12.13).
'Commit your life to the Lord – Psalm 37', John Michael Talbot, *Simple Heart* (Troubadour for the Lord, 2000, track 2).

PRAYER
http://www.spck.org.uk/classic-prayers/john-donne/.

TALK/ACTIVITY
1 When you ask the elderly if they have left a written record of their life for their families, many will say that they've just had an ordinary life, nothing 'exciting'. Yet we know from the hospice movement how affirming it can be for palliative care patients to have the chance to have their biography transcribed for their families or community. What a gift – a set of stories that no one else can tell, insights into another way of living, a glimpse of history seen through the eyes of someone who lived through decades of global and local change. Story-telling aids the process of life review, strengthens a person's sense of selfhood and allows them to realize that they have *contributed* to the world in a unique way – in other words, their lives, and they, *matter*.

   You may like to tell a personal story from your own life as a way of getting started; then, if numbers are small and you have a team with you, a small group time for sharing stories could follow – if a topic is needed to begin with, the stories may be about animals or siblings, where they grew up or went to school, memories of a war, world events, etc. It may take a while to 'catch on', but there is value in persisting with this and reinforcing the value of individual lives.

2 Although familiar, this Gospel story can still 'pack a punch'. It demonstrates a radical, risky form of giving, and the meeting place of vulnerability, grace and the glory of God dwelling in Jesus. The woman comes to the house knowing she is forgiven. She wants to express her gratitude to Jesus directly, but, having seen Jesus publicly humiliated by the absence of customary gestures of welcome (no water for washing, etc.) she empathizes with his situation and begins to weep (for a thorough commentary, see *Jesus Through Middle Eastern Eyes*, Kenneth E. Bailey, SPCK, London, 2008, pp. 239–51). A way forward opens for her to provide the customary hospitality, not with the water set aside for that purpose, but with her tears. Jesus allows her gesture, for he knows what it has cost her; he knows

too that she realizes that it is right that he be treated with respect and courtesy, for he is God's Holy One.

3   The Psalms provide a glimpse into the stories of a particular person – King David. The ups and downs of his life are captured in the material he has left us and show us how vital it is to be open and honest before God. Psalms can be found beyond scripture too – contemporary psalms are being written which continue the tradition of direct, honest communication between the writer and God about ordinary events and the feelings they evoke in the writer's life. It is worth getting a volume of such psalms as a resource, for example:

- Joy Cowley has written three volumes, *Aotearoa Psalms*, *Psalms Down-under*, and *Psalms for the Road* (available through online booksellers) in which she communicates directly with God about things as diverse as spring-cleaning, morning, loss, roads, bridges.
- Peter Owen Jones, *Psalm*, a slim, superb volume re-writing several psalms, (published by O Books, Winchester, 2005).
- You could have a group psalm-writing session with those present if they are able!
- Psalms are also being set to contemporary music, e.g. John Michael Talbot (details above) and the group Sons of Korah, (see, e.g., *Redemption Songs* (WACD001, 2000) and *Resurrection* (WACD003, 2005), both produced by Wordsong Artists, a division of CMC Australia), who set the text of psalms to original music to provide a fresh perspective and aid memory.

Evening Prayer: Stories

Truly I tell you, wherever the good news is proclaimed in the whole world,
what she has done will be told in remembrance of her.
(Mark 14.9)

Storytelling is part of every culture. You will have inherited family stories and may have passed them on to your wider network, along with new stories fashioned out of daily events and memorable moments of humour, sadness and celebration. Some stories you will have kept as secrets, mindful that they deal with the harder aspects of life, the hurts and the disappointments, the failures and the fears. The shape of your life is unique, known fully only to you and to God who, as the Holy 'Ghost writer', co-authors your life story.

MUSIC
'Here am I, Lord, I've come to do your will' (Sacred Weave).

PRAYER
**O God, you are the co-author of all our stories,
you walk with us as each chapter unfolds,
you hold us steady when struggles unsettle us,
you laugh and you weep with us,
you know all the beginnings
and all the endings, woven through
the ordinary events of each day.
Be with us now as we reconnect
with the greatest story in the world:
your radical writing of yourself into each
of our stories, to bring us life and hope,
through Jesus Christ. AMEN.**

HYMN
1 Tell me the old, old story, of unseen things above,
of Jesus and His glory, of Jesus and His love;
tell me the story simply, as to a little child,
for I am weak and weary, and helpless and defiled ...
    Tell me the old, old story, tell me the old, old story,
    tell me the old, old story, of Jesus and His love.

2 Tell me the story slowly, that I may take it in –
   that wonderful redemption, God's remedy for sin;
   tell me the story often, for I forget so soon,
   the 'early dew' of morning has passed away at noon.
      Tell me the old, old story …

3 Tell me the story softly, with earnest tones and grave;
   remember I'm the sinner whom Jesus came to save;
   tell me the story always, if you would really be,
   in any time of trouble, a comforter to me.
      Tell me the old, old story …

4 Tell me the same old story, when you have cause to fear
   that this world's empty glory is costing me too dear;
   and when the Lord's bright glory is dawning on my soul,
   tell me the old, old story: 'Christ Jesus makes thee whole.'
      Tell me the old, old story …
   (lyrics Katherine Hankey, 1866, music Bishop Doane)

GOSPEL
The woman who wiped Jesus' feet with her hair (Luke 7.36–50).

REFLECTION
Have you ever done something that made you vulnerable?
How might you talk to Jesus, to God, about that moment?
What psalm might you write to express your feelings and thoughts to God?

Leader: Words of encouragement.

Leader: We thank you for our life stories –
           they are made up of hard times and of joy,
           stories of birth and death
           and everything in between;
           together they make a library of love,
           a legacy for our families,
           a gift to strengthen the fabric of our community.
           Thank you for making each of us a 'first edition',
           priceless to you. AMEN.

THE LORD'S PRAYER

MUSIC
Commit your life to the Lord.
Trust in him, he will protect you.
Be still before God, wait in patience.
Commit your life to the Lord. (John Michael Talbot, based on Psalm 37)

CLOSING PRAYER
Bring us, O Lord God, at our last awakening
into the house and gate of heaven
to enter into that gate and dwell in that house,
where there shall be no darkness nor dazzling, but one equal light;
no noise or silence, but one equal music;
no fears or hopes, but one equal possession;
no ends or beginnings, but one equal eternity;
in the habitations of thy glory and dominion,
world without end. AMEN. (John Donne)

BLESSING
May God bless the closing chapters of *this* life's story and, in God's perfect time, may God reveal the opening chapters of the *next*, as you journey with Jesus into eternal life. AMEN.

Sacred Space

These simple services are designed to be offered at any suitable time of day, so they lend themselves to fitting in with care-home routines and requirements. Because they include less formal language and don't expect participants to know old forms of liturgy, they are particularly appropriate as a 'way in' for those new to faith and prayer.

The services incorporate a key verse, a brief litany, a story from scripture, time for reflection, silence, music, poetry and prayer. Generally the words, music and readings will speak for themselves so there is no homily or talk. The Sacred Space services will require some preparation to ensure that you have the suggested 'props' or focus items, but it is worth the effort! Full details of materials, music and any specific suggestions are provided on the following pages.

Often these services will use familiar things in a new way, modelling the reality that God can use anything at all to communicate with us, even if we are surprised by the ordinary suddenly pointing us to the divine. This is what Jesus did, of course, using the very ordinary things of life. A missing sheep, lost coins, a measure of flour and leaven, a pearl of great price, a treasure hidden in a field, wild flowers, birds of the air and more were pressed into service by Jesus to help people learn more about the nature of God and their own value in God's sight.

A variety of music is offered – a chant is used before and after the time of silent prayer before the leader takes a time of vocal prayer.

The key feature which may be new to the care-home residents and perhaps to you, is the substantial period of silence for reflection. Ten minutes' silence can help people to go beneath the surface of their normal thoughts. However, for the elderly or the very tired, such a lengthy silence can aid nodding off! It may work best to introduce silence gradually, starting with a couple of minutes (most will have experienced two minutes' silence as a mark of respect on Remembrance Day, for example) and then gradually building up their 'alert silence' capacity until they can manage ten minutes. If you have also been using the Evening Prayer services then you will have been offering time for reflection there as well, so this will help people feel more comfortable with silence.

If you are concerned about offering silence, then talk to the group about it and, as a way of ensuring that people are not associating silence with punishment or withdrawal of love, introduce the silence as being a gift to help them listen more closely to the voice of God and their interior monologue. In other words, silence enables deeper connection with God and oneself.

For all services, you will need:

- a portable altar, i.e. a trolley with suitable cloth, cross and a support for the focus picture
- copies of the service sheet for everyone
- the 'props' listed for the particular service

- special music: iTunes, Google Play or YouTube will hopefully help you to source most of the suggested tracks or you can choose your own and amend the service sheets accordingly.

On the accompanying CD and in Appendix 1, you will find six Sacred Space service sheets, on which are printed a litany, reading and music details, a psalm and/or poem, and sometimes a short commentary or questions to use during the service if you wish. Any pictures suggested for use in a Sacred Space service are in the Photo Appendix in black and white and in the Photofiles on the CD-Rom in colour.

Materials, music etc. for Sacred Space services

Sheets for six Sacred Space services can be found in Appendix 1.

Spring and Hopefulness

- Newspaper.
- Fragrant spring flowers.
- Butterfly picture.
- Music: 'Hymn to Hope', Secret Garden, *White Stones* (Polygram: Norway, 1997, 534605-2, track 3).
  'O Lord hear my prayer', Taizé, *O Lord Hear My Prayer* (Kingsway, 1994, KMCD 736, track 1).
  'Ubi caritas', Taizé, *O Lord Hear My Prayer* (Kingsway, 1994, KMCD 736, track 13).

Friendship

- For each person a palm-sized red cardboard heart on which is written: 'Friend of God'.
- Basket to collect and offer these 'hearts' as part of the service.
- Music: 'O Lord hear my prayer', Taizé, *O Lord Hear My Prayer* (Kingsway, 1994, KMCD 736, track 1).
  Text of 'You've Got a Friend', James Taylor, for reading aloud before you play the song. For a version of the song with lyrics, see http://www.youtube.com/watch?v=dDzNAxpOaYo (accessed 2.2.14).
  Alternatively, use the familiar nineteenth-century hymn, 'What a friend we have in Jesus', amending the service sheet and printing off copies of the lyrics for people to take away with them.
  N.B. The service ends with a sung Grace – you may need to teach this before the service starts:
  May the grace of our Lord Jesus Christ, and the love of God our Father, and the fellowship, the fellowship of the Holy Spirit, be with us, for evermore and evermore and evermore. AMEN. (If you can't locate a tune for this, then make one up yourself.)

God Knows …

- Laptop/tablet computer.
- Bible.
- Large eternity ∞ symbol.
- Music: 'Come my way, my truth, my life', Margaret Rizza, *River of Peace* (Kevin Mayhew: Suffolk, 1999, 1490050, track 2).
  'My soul is at rest in God alone', Taizé, *My Soul is at Rest: Songs of Taizé, Vol. II* (Kingsway, East Sussex, 1995, KMCD 841, track 6).
  'The Call of Wisdom', Will Todd, *The Call of Wisdom* (Signum, SIGCD298, 2012, track 3).

The Light of the World

- A NO ENTRY sign.
- A large question mark, 12″ high.
- A door-knob.
- Large copy or projected image of 'The Light of the World', Holman Hunt (St Paul's Cathedral).
- Music: 'The Lord is my light', Taizé, *O Lord Hear My Prayer* (Kingsway, 1994, KMCD 736, track 4).

Frailty and Fatigue

- Check that you can 'borrow' a walking-frame from someone to use at the start of the service.
- Several pill containers or bottles or medical aids.
- Picture or sculpture of praying hands.
- Music: 'It was a Very Good Year', Frank Sinatra – widely available.
  'Lord, now lettest thou thy servant depart in peace', *Rachmaninoff Vespers*, Tenebrae (Signum Classics, UK, 2005, SIGCD054, track 5).
  'My soul is at rest in God alone', Taizé, *My Soul is at Rest: Songs of Taizé, Vol. II* (Kingsway, East Sussex, 1995, KMCD 841, track 6).

Rocks and Stones

- Rocky Road confectionery, recipe: http://candy.about.com/od/kidfriendlytreats/r/rockyroad.htm.
- Fist-sized rocks/stones.
- A 'GONE FISHING' sign.
- Music: You may already have a recording of 'Rock of Ages' or be able to sing it with your team, but if not, you can download as video or music a simple but effective version with text on screen: 'Rock of Ages' (Augustus M. Toplady, 1775) sung in the video by the Antrim Mennonite Choir, http://www.youtube.com/watch?v=gM7gt_cSxjw (accessed 2.3.14).

'You raise me up', Secret Garden, *Once in a Red Moon* (Universal Music Australia, 548 678-2, 2002, track 2).

N.B. The poem 'Footprints', though widely attributed to 'Anonymous', is now recognized as the work of the late Mary Stevenson and copyrighted to her estate. Consequently it cannot be included in the text of this service. However, please look it up and read the text to those attending – perhaps telling the story of the woman who wrote the poem: a story of loss and struggle and finally of recognition. http://www.footprints-inthe-sand.com/index.php?page=Bio.php (accessed 2.3.14).

Reconnecting with Old Treasures: Music and memory

Neurological research over the past decade has been exploring the connection between music and memory,[6] trying to discover why music might be an important way of connecting with people affected by dementia. One of these researchers, Peter Janata, associate professor of psychology at UC Davis' Centre for Mind and Brain, believes that:

> The region of the brain where memories of our past are supported and retrieved also serves as a hub that links familiar music, memories and emotion. The discovery may help to explain why music can elicit strong responses from people with Alzheimer's disease. The hub is located in the medial prefrontal cortex region – right behind the forehead – and one of the last areas of the brain to atrophy over the course of the disease.

Music remains important for people as their mental functioning deteriorates, and for those who have suffered strokes, depending on the location of the clot and the level of damage done, music may still provide some comfort, as this story illustrates:

> *'Sarah' had lost most of her powers of communication following a major stroke. Like many, I struggled to understand her, but there was one graced encounter when she managed to say 'walk' and 'garden' and the Spirit prompted my recollection of the song 'In the Garden'.[7] When I sang it with her, tears came for us both. I discovered later that in planning her funeral, when she was well, she had specifically wanted to include this song.*

---

6 See, for example, http://www.news.ucdavis.edu/search/news_detail.lasso?id=9008, *Study Finds Brain Hub That Links Music, Memory and Emotion*, Peter Janata (accessed 6.3.14) http://www.livescience.com/5327-music-memory-connection-brain.html (accessed 8.1.14) and http://www.strokeassociation.org/STROKEORG/LifeAfterStroke/Regaining Independence/CommunicationChallenges/From-Singing-to-Speaking-Its-Amazing-To-See_UCM_310600_Article.jsp (accessed 24.1.14).

7 Austin Miles, 1912, written after the author's personal vision of the post-resurrection meeting between Jesus and Mary (John 20.11–18).

I come to the garden alone,
While the dew is still on the roses,
And the voice I hear falling on my ear
The Son of God discloses.

Refrain:
And He walks with me, and He talks with me,
And He tells me I am His own;
And the joy we share as we tarry there,
None other has ever known.

At the time of our meeting, what was so comforting was that she remembered this song in spite of her stroke, it gave her an emotional connection with her Lord, somehow brought to mind walking 'in the garden with Jesus', and it sustained her through to a peaceful dying.

The second memory is of a resident with some episodes of visual hallucinations which occasionally unnerved him and the staff. However, there was something special going on for him with the 'songs in his head' and they caused him no distress. As I was thinking about 'Paddy', this poem emerged:

Paddy has songs in his head
the young nurse reports
and looks for a psychologist's note.

I ask Paddy about the songs,
the first one is from my mother
he says
and sings a lullaby
haunting, simple,
all the words in their place
to tell the story of life
and loving
and sleeping
in peace.

'Three songs a day,' I whisper in his ear,
'like a tonic, a salve for your soul.'
Paddy grins. 'God bless you,' I say.
'God bless you,' he sings
to a melody of Love's own making.

The song he had playing in his mind had been laid down with feelings of security, love, peace, warmth and belonging, embodied in the person of his mother, when Paddy was very young. Here the lullaby was, decades later, as fresh as ever and able to bring deep comfort to a man whose connection with those around him was limited.

When we are with the elderly, if we are aware that music and emotional memory are intertwined, songs and singing, rhythm and melody may form part of our ministry in gentle, life-giving ways.

The extent to which you will be able to offer some sort of music ministry in the aged-care context will depend on the time and skills you and your team possess and the opportunities which you can engineer for some musical input into the care-home routine. Liaising with the diversional therapist or a senior clinical nurse may help you assess how often live musical entertainment is provided, or whether music DVDs which many older folk appreciate (for example of André Rieu, Daniel O'Donnell) are available. There may be someone in your network for whom a care-home music ministry could be an ideal option. Some possible ways into such a ministry follow:

Form a choir

You may like to watch *Young@Heart*, a British documentary (2008) which follows a group of New England senior citizens as they learn and perform music which shatters stereotypes of docile old ladies singing songs from the Second World War! While there is a growing interest in choirs made up of elderly people, with the World Choir Games and other competitions having a Senior Choir section, few of us have the time, skill, energy or resources to take this particular path – nor is it necessary, because a choir in an aged-care home does not have to perform to concert standard. Instead it can:

- be fun, inclusive and not take itself too seriously, i.e. no auditions
- value participation over and above the quality of the performance
- tap into a vast reservoir of musical memory among members of the choir
- include singers with some memory loss or early/mid-stage dementia
- offer entertainment to fellow residents or to the elderly in other institutions
- foster good links with others such as a local school or church.

Such a regular gathering for singing builds up members' personal self-esteem, gives people a purpose and contributes to the well-being of the care-home community as a whole. And it's a lot of fun!

Making music together

If you can keep time musically, consider making music with a group of residents. For those with later-stage dementia in particular, engaging with a range of musical instruments (visit your local Fair Trade shop or online equivalent, e.g. http://www. siestacrafts.co.uk which stocks pipes, drums, shakers, finger pianos, didgeridoos, whistles, etc.) can produce astonishing alertness and participation in people thought to be beyond communication. Together you will be living out the psalmist's vision of making a joyful noise to the Lord (Psalm 98.4–6).

Spiritual conversation around the place of music in someone's life

When in small group or one-to-one conversation, consider using one of these starter questions:

'What part has music played in your life?' or
'What's your favourite song/piece of music?'

The answers may well lead into spiritual reminiscence – shared memories of how music has connected them to other people, to their faith, their community or country. Additional starter questions might be:

'What music makes you happy/warms your heart?'
'Where did you experience music when you were growing up?'
'What music makes you feel close to God?'

For those who do not 'feel' the presence of God, it may be worth asking what happens to them when they sing or listen to beautiful music. Some people find that music is the door to encounter with the sacred and may lead them to conversation with God, to thanksgiving for music, to sharing how they feel when a piece of music has moved them to tears or great joy, to sensing God alongside them in the sounds, words, voices and emotion of the music.

Music can be a vehicle of God's consolation in the midst of loss. I remember several weeks after my mother died discovering 'Be still my soul' set to the tune 'Finlandia'. It soothed me then, and still does.

🕯 You may like to reflect on your experience of music during times of stress, loss or celebration.

Praying with scripture

It is sad to see old Bibles piled up on tables at second-hand book fairs. It is even sadder to pick one up and find that it bears no signs of having been a friend to someone, no pencilled questions, under-linings and exclamation marks, nothing to hint at a life lived supported by scripture.

In aged-care ministry we will meet people who have never picked up a Bible; others who may have tried to read the Bible from start to finish but who gave up somewhere in Genesis when they encountered names too difficult to read, let alone pronounce; some who have read their Bible occasionally; and a few, a very few, for whom scripture is indeed a familiar friend with verses settled in their psyche, available to be recalled, used by the Spirit to offer guidance and consolation.

How do we start helping people engage with scripture in a constructive way if they have little experience, can't concentrate for very long, or can't read the text for themselves?

This is where the ancient practice of *lectio divina* (sacred reading) comes into its own, either with an individual or a small group, in a care-home context or in a parish setting. This simple ten-minute process[8] consists of:

- *lectio (reading)*: the slow reading aloud of a **small** portion of scripture, two or three verses
- *meditatio (reflecting)*: a few minutes spent pondering how that scripture might connect with our personal circumstances, noticing associations, emotions and related experience
- *oratio (responding)*: talking to God about what has been discovered, or any questions or thanksgiving which have surfaced
- *contemplatio (resting)*: stepping back from analysis or mental reasoning, we spend time quietly being with God, like a contented cat sitting on God's lap.

> A small group may pray with scripture together and, after the time spent in quiet contemplation, can choose whether or not to share a little about what they have discovered or 'heard' from God.

Suitable scriptures are those which bring encouragement, connection, assurance of forgiveness, etc. For example

- 'My grace is sufficient for you, for my power is made perfect in weakness' (2 Corinthians 12.9).
- 'Cast all your anxieties on me, because I care for you' (1 Peter 5.7 – changed to first person from third).

---

8 Ideally *lectio divina* is spread over a longer period, from 20 to 30 minutes, but initially it is preferable for a shorter time to see how those who attend manage the experience. If they are comfortable with more time to reflect or rest in God, the time can of course be extended.

- 'Ask, and it will be given you; search and you will find; knock and the door will be opened to you' (Matthew 7.7).
- 'O give thanks to the LORD for he is good, for his steadfast love endures for ever' (Psalm 107.1).
- '... nothing in all creation will be able to separate us from the love of God, in Christ Jesus our Lord' (Romans 8.39).
- 'Come to me, all you that are weary and are carrying heavy burdens, and I will give you rest' (Matthew 11.28).
- 'The thief comes only to steal and kill and destroy. I have come that you might have life, and have it abundantly' (John 10.10 – changed to second person).
- 'Jesus began to weep' (John 11.35).
- 'Do not fear, for I have redeemed you; I have called you by name, you are mine' (Isaiah 43.1b).

A second and equally valuable way of praying with scripture is to engage with it *imaginatively*, either by putting oneself as fully as possible in the biblical context, or by bringing the characters and events forward into your own setting. For example, if you were using Luke 1.26–38 (the annunciation) you might either imagine the scene in Mary's context in Roman-occupied Palestine, or bring the event into the twenty-first century, as if the angel Gabriel were coming to you in *your* context – be it kitchen or garden, factory, office or car – to speak to you of something that God wants to bring to birth in your life.

Some of us, those in care homes included, may have grown up with parents or influential adults who denied the value of the imagination or actively dismissed it. However, we can be assured that our imagination is part of God's good creation. We can ask the Holy Spirit to sanctify our imagination and use it to help us engage with scripture and draw closer to God.[9]

When selecting a passage to use for imaginative prayer with an individual (for example during a pastoral communion) or with a small group, choose a Gospel story in which Jesus has a personal encounter with someone. Familiarize yourself with the passage before you read it through to those present, slowly. Then guide them into an imaginative encounter which culminates in a one-to-one meeting with Jesus and time in his presence. End the process after a few minutes of silence by playing some gentle music, gradually increasing the volume to bring them back to this place and time.

Taking, for example, Matthew 20.29–34 (Jesus heals two blind men), a guided meditation might proceed like this:

I am going to read a short passage from the Gospel of Matthew in which two blind men seek healing from Jesus. After I've read it through so you have an overall sense of the story, I'm going to guide you slowly through an imaginative engagement

---

9 It is not advisable to use guided imaginative prayer with anyone who has difficulty telling the difference between what is real and what is in the imagination, for example anyone with serious mental health issues or those with advanced dementia.

with the passage. As you listen, be alert for any sense of connection with someone in the story.

Read the passage slowly, then begin with prayer:

Loving God, you gifted us with imagination; please sanctify that gift for our use now as we enter more closely into the reality of one of your healing encounters. AMEN.

Settle yourself into as comfortable a position as you can and close your eyes so that you can concentrate on listening. Don't struggle to make something happen – some people form mind pictures easily, while others have more of an inner impression without a lot of detail. Just let the story unfold and see what happens.

Here we are, part of a large crowd following Jesus as he leaves Jericho, and moves into the desert on a dusty road. Take a few moments to allow your senses to fill out the details of that scene – feel the dry heat, hear the bustle of feet and murmuring of people around you … Just let yourself be with the scene as best you can, and let God do the rest.

As you walk along, notice where Jesus is – is he nearby? Is he up ahead a little?

You hear voices calling out, 'Lord, have mercy on us, Son of David.'

As you look in the direction of the voices, you see two blind men getting to their feet. Then, stern voices are raised, telling them to be quiet. How do you feel? What are you thinking now?

The blind men call out again, asking for mercy, and this time you see Jesus stop, turn and call them to his side.

Imagine that Jesus has stopped his journey just for you.

Imagine that he is calling you to his side, that he is looking at you and, with a voice full of compassion, saying: 'What do you want me to do for you?' *(Repeat this question gently.)*

Spend a few minutes with Jesus; feel his compassionate love warming and encouraging you. Let yourself form a response to his question as honestly as you can, bringing your deep desire to him. *(Give five minutes to this process if you can.)*

Walk with him for a little while, perhaps talking, perhaps in companionable silence until you hear the quiet music and gently begin to reconnect with this place and this time.

(If time permits and it seems appropriate for the group, invite them to share briefly with their neighbour or with the group as a whole, depending on numbers, anything they want to about the experience.)

Honouring Special Days

In this section you will find leader's resource sheets and service sheets for a range of services relevant to aged-care ministry and easily undertaken in a care home or church context. On the CD-Rom these services are available in a larger font and in a format for ease of printing.

The services are for:

Ash Wednesday
Good Friday
A Memorial Service for use e.g. when a lot of residents or parishioners have died
All Souls: acknowledging those who have died during the previous twelve months
Remembrance Sunday or similar national commemoration, e.g. Anzac Day

Again the emphasis is on simplicity, relevance, reverence and building connection with God. You can easily adapt the pattern of these services for other commemorations, for example of saints' days or when calling a congregation to prayer for a particular purpose relevant to your context.

Leader's Resource Sheet: Ash Wednesday

This short liturgy can be included in a service of Holy Communion before the Gospel reading or used as a stand-alone service. You will need to source 'ashes' – traditionally these are the burnt remains of last year's palm crosses. Mix the ashes with a little holy oil to make it easier to sign the cross in ash on each person's forehead. Note that this is only done *with the individual's express permission*. We do not 'impose' ashes on anyone; they need to give their assent and we respect their right not to participate.

The young family in the story can be seen on TV3 Campbell Live website for verification: http://www.3news.co.nz/Termite-tragedy-for-one-Waikato-family/tabid/817/articleID/333979/Default.aspx

MUSIC

'Come back to me', e.g. by John Michael Talbot, *City of God* (Troubadour for the Lord, AR, 2005, TDD 4637, track 9), inspired by the book of Hosea. It may pay to read the lyrics aloud before playing the track.

Taizé – *Instrumental 2* (GIA, 2005, CD 651), guitar and flute, or *Icons 1*, Margaret Rizza (Kevin Mayhew, Suffolk, 2003), instrumental versions of her chants.

'Nine-fold Kyrie' from the Communion Service in F major, Darke, in *Music for Lent, The King's School, Ely* (Lantern, 2008, LPCD26, track 1), or a similar Kyrie from another source.

'HE WILL WALK • WONDER AND STARE • ALLELUIA', Iona Community (1995, CD-355, track 11), a spoken/sung journey with Jesus to Jerusalem, the cross and the resurrection.

Ash Wednesday Liturgy for Receiving the Cross of Ashes

(as part of a Communion service or as a stand-alone rite)

Leader: In the Christian tradition, ashes have long been associated with repentance and a reminder that we are 'made out of dust'. Ash Wednesday
marks the beginning of the season of Lent. During this period of penitence
we reflect on our own failures, regrets and sinfulness. With confidence in
God's forgiveness and mercy, we bring these to God as we prepare for a
holy celebration of the great mysteries of Easter. For on Easter Day we
are reminded that God's desire is:

To console those who mourn in Zion,
To give them beauty for ashes,
The oil of joy for mourning,
The garment of praise for the spirit of heaviness;
That they may be called trees of righteousness,
The planting of the LORD, that He may be glorified. (Isaiah 61.3, NKJV)

MUSIC
We listen to 'Come back to me' (John Michael Talbot).

Leader: We pray some verses from Psalm 51 in penitence and trust.

PSALM 51
  1 Have mercy on me, O God, according to your steadfast love;
      according to your abundant mercy blot out my transgressions.
  2 **Wash me thoroughly from my iniquity**
      and cleanse me from my sin.

  6 You desire truth in the inward being;
      therefore teach me wisdom in my secret heart.

10 Hide your face from my sins
      and blot out all my iniquities.
11 **Create in me a clean heart, O God,**
      and put a new and right spirit within me.

16 For you have no delight in sacrifice;
      if I were to give a burnt offering, you would not be pleased.
17 **The sacrifice acceptable to God is a broken spirit:**
      a broken and contrite heart, O God, you will not despise.

MUSIC
'Nine-fold Kyrie' (Lord have mercy, Christ have mercy, Lord have mercy).

Silence.

MUSIC
Instrumental chant music will play in the background.

Leader: Please stay seated. We will come to where you are sitting, and, if you agree, will make the sign of the cross on your forehead with the ashes, as we say:
'Bear this cross as a reminder of Jesus' passion.'

Silence is held for a few moments once all have been signed with the cross in ashes.

SHORT TALK
Leader: With modern heating systems we don't come across *ashes* much in everyday life, and most of us do our best to keep our homes free from accumulating *dust*!

But *ashes and dust* became horribly real for a young family who recently bought what they thought was the ideal family home. Two months after taking possession they were horrified to discover that the house was so riddled with termites that behind the wallpaper the wood was crumbling, literally turning to *dust* in front of their eyes. Their dreams were turning to *ashes* and they were facing bankruptcy. A television station took up their plight, and within two weeks funds had been raised to demolish the house and clear the land, and a building firm offered to project-manage them into a new home. They would still have a mortgage, of course, but now they had a brighter future. Theirs is a story of *dust* and *ashes* being transformed into a 'resurrection'. From despair, hope emerged, thanks to the kindness of thousands of strangers.

This family walked the road of despair, not knowing what lay ahead.

Jesus walked the way to the cross, knowing all too well what lay ahead – a dreadfully painful death, yes, but more than that, the indescribable taking upon himself of the sins of the world. He who knew no sin, became sin for us (2 Corinthians 5.21).

BUT – he came through that hell to the resurrection – to bring us all to new life …

MUSIC
'HE WILL WALK • WONDER AND STARE • ALLELUIA' (Wild Goose Worship, Iona)

Leader:
We are walking with Jesus towards the cross, and towards the resurrection. The next 40 days provide us with time to reflect on our own journey, time too to bring to God anything that weighs heavily on our conscience, anything we wish we'd done differently.

Remember that Jesus died to set us free from the burden of sin and guilt.

Have no hesitation in bringing your pains or failures to God – he will listen to you with the utmost patience and compassion. And when you have got everything off your chest, God will assure you of his forgiveness and ongoing kindness. You will be free.

Free to love others and to love yourself.

BLESSING
May God our Creator, Father and Mother of us all,
walk with us during this season of Lent.
May we enter more deeply into the passion of Jesus
and come to depend more completely on his Spirit,
that we may live a life that sparkles
with the light of the resurrected Christ. AMEN.

Leader's Resource Sheet: Good Friday Reflection

As this service is based on the Seven Last Words of Christ you will probably be familiar with the overall structure. I have included a simplified version, with short responses and silences – by honouring the silence (30 seconds) the service can proceed at a gentle pace more suited to older minds. The picture below illustrates how the focus is set up.

You will need to gather:

- Candles and candle-snuffer. The six candles on the right are on a plate so they can be taken around for capable residents to extinguish – they appreciate being able to do this. The large single candle on the left is the last one to be extinguished by the leader.

- Choose a large image of Christ crucified as the central focus for this service. An internet search will help you find something suitable.
- In front of this picture, on a small table covered with a dark cloth, is a basket for the stones.
- Enough stones for each person present. It means a great deal to individuals to be able to come forward at the end to place the stone in the basket themselves. Even if this is very difficult for them and slow, resist the urge to do it for them, unless they really cannot manage. The chant at the end is over six minutes long and may need to play through at least twice to enable people to place their stones and leave without being hurried.
- Music: 'Jesus remember me', *Songs of Taizé, Vol. II, My Soul is at Rest* (Kingsway, 1995, KMCD841, track 11; Adoramus Te Christe', same album, track 2).

On the CD-Rom the full service is provided as four A4 pages, which can then be printed off on A3 paper to form an A4 booklet (portrait orientation).

A Service of Reflection for Good Friday
Based on the Seven Last Sayings of Jesus

(As they come in for the service, each person is given a stone to be laid at the altar as the service ends.)

We gather to remember the last hours of Jesus' earthly life.
We will spend time listening to the last words Jesus spoke from the cross and come closer to understanding a little more the true depths of his suffering for us.
And at the end of the service we will bring to him our own struggles and weakness, knowing that this is what Jesus came for, to free us from fear, guilt, sadness and shame, and re-connect us with our God.

HYMN
When I survey the wondrous cross

1   When I survey the wondrous cross
    on which the Prince of Glory died;
    my richest gain I count but loss,
    and pour contempt on all my pride.

2   Forbid it, Lord, that I should boast,
    save in the death of Christ, my God;
    all the vain things that charm me most,
    I sacrifice them to his blood.

3   See, from his head, his hands, his feet,
    sorrow and love flow mingled down.
    Did e'er such love and sorrow meet,
    or thorns compose so rich a crown.

4   Were the whole realm of nature mine,
    that were an offering far too small;
    love so amazing, so divine,
    demands my soul, my life, my all.

THE FIRST WORD
Luke 23.33–34.

> When they came to the place called Golgotha (the Skull), they nailed Jesus to the cross there, and the two criminals, one on his right and one on his left. Jesus said, 'Father, forgive them! They do not know what they are doing.'

Lord Jesus – you lived true to God's call on your life, even unto death.
May we be brave enough to follow God's call wherever it may lead.

WE HOLD SILENCE AS THE FIRST CANDLE IS EXTINGUISHED.

✠

THE SECOND WORD
Luke 23.39–43.

> One of the criminals hanging there threw insults at him: 'Aren't you the Messiah? Save yourself and us!' The other one, however, rebuked him, saying: 'Don't you fear God? Here we are all under the same sentence. Ours, however, is only right, for we are getting what we deserve for what we did; but he has done no wrong.' And he said to Jesus, 'Remember me, Jesus, when you come as King!' Jesus said to him, 'I tell you this: Today you will be with me in Paradise.'

Lord Jesus – you offered hope even in the midst of your suffering.
May we recognize the hope you offer us whenever we turn to you.

WE HOLD SILENCE AS THE SECOND CANDLE IS EXTINGUISHED.

We listen to the chant, 'Jesus remember me, when you come into your kingdom' (Taizé).

✠

THE THIRD WORD
John 19.25–27.

> Standing close to Jesus' cross were his mother, his mother's sister, Mary the wife of Cleopas, and Mary Magdalene. Jesus saw his mother and the disciple he loved standing there; so he said to his mother, 'Woman, here is your son.' Then he said to the disciple, 'Here is your mother.' And from that time the disciple took her to live in his home.

Lord Jesus – you thought of your dear ones, even as you died.
May we think of others and their needs, even as our lives draw near their end.

WE HOLD SILENCE AS THE THIRD CANDLE IS EXTINGUISHED.

CONFESSION AND INTERCESSION
As Jesus cared about the well-being of his beloved mother, so, in a minute's silence, we bring to God all those for whom our hearts ache, all those in our family or our network of friends who are unwell in body, mind or spirit.

Silence.

We bring to you our own needs for this day, and the needs of those around us.

Silence.

Lord, we know that you hear us: **We know that you hear us always.**

Lord have mercy,   **Lord have mercy,**
Christ have mercy,   **Christ have mercy,**
Lord have mercy.   **Lord have mercy.**

Confident of the breadth of God's forgiveness and the depth of God's love, we bring to God our regrets and failures, our weakness and our wilfulness.

Silence.

Know that God hears and forgives. Be at peace.

THE FOURTH WORD
Mark 15.33–34.

> And when the sixth hour had come, there was darkness over the whole land until the ninth hour. And at the ninth hour Jesus cried with a loud voice, 'Elo-i, elo-i, lama sabach-thani?' which means, 'My God, my God, why hast thou forsaken me?'

Lord Jesus – for our sake you felt the darkness of separation from God.
May we be kept from such terror, by the power of your Spirit.

WE HOLD SILENCE AS THE FOURTH CANDLE IS EXTINGUISHED.

We sing   O Sacred head, surrounded by crown of piercing thorn!
quietly: O bleeding head, so wounded, so shamed and put to scorn!
           Death's pallid hue comes o'er thee, the glow of life decays;
           Yet angel-hosts adore thee, and tremble as they gaze.

THE FIFTH WORD
John 19.28.

    After this, Jesus, knowing that all was now finished, said (to fulfil the scripture),
    'I thirst.'

Lord Jesus – you knew a human body's yearning for relief from pain and thirst.
You understand our suffering and stand with us in our pain.

WE HOLD SILENCE AS THE FIFTH CANDLE IS EXTINGUISHED.

THE SIXTH WORD
John 19.29–30.

    A bowl was there, full of cheap wine mixed with vinegar, so a sponge was soaked in
    it, put on a stick of hyssop and lifted up to his lips. When Jesus received the wine,
    he said, 'It is finished.'

Lord Jesus – in your dying, you gave to us new life.
May we open ourselves to receive this gift, purchased with your blood.

WE HOLD SILENCE AS THE SIXTH CANDLE IS EXTINGUISHED.

We sing   **In this thy bitter Passion, Good Shepherd, think of me**
quietly: **with thy most sweet compassion, unworthy though I be:**
           beneath thy Cross abiding, for ever I would rest,
           in thy dear love confiding and with thy presence blest.

THE SEVENTH WORD
Luke 23.46.

Then Jesus, crying with a loud voice, said, 'Father, into thy hands
I commend my spirit!' And having said this, he breathed his last.

Lord Jesus – at the last you gave yourself to God.
When the time comes for our dying, may we trust enough to do the same.

WE HOLD SILENCE AS THE SEVENTH CANDLE IS EXTINGUISHED.

BLESSING
May you find in the cross a sure ground for faith, a firm support for hope, and the
assurance of sins forgiven. And the blessing of God Almighty, Father, Son and Holy
Spirit, be with you and those whom you love, now and always. AMEN.
(NZPB, p. 536)

The Taizé chant in Latin (English translation below):

Adoramus Te, Christe, et benedicimus Tibi,
Quia per crucem Tuam, redemisti mundum.

We adore Thee, O Christ, and we bless Thee,
who by your Holy Cross have redeemed the world.

**As we leave, in our own time, we take our stone and put it in the basket, in front of
the picture of the crucified Christ. In doing this, we identify with the struggles and
pain of our Lord, and we offer to God all that is hard about our lives: our disappointments, our selfishness, our doubt and our weaknesses – for Christ died to free
us from such burdens.**

Reproduced by permission. © Sue Pickering 2014.

Leader's Resource Sheet: A Memorial Service

Following a request from residents who found it impossible to attend funerals, I began to offer a Memorial Service when there had been a run of deaths of residents at the care home, or in the retirement village, in a short space of time. Losing people like this can be very unsettling and sad for those left behind who shared their tables in the dining-room, had formed unexpected friendships, or reconnected with folk they had gone to school with many years ago! A Memorial Service creates a space in which to remember those who have died, and gives those who mourn them a chance to be together, to receive comfort and an assurance that their grief is recognized.

The simple service, as it appears in this resource, uses contemporary music, well-known readings and time for reflection – the picture will give you an indication of how the space is arranged and used. A printable service can be found on the CD-Rom as 2 × A4 pages.

You will need the following:

- Pictures of those who have died or service sheets from each of the funerals of those whom you are remembering from the village or care home. If these are not available, then printing off their names in large print and putting them on colourful cards arranged on a board can provide an attractive visual focus for those attending, and ensure that each person has equal recognition.
- A large, flat basket filled with flowers such as camellias (winter) or roses (summer) which include some that are buds, some starting to open, some fully open and some beginning to fade or drop petals – i.e. to indicate the life of the flower and draw parallels with our lives. If no suitable flowers are available try to source fresh rosemary – the herb traditionally associated with remembrance.
- Two small tables on which to place two large platter-type pottery plates or similar to receive the flowers when it comes time for members of the congregation to pay their respects.
- A dark cloth to cover the altar, e.g. old black velvet curtain, a dark navy sheet, etc.
- Enough copies of the service for each person present.

- Large-print copy of the readings, especially if you are going to ask a resident to read.
- Suitable music – use your own preferences or see suggestions below for a mix of contemporary and traditional which speak of homecoming, etc.
  'Home', Elizabeth Marvelly, *Home* (EMI: NZ, 2010, 50999 0943462 2, track 1). This begins with the line, 'Look over to the horizon …'.
  'Abide with me' – choral version.
  'Amazing Grace', choral version, or Katherine Jenkins, *Living a Dream* (UCJ: EU, 2005, 476 306-3, track 9).

REFLECTION

These few words can focus on one of the following themes, for example:

- 'Seeing beyond the horizon' and 'going home to where love is' (in 'Home' and 'the Ship') to a new life in the fullness of Christ. For now we can only glimpse this life through the example of Jesus, and other people whose living reflects the glory of God, i.e. they are fully alive, making abundant use of their giftings in spite of their weaknesses, *or*

- The cycle of life – new buds grow alongside full blooms and fading flowers. All are valued as part of life – as we age and fade, children are being born who will take the world forward, *or*

- The John 14.1–6 reading in which Jesus assured his disciples that he was going on ahead to prepare a place for them – and for us. The closer we get to Jesus in this world, the more certain we can be of the truth of his assurance that he is with us always, *or*

- We can remind people of the nature of God as Love – those who have died have been received into that great Love from which they came, the same Love in which we 'live and move and have our being'. We are all one in the love of God.

A Memorial Service to Honour Those of Our Community Who Have Recently Died

WELCOME
We listen to: 'Home' sung by Elizabeth Marvelly.

We listen to the reading:

'The Ship' or 'What is Dying' (Bishop Brent)

I am standing upon the foreshore,
a ship at my side spreads her white sails
in the morning breeze and starts for the open sea.
She is an object of great beauty and strength,
and I stand watching her sail,
till at last she fades on the horizon
and someone at my side says: 'She is gone.'

Gone! Where? Gone from my sight – that is all.
She is just as large in the masts,
hull and spars as she was when she left my side,
and just as able to bear her load
of living freight to its fullest,
her diminished size and total loss of sight
is in me, not in her.
And just at the moment
when someone at my side says:
'There! She is gone',
there are other eyes watching for her coming,
and other voices ready to take up the glad shout:
'There she comes!'
– and this is dying.
The horizon is just the limit of our sight.
Lift us up, O Lord, that we may see further.

121

We take some time to reflect:

ACT OF REMEMBRANCE

We remember those who have died from our community over the last few weeks – each person's name is read aloud and then we share a minute's silence in their memory.

We remember too other friends or family who have also died recently – please feel free to name them aloud or to name them before God in the silence of your hearts.

Music for personal reflection is played, during which time a basket of flowers will be passed around for you to take to use later in the service.

PSALM 23.1–4, 'THE MESSAGE VERSION'

God, my shepherd!
I don't need a thing.

You have bedded me down in lush meadows,
you find me quiet pools to drink from.

True to your word,
you let me catch my breath
and send me in the right direction.

Even when the way goes through Death Valley,
I'm not afraid when you walk at my side.

Your trusty shepherd's crook
makes me feel secure.

READING
John 14.1–6, 26–27.

PRAYERS OF THANKSGIVING AND FAREWELL

MUSIC
We listen to 'Amazing Grace'.

BLESSING

While the music continues to play, please go forward and place your flower/rosemary on the altar table in a personal act of farewell, thanksgiving and remembrance. Then leave when you are ready.

Leader's Resource Sheet: All Souls

If the care home is involved in the keeping of Hallowe'en (pumpkins, witches' hats, goblins and all) then it is important that we make an attempt to present another way of approaching a commemoration of the dead! People may not realize that Hallowe'en is derived from the eve of All Hallows (All Saints) which begins a time of Christian remembrance of the dead. The All Souls service is traditionally set down in the Church's calendar for 2 November of each year, although it is often moved to the first Sunday in November. All Souls gives us an ideal chance to remember all those who have died at the care home during the preceding 12 months (you may already hold such a service in the parish but, if not, then this service would work well in both contexts).

The key to this service is to keep a list of the contact details of next-of-kin through the year as the deaths occur; for example, for the 2015 All Souls service you begin to keep a list from October 2014. This enables you to send *personal* letters to the next-of-kin, naming their loved one and issuing an invitation to the service *and* to an afternoon tea immediately beforehand. For those who have lost loved ones during the year, this invitation to return and remember their loved one in the care-home context can be a significant step on their journey of healing. When you first introduce this service, only one or two families may attend, but it is worth the effort just for them and, over the years, the response will increase. A general invitation to attend is also issued to staff.

You will need the following resources:

- List of names and date of death of those who have died since the end of October in the preceding year, this list to be read aloud at the All Souls service.
- Two purple candles and a picture which symbolizes the mystery of death and the hope of resurrection as a focus of prayer.
- Two large candles – one to light for those from the care home who have died, the other to light for others known to those in the congregation who have died during the year.
- Copies of the service sheet with the hymn/s and the reading, and the translation of any chants.
- Music: someone to play for the two hymns and two other evocative pieces:
  'God be in my head, and in my understanding', e.g. sung by Kenneth McKellar, *Hymns and Anthems Vol. 1: All Things Bright and Beautiful* (Decca, CD1 448 682-2, 1995, track 11).
  'In Paradisum', from Fauré's *Requiem*, available on compilations, e.g. *Agnus Dei* (Erato, 0630-14634-2, 1996, track 11).

- Something for people to take away as a remembrance of their loved one – choose a different item each year and amend the service sheet accordingly. Depending on numbers, this could be something simple such as:
  - a blue glass pebble to keep in their pocket (available from novelty/florist shops)
  - a piece of rosemary (traditionally rosemary is the herb for 'remembrance')
  - a bookmark with an appropriate prayer and comforting image from nature
  - a piece of velvet ribbon to keep in their Bible or by a loved one's photo
  - a small candle to light on the anniversary of their loved one's death or birthday.

Another helpful practice is to keep a Memorial Book into which is placed, for each resident who has died, the death notices, service sheet and, for families who wish it, a copy of the eulogy/biography. Memorial Books take little time to keep up-to-date and, at the All Souls afternoon tea, are always sought out by relatives of those whose deaths are recorded in these books. They are also appreciated by other residents who are unable to attend funerals.

All Souls' Memorial Service

A warm welcome to this service at which we honour those who have lived and died among us here at *(insert name of care home/retirement village)* over the past 12 months. We also remember others known to us who have died – family members, friends or work colleagues whose lives have touched our own. So let us begin, and may the music, readings and prayers bring comfort and hope to those who mourn.

ABIDE WITH ME
Abide with me; fast falls the eventide;
The darkness deepens; Lord with me abide.
When other helpers fail and comforts flee,
Help of the helpless, O abide with me.

Swift to its close ebbs out life's little day;
Earth's joys grow dim; its glories pass away;
Change and decay in all around I see;
O Thou who changest not, abide with me.

I fear no foe, with Thee at hand to bless;
Ills have no weight, and tears no bitterness.
Where is death's sting? Where, grave, thy victory?
I triumph still, if Thou abide with me.

Hold Thou Thy cross before my closing eyes;
Shine through the gloom and point me to the skies.
Heaven's morning breaks, and earth's vain shadows flee;
In life, in death, O Lord, abide with me.

For some here today, grief is still new and raw, and there is a daily awareness of the loved one's absence. Some days it's hard to believe they have gone; some days the roller-coaster of emotions takes us by surprise.

God is with us in these moments of sadness and separation, even if tears blur our sight. The love and care of friends are part of the way God brings us comfort and hope.

For others, the years have passed, some slowly, some quickly; photographs and stories help keep alive the uniqueness of a mum or dad, a spouse, or friend. Grief may be less of a sharp stab in the side, and more of a quiet remembering or a deep sense of absence at a family gathering.

> *It takes time and a thousand tears to accept the death of someone you love ... Your tears are holy water from the deep place of your loving ...*
>
> *Love will be found in the hearts of those who surround you and care for you. People who have been in a place of sadness, where you are now will be there for you ...*
>
> *Gradually you will begin the sacred daily ritual of remembering and begin to move through the valley of suffering step by step, until in time the veil of sorrow will lift and peace will come to your heart ...*
>
> (Susan Squellati Florence, When you Lose Someone You Love, Helen Exley, 2002, p. 2, adapted)

Our faith also tells us that we are held close to God, no matter what we have to face, no matter where we go, in life or in death. Some verses of Psalm 139 emphasize God's ongoing presence with us ...

PSALM 139.1–3, 7–10
O LORD, you have searched me and known me.
You know when I sit down and when I rise up;
you discern my thoughts from far away.
You search out my path and my lying down
and are acquainted with all my ways.

Where can I go from your spirit?
Or where can I hide from your presence?
If I ascend to heaven, you are there;
If I make my bed in the grave, you are there.

If I take the wings of the morning and settle at the
farthest limits of the sea,
even there your hand shall lead me
and your right hand shall hold me fast.

So, we can never go beyond the reach of God. We – and our loved ones who have died – are all held in the loving arms of God. For now, our dead rest from their labours; one day they – and we – shall rise in glory, with a resurrection body that will herald the start of a new life in a new heaven and a new earth.

We light the first candle in memory of *(name of care home)* residents who have died during these past 12 months. As their names are read out, let us give thanks for all that they have meant to us as part of the *(name of care home)* family.

We light the second candle, and in a minute's silence, we bring to mind other special people whom we have loved and lost recently and in the passage of many years.

As we listen to 'God be in my head' and 'In Paradisum' from Faure's *Requiem* please come forward and take a *(name the symbol you are using, e.g. 'glass pebble as a touchstone')*, a reminder of the loved ones you carry in your heart. Take one for each person whom you are remembering today. Keep it in your pocket or on your table beside a favourite photo, or put it in a special place in your garden. *(Adjust this last sentence according to the chosen symbol.)*

God be in my head
God be in my head, and in my understanding; God be in my eyes and in my looking; God be in my mouth, and in my speaking; God be in my heart and in my thinking; God be at my end, and at my departing. (Pynson's *Horae*, 1514)

In Paradisum
In paradisum deducant te Angeli; in tuo adventu suscipiant te martyres, et perducant te in civitatem sanctam Ierusalem. Chorus angelorum te suscipiat, et cum Lazaro quondam paupere æternam habeas requiem.

May the angels receive thee in paradise; at thy coming may the martyrs receive thee, and bring thee into the holy city Jerusalem. There may the choir of angels receive thee, and with Lazarus, once a beggar, mayst thou have eternal rest.

READING
John 14.1–6, 27.

[1]'Do not let your hearts be troubled. Believe in God, believe also in me. [2]In my Father's house there are many dwelling places. If it were not so, would I have told you that I go to prepare a place for you? [3]And if I go and prepare a place for you, I

will come again and will take you to myself, so that where I am, there you may be also. [4]And you know the way to the place where I am going.' [5]Thomas said to him, 'Lord, we do not know where you are going. How can we know the way?' [6]Jesus said to him, 'I am the way, and the truth, and the life. No one comes to the Father, except through me.' … [27]'Peace I leave with you; my peace I give you. I do not give to you as the world gives. Do not let your hearts be troubled, and do not let them be afraid.'

PRAYERS
Father in heaven,
your Son Jesus Christ wept at the grave of Lazarus.
Show your compassion now to those of us who mourn.
Supply our needs, and help us trust in your
fatherly care and companioning love. AMEN. (Adapted from NZPB, p. 860)

Loving God, we recognize that,
with the birth of each child,
hope comes into the world.
Help us keep this truth in mind
whenever we lose someone we love.
Help us celebrate new life,
new energy and vision
wherever we find them …
for these are signs of your creative life
among us.
This we ask through Jesus,
who taught us to pray:

Our Father, which art in heaven,
hallowed be thy name,
thy kingdom come; thy will be done
on earth as it is in heaven.
Give us this day our daily bread
and forgive us our trespasses,
as we forgive those who trespass against us.
And lead us not into temptation,
but deliver us from evil.
For thine is the kingdom, the power and the glory.
For ever and ever. AMEN.

THE 23RD PSALM
(tune Crimond)

1 The Lord's my Shepherd, I'll not want; He makes me down to lie
in pastures green; He leadeth me the quiet waters by.

2 My soul He doth restore again, and me to walk doth make
within the paths of righteousness, e'en for His own name's sake.

3 Yea, though I walk in death's dark vale, yet will I fear no ill;
For Thou art with me, and Thy rod and staff my comfort still.

4 My table Thou hast furnished in presence of my foes;
My head Thou dost with oil anoint, and my cup overflows.

5 Goodness and mercy all my life shall surely follow me;
And in God's house for evermore, my dwelling place shall be.

BLESSING
May God who holds the living and departed in a single embrace
bless you and keep you always close to his heart, close to Jesus. AMEN.

Leader's Resource Sheet: Remembrance Sunday

(The second Sunday in November)

We do well to honour the memories of those who have made the ultimate sacrifice in times of war. In care homes there will still be some very elderly folk who served in the Second World War and conflicts thereafter. There may also be residents who lost beloved family members in wartime. They too value a service and the remembering that goes with it.

For readers in the United Kingdom, Remembrance Sunday is the traditional time for such remembering to be made, the Sunday nearest the signing of the armistice at the end of the First World War. When 11 November does not fall on a Sunday, there is a traditional two-minute silence kept at the eleventh hour. Communities across the nation, and in European countries affected directly by that conflict, will gather to pay their respects in various ways around this time, and so it is natural to offer a short service to those whom you serve.

A full Remembrance Sunday service can be found at http://www.ctbi.org.uk/233 (Churches Together in Britain and Ireland website) suitable for general parish use but too long for care-home use. The shorter service which follows keeps all the main elements, is designed for a British/European context, but can be adapted for Anzac Day (25 April) remembering Australia and New Zealand Army Corps (especially the First World War and the disastrous Gallipoli campaign), and all wars thereafter in which 'Aussies' and 'Kiwis' have served together. For readers in other countries, the main elements can easily be adapted to your contexts.

You will need the following resources:

- A cross to which poppies can be attached (you can use the one mentioned for the flowering of the Cross on Easter Sunday) *or* use a wreath instead and amend the text.
- An altar table or stand against which can be laid the poppy-cross/wreath.
- Enough poppies and service sheets for all present.
- A trolley or similar to use to take the cross/wreath around to the residents – it's a good height for them and easy for you to manage moving between rows.
- A national flag – depending on where you are holding this service and whom you can arrange to support you, it may be possible to incorporate a flag-raising and lowering ceremony as part of the service. Local Veterans or Returned Services Associations are worth contacting to see if anyone is available to assist and to ensure that correct protocol is followed.
- Similarly it can be helpful to have someone speak who is a member of the Armed Forces – not necessarily an 'old soldier' but someone who understands the ethos of the defence forces and is able to speak about such things as service to Queen and country.

- A CD track of 'The Last Post' (better still if you can find a live musician!).
- I have not specified the music to be played in the background while you are taking the poppies around to make the cross/wreath. It would make sense to use something like 'I vow to thee my country' but I am aware that some controversy has arisen in Britain in recent years over the appropriateness of the text of this popular patriotic hymn. If this is an issue for you, then using an *instrumental* version would be one way of incorporating the music in the service, so that those who know and value the hymn would not miss out completely.
- Alternatively you may like to introduce something quite different by the boy sopranos' group Libera. 'We are the lost' (track 11 from their album *Visions*, EMI, 2005, 0946 3 39862 2 0) is a respectful and beautiful sung compilation of words adapted from 'In Flanders Fields' by John McCrea and 'O God, our help in ages past' by Isaac Watts.

Remembrance Sunday

Leader: We gather today to remember all those who have given their lives in the service of others, particularly those who have died during times of war or national threat, during times of civil unrest or attacks of terror. We think of servicemen and women, many of them young, who left these shores never to return. Some live on in the minds of their families; all are alive in your mind, O God, in your heart and keeping.

All: **No-one has greater love than this, to lay down one's life for one's friends.**
(John 15.13)

HYMN

O God, our help in ages past, our hope for years to come,
our shelter from the stormy blast, and our eternal home;

Beneath the shadow of thy throne thy saints have dwelt secure;
sufficient is thine arm alone, and our defence is sure.

Before the hills in order stood, or earth received her frame,
from everlasting thou art God, to endless years the same.

Time, like an ever-rolling stream, bears all our years away;
they fly forgotten, as a dream dies at the opening day.

O God, our help in ages past, our hope for years to come,
be thou our guard while troubles last, and our eternal home.

Leader: We move now into a time of silence, two minutes in which to remember those we have lost through war and the freedom we experience because of their sacrifice.

Two minutes' silence is kept.

Leader: We give thanks to you, O God, for those who have given their lives for their families and countries, for freedom and for peace.

All: **Help us to use wisely that freedom, to keep persistently that peace, so their sacrifice will not have been in vain. Empower us with your Spirit, in Jesus' name. AMEN.**

Leader: In preparation for the Act of Remembrance, you are invited to place a poppy in the cross as it is brought around to where you are sitting.

The trolley with the cross will be brought to where you are sitting so you can put your poppy in place.

Leader: Let us now make our Act of Remembrance – standing or sitting as you are able.

All: **They shall grow not old, as we that are left grow old:**
            age shall not weary them, nor the years condemn.
            At the going down of the sun and in the morning,
            we will remember them.
            We will remember them.

The poppy-filled cross is brought to the front and laid against the altar table in full view of those present.

The Last Post is played.

READING

… and many nations shall come and say: 'Come, let us go up to the mountain of the LORD, to the house of the God of Jacob; that he may teach us his ways and that we may walk in his paths.' For out of Zion shall go forth instruction, and the word of the LORD from Jerusalem. He shall judge between many peoples, and shall arbitrate between strong nations far away; they shall beat their swords into plowshares and their spears into pruning hooks; nation shall not lift up sword against nation, neither shall they learn war any more; but they shall all sit under their own fig trees, and no-one shall make them afraid; for the mouth of the LORD has spoken.'
(Micah 4.2–4)

REFLECTION

Leader: Let us pray.
            God of justice and deep compassion,
            you weep when you see what we do to each other, sometimes, even,
            in your name.

Be with us now, as we pray for your grace for those affected by conflict around the world.

Leader: We pray for those who face exhausting and frightening situations every day,
for those who are trying to keep their children safe,
for those who have lost homes and livelihoods.

All: **Guide, guard and strengthen them, we pray.**

> '**When you go home, tell them of us and say, for their tomorrow, we gave our today.**'
>
> The Kohima epitaph
>
> John Maxwell Edmonds (1875–1958) written c.1916

Leader: We pray for those who help the wounded as hospitals are bombed,
for those who try to house the dispossessed, the refugee,
for those who keep believing in a better future.

All: **Guide, guard and strengthen them, we pray.**

Leader: We pray for all men and women of good will,
for they are your peace-makers.

All: **Guide them by your Spirit,**
give them courage and determination,
help them to bring stability to countries torn apart,
to bring sanity in the midst of madness,
to bring calm in the midst of chaos,
to bring hope in the midst of despair.
Remind us to uphold them in prayer day by day.
Through Jesus, our Saviour, brother and friend,
with whom we dare to hope for a world renewed. AMEN.

The National Anthem is sung.

The service concludes with this verse of scripture as a blessing:

Leader: Jesus said, 'Peace I leave with you; my peace I give to you. I do not give to you as the world gives. Do not let your hearts be troubled and do not let them be afraid.' (John 14.27)

2

Pastoral Practices

Safety net scriptures

If you spend the bulk of your ministry one-on-one with the elderly, their families and staff, then you will already know that this is no 'walk in the park', that this ministry asks of us all we have to offer and more, and draws us into pain and partings. What keeps us afloat when we are faced with attaching and losing time and time again, as those we serve with our best endeavours, inevitably diminish and die?

This is a question we each answer in our own way. Over the years, I have made more time to spend time in silence before God, quietening my spirit, welcoming the guiding strengthening Spirit before I venture out to the care home where I am chaplain. Over the years too, key scriptures for aged-care ministry have woven themselves into a safety net, strong enough and far enough above the sea of loss and exhaustion to keep me from sinking, so I'll share them with you.

> Nothing can separate us from the love of God in Christ Jesus our Lord.
> (Romans 8.39)

Romans 8.38–39 begins: 'For I am convinced …' and goes on to list those things which *cannot* get in the way of the love of God made visible in Jesus Christ. If we were to rewrite that list in the context of pastoral ministry with the elderly, it might look something like this:

> For I am convinced that neither major stroke, nor dementia, nor pain, nor coma, nor dying, nor bodily weakness, nor amputation, nor disfigurement … nor my own fear and anxiety, nor my need to be needed, nor my lack of experience or time … nor family tensions, nor staff interruptions … *nor any other thing* … will be able to separate us from the love of God in Christ Jesus our Lord.

🕯 Take a few minutes to reflect on the above and then rewrite it to make it your own.

If we truly believe that *nothing* can separate us from God's love, then we can also believe that the essential person remains with us and accessible right to the time of his or her dying. Whether or not they can communicate with us, we will sit with them and pray with them and laugh and cry and sing with them, trusting that, in ways we may, as yet, not understand, the love and care offered them touches their innermost being. We can do this only if we ourselves are attentive to the Spirit; only if we are aware of our inner questions and personal weaknesses and bring them before God so they do not clog up the channels of God's love moving through us. The story below I hope illustrates how this process looks in practice:

> *'Jessie' had a severe stroke, and as she had no family nearby, I went up to A&E to see her. Standing beside her trolley in a quiet corridor, I felt overwhelmed by her apparently inaccessible state. What could I do? How should I pray? But then Wisdom whispered, 'It's not about you.'*
>
> *I realized that instead of being **with** Jessie, approaching her situation from a contemplative stance (ego-chatter quietened, attentive to the 'still, small voice', confident that God was present), I was self-focused. Chastened, I named before God my sense of helplessness, my need to be **doing** something, and shifted my focus to what God might want for this faithful woman. I was freed to listen to the Spirit's leading, right there and then.*
>
> *That shift in focus made an extraordinary change to the quality of my presence with her: instead of fretting with something akin to performance anxiety, I leant back against God and invited God's wisdom, words and action into the situation. It soon became clear that I was to anoint her and pray for her healing in the name of Jesus, so that is what I did. There was no visible response, but I trusted that something was happening, that God was at work, whatever the outcome might be.*
>
> *Jessie recovered sufficiently to be able to communicate with those around her, before she died some weeks later. My enduring memory was the absolute love shining from her eyes, as her only relative arrived to keep vigil with her. Nothing could get in the way of the love that flowed between them.*

Jessie's brief 'resurrection' was of course a precious outcome. However, I've also been prompted and prayed with other people in similar circumstances, and they have died in a matter of hours or days, without regaining consciousness. I am sure that God was at work in these women just as much as in Jessie. Naturally the 'Why' question arises, but the 'Why' is God's domain, not mine: I have learned that I do not need to know the answer. I am simply – on a good day – a vessel of grace, no more and no less. Surrendering to the greater purposes of God brings its own freedom.

> The Helper, the Holy Spirit, whom the Father will send in my name, will teach you everything and remind you of all that I have said to you. Peace I leave with you, my peace I give to you … Do not let your hearts be troubled, and do not let them be afraid. (John 14.26–27)

If we are new to pastoral or any other ministry, we look for support from mentors, read books, undertake courses such as CPE (Clinical Pastoral Education) and watch what others have done – successfully or otherwise. There is value in this building up of skills and understandings, but the more we engage in pastoral ministry, the more we find that much of it happens in situations that require us to respond immediately, without a lot of time to prepare and often in situations we've never studied or practised. This is where we need the grace of God to help us build on what we've learned and minister in the unpredictable situations we face. Letting go of *needing to know* exactly what to do and learning *how to be* with people, is part of trusting the Holy Spirit's work in and through us and another aspect of the perfect freedom we can know when serving God.

'Mathilda' was a diabetic who had already lost toes on one of her feet as her circulation began to fail. I visited her in hospital to find she had learned that another dying toe needed to be amputated. I sat with her and listened to her – Mathilda was angry, embarrassed and anxious, but she had a faith and a connection with Jesus, so it was natural for us to pray about the surgery she was facing the next day. We prayed for skill for her surgeon, vigilance for her anaesthetist, compassion for all those caring for her and for the grace she needed.

As we were closing our prayer time the word 'footwashing' came to mind unbidden, like a pure bubble of spring water welling up from the deepest earth: the passage in John 13, when, one by one, Jesus washes his disciples' feet in an act of service and as a ritual of farewell. I hesitated. Should I raise this with Mathilda? What if she thought I was being insensitive? But then I stepped back from 'my stuff' and prayed my way into our conversation:

'Mathilda,' I said, 'as we were praying, the story of Jesus washing the feet of the disciples came to mind. You know that story – the night that Jesus shared the Last Supper with his friends – he wanted to wash the feet of each one of them to remind them they were called to be servant leaders but also to make a personal connection with each one of them because he loved them.' (I paused for a minute ... she was listening intently.) 'I wonder whether, after I leave, you might like to spend a little time putting yourself in that picture ... being there with Jesus ... letting him come to you with towel and basin?' We looked at each other in silence for a moment. Then, slowly, she smiled and her eyes lit up. I didn't say any more, just squeezed her hand and left. I knew that she had heard the invitation, and where she went from there was between her and her God.

I wanted to share this story with you because I hadn't gone to see Mathilda thinking about what I might say or what a 'good scripture' passage might be for her. I had just gone to be with her, where she was. We do not have to have all the answers, but can rely on the Spirit of Jesus to be with us, and, if we are listening, to show us a way forward that may be just right for the person in need.

> If we confess our sins, he who is faithful and just will forgive us our sins and cleanse us from all unrighteousness. (1 John 1.9)

In any ministry context we will make mistakes. There are days when we simply do not have the energy or the will to go and see someone we know we 'should' visit. There will be times when we carelessly say a word that is far from kind to a harried staff member and we do *not* say the words that could have soothed a daughter, battered by a domineering, demented parent's 'Go to hell!' We forget a hymn at a funeral service or call people by the wrong names. We don't pass on a message, we avoid a confrontation with a difficult person, and so it goes on. We recognize, with a deep inner pain, the truth of the lines in the prayer of general confession which read: '… we have left undone those things which we ought to have done, and we have done those things which we ought not to have done' (BCP, Penitential Rite 1).

But, thank God, we do not need to be weighed down by our failures; we can choose to share our sins of omission and commission with God and be assured of God's astonishing forgiveness. Psalm 32 tracks David's inner journey of repentance:

> While I kept silence, my body wasted away
>   through my groaning all day long …
> Then I acknowledged my sin to you,
>   and I did not hide my iniquity;
> I said, 'I will confess my transgressions to the LORD',
> and you forgave the guilt of my sin. (verses 3, 5)

Our God forgives. Always. May we forgive ourselves. May we learn from our errors so they are not repeated. May we be gentle with others who make mistakes, and share with them our trust in God's mercy and faithfulness.

> God is love, and those who abide in love, abide in God, and God abides in them. (1 John 4.16b)

God is love: a summary of God's character, a reassurance of God's true nature, a message that our hurting world needs. Yet the nominated message-bearer, the institutional Church, has struggled to carry that message clearly and cleanly into the twenty-first century and is being challenged in post-Christian Britain, Europe and the West as never before. Rather than going into defence or maintenance mode, it is time for those of us who are part of the Church and who *know* God as love, to broaden our vision, to open our eyes to the myriad ways the mission of God is currently being expressed beyond traditional church communities. Yes, we have 'Missional Church' and 'Messy Church' and 'Fresh Expressions' and other valuable ways of Church interacting with community; but something else is happening, growing up from the 'grass roots': younger people are forming their own communities of faith devoted to justice and Jesus; movements in prayer are being carried around the globe borne on the wings of hope and social media; there is growing interest in contemplative prayer and a new monasticism; there is a discontent with systems that disempower the poor, and a desire to see a social gospel; there is a developing recognition that materialism favours the few and bankrupts both the spirit and the environment for everyone else.

Sometimes in mainstream churches we can behave as if we have a monopoly on God, but God is well and truly active *wherever* we care to look, if we have eyes to see. We trust that God is already at work with people everywhere, whether or not they are aware of God's presence, and, instead of 'taking God to the Godless', we begin to look for evidence of God's ways and wisdom.

How and where do we notice God's presence? 1 John 4.16b provides a starting point: 'God is love, and those who abide in love abide in God, and God abides in them.' If we take the incarnation of Christ seriously, then *we will find him in all people who love*: in family life, in sacrificial caring, in those who work for good in any context; we see him in wholesome creativity and innovation, in research and medical breakthroughs, in selfless service to a nation or our neighbour … we will discover the truth of the ancient chant, 'Ubi caritas et amor, deus ibi est' ('Where charity and love are, God is present').

In our pastoral encounters with the elderly, we are alert for intimations of the presence of this Christ of ours who took on flesh and paid the price of that embodiment. As we meet them in the privacy of their own rooms, we'll see the carefully selected or randomly grabbed remnants of a lifetime: unwritten memories, precious artefacts, photographs that hint at happier times, favourite music CDs, the presence or absence of religious pictures or reading material. The handful of personal items which co-exist with the walking and hearing aids, rails and call-bells and the button-driven bed, may provide us with clues about the state of the resident's 'God-connection' and can inform our conversation as we listen for memories still fragrant with Love, stories which shape a person's spirituality:

- the relationships that have been precious
- the desire to reconnect with disaffected or distant family
- a courageous letting go of what has been and opening to the work of the present moment
- early spiritual formation, spiritual experience and prayer practice
- thanksgiving for what has been significant in their lives
- the place of beauty, the arts, music and laughter
- things which bring them peace and comfort
- their relationship with the natural world, for example birds, the care-home cat, flowers and fragrance.

God is indeed present in each life revealed in the love given and received, but is also revealed in the suffering. When we love, we risk loss and pain, we make ourselves vulnerable, which is what God in Jesus did. So we find God in all grieving, in suffering and dying, and in the stricken souls of victims and perpetrators of violence, in whom the image of Christ is crucified anew with each act of brutality. In aged-care we will likely find people who have suffered, been betrayed or abused, lost loved ones too early, lost health and hope too soon. We need to be able to listen to stories of suffering if we are going to be of any use and bear witness to that key truth which is another part of our 'safety net':

> Look, the virgin shall conceive and bear a son, and they shall name him Emmanuel, which means, 'God with us'. (Matthew 1.23)

Christ is indeed God with us – the enormity of this truth is incalculable: the limitless God choosing to be limited by human form, yet in doing so, hallowing our person-hood and revealing the uniqueness of our faith: in Jesus we have a God who is *not* remote from human suffering but is there *with us* in it. In his humanity, Jesus felt what many human beings experience when faced with terminal illness and inevitable death. Ultimately the very thing that is the most abhorrent – Jesus' poignant journey to the cross and a terrible death – makes the most sense to people on their own final journey:

- Jesus anticipated his death with all its imaginings (Luke 9.22; 24.7).
- In Gethsemane he felt terror and isolation (Matthew 26.36–46).
- In his trial and crucifixion he felt pain, weakness, vulnerability and abandonment (Mark 15.34).
- Jesus shows us how to be in these dark and difficult places – even in extremity, he cries out to God, using the language of the psalms (Psalm 22) – honest, gutsy, desperate, real, intense emotion expressed within the covenant relationship with God (Luke 23.46).

In aged-care we especially value the Christ who is familiar with the marginal[1] places of life, with the pastorally difficult liminal spaces of ageing, transition and unknow-ing, with the waiting and the 'not yet, but soon' stage of life's ending. *God is with us* all the way to our own dying and beyond to the *resurrection* – we will not be left alone. We do not have to go through it by ourselves – Jesus has been down this road before and knows it step by anguished step. And so we listen for stories and memories that tell of being on the margins, stories and memories of suffering:

- betrayal and abandonment
- deep fear and anguish borne unsupported
- the hope of comfort dashed by painful judgement
- disappointments with others, with oneself, or with God
- accidents, guilt, blame and forgiveness
- the untimely deaths of family or friends.

---

1 Robert Lentz (icons and biographies), Edwina Gately (reflections), *Christ in the Margins*, Orbis Books, Maryknoll, NY, 2003.

Tragic losses may have made the elderly call into question God's nature or existence. Such events can throw an unexamined faith into the dustbin of despair, and not everyone has the will, opportunity or support to begin to rescue the shards and re-form them into a faith that is strong enough to deal with doubt and transcend trauma. If someone mentions such an event, gently encourage the elder to talk about it more fully with you. Listen very carefully for any sign of grace in the circumstances, or in the way the older person has dealt with the loss, for example:

'Paul' had an asthmatic adult daughter who had died years ago in a hiking accident, when a river suddenly flooded. A faithful Christian, he had taken comfort from the fact that the post-mortem showed she had not drowned, but had suffered a heart attack. To Paul, this was a sign of grace, for he could not bear the thought of his child struggling to breathe and being gradually overwhelmed.

If there seems to be only horror in the ending of a loved one's life, then encourage the person to tell God/Jesus/Mary (in your presence or in private) how they are feeling and what they are thinking, *even* if this means being angry with God, or using words that are not 'proper'. Such 'venting' opens up a line of communication between the hurting person and God, starts to release pent-up tension and begins to make possible a slow but definite move towards building a robust relationship with God. For this journey will lead them ultimately to *resurrection*, an emerging hope, a sign of new life and love:

'Jane's' son was killed overseas in dreadful circumstances. Her anger with God was palpable and she did not hesitate to voice her questions. 'How could God have let this happen?' I listened for a long time. Then we talked about her son, her mothering of him, how he had been an adventurous child. We talked about how hard it was for her as a mother to see him hurt and to know that she couldn't stop him making decisions which might put him in harm's way. She loved him with all her heart but, he had to live his life. We talked about God as a loving parent ...

Months later I 'happened' to see her in hospital. She was near death, hardly able to speak. I reached into my bag and drew out a holding cross. When I offered it to her, she clutched it to herself ... there was peace in her eyes.

She died the next day.

In the pages that follow are 12 pastoral practices drawn from the coalface of ministry with the aged. What is written here is the result of both action and reflection. I hope you will find that this material makes a positive difference to your ministry so you may be a *non-anxious presence* among the elderly, their families and the care-home staff or congregation, able to hold a sacred space of calm in the midst of chaos. Others around you absorb some of that inner peace even as the comings and goings continue; they are soothed by something they may not be able – yet – to name which enables you to be present to them in a time of loss or crisis or confusion. That 'something' within you is, of course, the Spirit of Jesus reaching out to them through you, through your kindness, your time spent with them, your listening, your very personhood in Christ.

We trust that the Spirit is with us and will guide us. We model that to others and they are blessed.

A word about dementia

Earlier in this book we considered the sacrament of the present moment and the way being fully present to another enables deep connection and spiritual conversation. This 'Right Now' focus is the key to being with anyone, but *especially with people with dementia* – whether their 'present moment' is rich with joy or full of despair and confusion. As educator Laura Bramly expresses:

> People living in the later stages of dementia are living in the present (and by the present, I mean now, this second) because there is nothing else ... (we) need to step into this reality and realize that all that matters is Right Now, not five minutes ago, and not half an hour from now. If you are able to bring joy into their Right Now, then you have done something wonderful. If, for one second, you were able to make them think, to use their cognitive abilities, to feel curiosity, excitement, wonder ... then you have increased the quality of their life for that one second. And because that one second is all there is, then you have done everything.[2]

Dementia itself is not an illness but a syndrome, a set of symptoms caused by certain diseases such as Alzheimer's, advanced Parkinson's, Creutzfeld-Jakob disease, injuries such as repeated head trauma, or behaviours such as long-term alcohol or substance abuse. These cause physical brain damage which leads to a range of symptoms which gather under the umbrella term 'dementia'. These symptoms include memory loss, confusion and disorientation, increasing difficulty in learning new tasks or using everyday items for their intended purpose, repetitive speech or actions, and 'confabulation' in which a person – with no intent to deceive – makes things up to compensate for gaps in memory.

Increasingly, health professionals are adopting a palliative care approach to dementia care, i.e. 'a supportive approach that aspires to improve the quality of life of a person and their families facing a terminal illness, according to the person's wishes and through the prevention and relief of suffering by early identification and treatment of pain and other problems, physical, psychosocial *and spiritual*.'[3]

---

2 Cathy Greenblat, *Love, Loss and Laughter: Seeing Alzheimer's Differently,* Lyons Press, Guilford, CT, 2011, p. 71.

3 http://www.fightdementia.org.au/common/files/NAT/18122013_PCA_Alzheimer_position_statement.pdf (accessed 8.3.14).

Good pastoral care depends on the quality of the connection we make with those we visit, whatever their situation. Key skills and attitudes for establishing a sound working relationship include being respectful and non-judgemental, listening actively, being present and attentive, noticing body language, sitting at the same level, reflecting both the feelings and the content of what we hear, asking open-ended or evocative questions, being comfortable with silence and the expression of a range of emotions.

These skills plus others identified by Goldsmith[4] paraphrased below, will enable us to minister to those who have dementia with compassion and appropriateness:

- Give time for the person to notice you are there before trying to interact with them.
- Start by saying who you are and what your relationship is with the person you are visiting rather than expecting them to remember, e.g. 'Hello, Alice, I'm Chaplain Sue.'
- Most of us speak quickly; we need to slow down and give the person time to respond.
- If someone does not answer right away, it does not mean they do not understand
- Use short sentences with one main idea.
- Avoid complex language.
- Avoid asking multiple questions.
- There is an important place for silence and for appropriate touch (see under 'Pastoral Practices').
- Pay attention to how the person seems to be feeling.
- If you are rebuffed, don't take it personally; come back another time.

I remember an old lady whom I will call Adele. I was new to my work and was introducing myself. 'I'm Sue, the new chaplain,' I said, loudly, as I had been told she had hearing loss. 'No you're not!' she said. And nothing I said would convince her. After months of popping in to see her, one day when I was visiting she looked at me and said, 'I'm in heaven.' I waited a moment and said, 'What's that like?' 'It's beautiful,' she said, and smiled, happily present to her 'heaven' moment, that single word conveying everything for her.

You may like to familiarize yourself with the Behavioural Staging Model of dementia care developed over many years by Dr Gemma M. M. Jones (see 'Further Reading'), a dementia care consultant and founder of the Alzheimer's Café movement in the UK. Her work helps us better to understand key behaviours and fears, as well as helping strategies appropriate to dementia, from mild confusion to end stage withdrawal. Remembering that no stage theory is set in stone and people will move back and forward at times, Jones' model helps us get a sense of an overall pattern of behaviours and fears as dementia symptoms escalate.

---

4 M. Goldsmith, *In a Strange Land: People with Dementia and the Local Church*, 4M Publications, Nottingham, 2004, pp. 89–90.

For example, in material prepared for caregivers and family members by Ruth Thomas,[5] the behaviours/fears and helping strategies of stage two of Jones' four-stage model look like this:

Stage 2 behaviours and fears[6]	Stage 2 helping strategies
Factual memories are very blurred and less important to the person. Emotions and how the person feels are more important now. They are disoriented to time and often to place. They cannot cover up their memory loss any more and are becoming disinhibited. Their conversation is hard to follow.	Encourage the person to talk about whatever they want to. Don't feel obliged to change the subject if it isn't 'happy'. Reminisce with them. Acknowledge the person's feelings and life experiences. Resist correcting mistaken facts. Encourage them to share their wisdom (ask questions like: 'What advice would you give to people wanting to get married/move overseas/change their job etc?'). Use touch, eye contact, music, singing and movement. Try to find another resident in the same stage for them to 'buddy' with.

Once we begin to realize that people affected by dementia are displaying 'normal reactions in an unusually perceived world as opposed to displaying strange and unexplained reactions in a normally perceived world'[7] we are on the way to a deeper appreciation of their reality and a more effective and compassionate ministry.

Interactions with different residents over a week help illustrate how varied the 'Right Now' moments can be with people with later stage dementia:

5 For helpful information, visit http://www.midlandmentalhealthnetwork.co.nz/page/160-midland-regional-dementia-advisor+dementia-dementia-care-information-leaflets (NZ, accessed 1.2.14); most countries will have organizations such as Alzheimer's Society or its equivalent. In the UK, visit the Alzheimer's Café website http://www.alzheimercafe.co.uk/; in Australia see, for example, www.fightdementia.org.au; in NZ contact your local District Health Board or the National Dementia Cooperative: http://ndc.hiirc.org.nz/section/19790/national-dementia-cooperative.

6 Ruth Thomas, *Behavioural Staging: Leaflet 3 – The different helping strategies for each stage*, 2012 (see first website in footnote 5 for further information).

7 Ruth Thomas, *Dementia Care* presentation, Midland Health, 22.1.14 (see first website in footnote 5 for further information).

- sitting with someone who is repeatedly folding and unfolding a large tea-towel, totally absorbed and silent
- meeting someone coming from her room, her face crumpled, her hands anxiously clenched, talking of something that happened in her youth. She clearly feels unsafe, so, taking her hands, I say, 'No-one can hurt you. You are safe here, you are safe.' I know of her long-standing faith, so I ask her, 'Shall we pray?' 'Yes,' is the clear reply. So I gently pray for her to feel the safety of Jesus' presence with her in that moment, his peace and his love, right now. It is not long before she relaxes and we go to get a cuppa
- at a Communion service, seeing a resident with arms raised high in worship, eyes closed, singing a favourite hymn
- someone linking her arm through mine and smiling as we walk towards the recreation room for a concert.

We may initially feel uncomfortable around people with dementia; part of that discomfort is because their emotional expression is no longer inhibited by convention or upbringing.

> I think of old 'Mary' whom I met early in ministry. I could never seem to find the right words or make some sort of connection. I would sometimes pass by her room and hope she was asleep. When I did make the effort to spend time with her, I found her language hard to deal with. I have to say I was relieved when she died. When I took my ambivalence about Mary to supervision, it became clear that what I had found uncomfortable were my powerlessness and frustration: I couldn't make things better. All the usual things I could do with someone were useless. That was when I began to learn about 'being', the ministry of presence.

If we find it difficult to notice and name *our* own feelings, if we normally keep a tight rein on our expression of anger, sadness, grief, frustration, confusion, desire and so on, we may struggle to know how to respond when we are with people who openly express *their* feelings, use language we wouldn't want to repeat, and may exhibit sexual interest or behaviours that we might deem inappropriate in someone of advanced age! In some ways, those with late-stage dementia unknowingly confront us with our 'shadow' selves, the parts of ourselves that we keep hidden.

When we struggle to be alongside residents for any reason, fear is at work in us, '... but perfect love casts out fear ...' (1 John 4.18a). And so we are brought back to the fundamentals of our faith and ministry practice: our dependence on the Spirit of Jesus right now, each moment.

Listening

Threefold listening informs all pastoral encounters. We listen to the person we've come to see, of course, but we also listen to ourselves and to God.[8] It's a complex dance of paying attention to the 'still, small voice' and the nudges we have come to recognize as the Spirit at work, moving in harmony with (or sometimes pulling against) our own ideas and agendas, while all the time keeping in step with the rhythm of the other person's clumsy or skilled story-sharing. When we are listening well, God's creative energy flows through us into the situations we meet, giving us ideas and guiding our ministry.

However hard it may be, this life-listening dance opens up the possibility of real connection with another person and with the reality of God, so long as we do not trip them up. To avoid blocking the Spirit's flow, we need to take seriously the story of the mountain-top transfiguration of Christ. In the synoptic[9] Gospel accounts (Matthew 17.1–8, Mark 9.2–8 and Luke 9.28–36) there is surprising agreement on what God had to say to the stunned disciples as Jesus' glorious nature mysteriously emerged before their startled eyes. They heard God first affirm Jesus as beloved Son, the Chosen, and then tell the disciples what they needed to do: '... *listen to him*.'

That's what God told them to do *then*, and tells us to do *now*: 'Listen to Jesus', for he is the answer to all our questions, the port in any storm, clearer of the way, author of truth, life-bringer (John 14.6).

So how do those of us who offer ministry in his name, 'listen to Jesus'?

- Ask for the grace to begin to 'hear' or 'see' the Son, the beloved, whom God has chosen.
- Notice synchronicity, answered prayer, God-given openings and perfect timing.
- Read aloud the Gospel stories of Jesus, the Acts of the Apostles which witness to his Spirit.
- 'Read' the book of creation – the ways the natural world 'speaks' to us of God.
- Pray in silence, opening ourselves to the influence of the Spirit of Jesus.
- Keep a spiritual journal in which we listen to our lives and note signs of God's presence.
- Reflect on our spiritual experience with a trusted minister, soul friend or spiritual director.
- Watch for and expect hints of God's activity among those we visit.
- Be still enough to pay attention to the inner promptings of the Spirit even if they take an unusual form, as this story shows:

---

8 For a much fuller treatment of 'Listening to God, to ourselves and to others' in a pastoral context, see my *Spiritual Direction: A Practical Introduction*, Canterbury Press, Norwich, 2008 (also available in Kindle edition, 2011).

9 *Synoptic* – from the same viewpoint – is the name given to the first three books of the New Testament: Matthew, Mark and Luke – which have much common material, whereas the Gospel of John contains much that is not mentioned in the other Gospels and has its own particular perspective on telling the Jesus story.

We were about to leave home to visit friends hospitalized following a bad car accident, when I had a very distinct impression that I was to take with me the large teddy bear which usually sat in my office. My husband raised an eyebrow but kindly chose not to question what I was doing, and we headed off.

He went to see 'Ted' in one ward, and I went to see his wife 'Nellie' in another ward. I got to the door of her room, rather gingerly holding the teddy bear in front of me. Nellie's face lit up, 'How did you know?' were her first words as she reached out with her good arm for the bear. 'Know what?' I said, as I handed it over. Snuggling it to her body, she said, 'Whenever Ted's away, I always take a teddy bear to bed with me to hold on to. He's in another ward and we can't get to each other at the moment. This will help me feel close to him.' I was stunned. 'Well,' I said, 'I didn't know that … but God certainly did!' And I told her what had made me bring the bear to her.

She was amazed that God might care for her in this way, and to this day she still speaks of God's teddy bear.

Spirit-prompts to action enable God to work in and through us if we are listening and willing to respond. But of course that isn't always the case:

My mum went into hospital voluntarily for a revision of her hip replacement at the age of 80. As she was in a lot of pain, she was keen to have the surgery and was in a positive mood when I left her in the hospital ward. I had gone only a few yards down the corridor when the prompt came: 'Go back and give your mum a hug.' I hesitated. We'd said 'Au revoir', as you do before surgery, without too much fuss. But the prompt was insistent, so I went back to her room. When I arrived, the door was closed: the 'Isolation' sign was up, as was the practice 20 years ago prior to surgery. I looked through the little glass window and could see Mum chatting away animatedly to a nurse. She seemed fine. Back then I wasn't one to 'buck the system' and insist on seeing her. So I turned and went back down the corridor. Mum died during surgery the next day.

I don't think that the prompt was for her so much as for me. We'd had an ambivalent relationship which had only recently started to reconcile. Perhaps God knew that a hug would be something special, a gift for me to hold on to as I grieved. I regretted I had not been more obedient.

All of us have the chance to be guided by the Spirit. Sometimes we listen and sometimes we don't. Who knows how differently individual, or even national history might have unfolded, had someone listened and obeyed a clear invitation from God to act. Listening for the 'still, small voice' which we learn to recognize as coming from all that is good, and holy, and loving and just – from God – is the responsibility of all who follow Christ.

🕯 Think back to an experience you have had when you have responded to, or ignored, a Spirit-prompt and the consequences.

When we are in a pastoral setting in home, hospital or care facility, we listen to the person before us, in spite of interruptions. We tune out distracting noises, listen with our eyes as well as our ears, we notice small clues that hint at people's faith or fear, we pick up factual information about their life, and we 'read between the lines', listening for what is *not* said, the feelings behind the words.

We might feed back to the person a summary of what we think we have heard so the person knows that we are 'onto it', we've *heard* them. Being heard in itself brings healing and comfort. We don't have to 'fix' things, we don't have to give deep theological answers; we do have to trust God and *believe* the scripture in which the Lord says to Paul – and to us and those we serve: 'My grace is enough; it's all you need. My strength comes into its own in your weakness' (2 Corinthians 12.9, *The Message*).

We listen particularly to the way people speak about God or the sacred or that which is central to their well-being. Much of our language about matters of faith is *metaphorical* because mystery and divinity, the truth and shape of eternal life, the unknown reaches of mercy and justice which God inhabits, demand reverence and resist definition. *Metaphors and similes* pepper people's speech in everyday conversation too, and we do well to listen for such word pictures or potent phrases, because they can provide a way into a person's felt experience when other methods of enquiry, even open-ended questions, prove fruitless. Consider this example of how a dying man approached the time of 'waiting':

> *'T' was nearing death and was very tired. He was comfortable and seemed accepting of the inevitable outcome, looking forward to being reunited with his wife, who had died several years earlier. When asked what it was like waiting, he described it as 'like being on a railway platform'. This was a natural simile from his working life. When invited to say a little more, he said he always enjoyed the anticipation of a train coming in, thinking about where it had come from and where it was going. This opened up more conversation around the destination of the train he would get onto: '... heaven ...'*
>
> *'So what's it like being on the platform now?'*
> *'Just fine,' he whispered. A thumbs-up sign. A smile.*

Metaphor also turns up as people try to make sense of what is happening to them medically:

> *'Sandra' was experiencing a series of small TIA's.*[10] *She talked about these attacks being 'like an earthquake – you never know when it's coming, how long it will last or how bad it's going to be'.*

---

10 'Trans-ischemic attack' or 'mini-stroke', usually resolves quickly, and may not cause lasting damage, i.e. tissue death.

This metaphor, particularly relevant to experience in New Zealand over recent years as the ground beneath our feet shifts and shakes, was a perfect description of her uncertainty and allowed her to name with great precision the process she was experiencing, so those around her got a sense of what it was like for her.

Continuing the metaphor, we could ask her, 'What's it like to be on such shaky ground?' or 'How does it feel when everything around you starts shaking?' To go deeper we might ask, 'Sandra, where is God in this uncertainty?' Such a question could help her give voice to her spiritual strength or alert us to her spiritual needs.

Sometimes, although we are listening attentively, it is literally hard to hear what people are saying. As dementia reaches its later stages speech gets muddled and can all but disappear, strokes can make unravelling a person's conversation challenging, those near death may speak very quietly. We can do our best to listen; we can say, 'I'm sorry, but I didn't quite catch what you said. Can you tell me again, please?' But sometimes we just won't be able to understand, and that's hard for us and for them. We can only commend the person to God and trust that inwardly they are able to say what they need to say to the One to whom they will return.

Listen to God, listen to others – and listen to ourselves. It is important that we pay attention to:

- our strong reactions to people or situations – these can hamper our pastoral effectiveness and hint at unfinished emotional work which will need working out in counselling or supervision
- persistent anxiety, feelings of sadness or inadequacy, exhaustion and weepiness can all be signs of depression or the onset of burnout/compassion fatigue: seek professional support
- how we are spiritually 're-charged' – take an annual week's retreat as well as quarterly retreat days and keep up a daily pattern of life-giving prayer
- how we are resourced physically and emotionally – sleep, exercise, healthy eating, regular medical checks, and good friends and family with time out for fun and a hobby or two!

'Are your ears awake? Listen. Listen to the Wind Words, the Spirit blowing through the churches' (Revelation 3.22, *The Message*).

Befriending silence

In silence, trees put down deep roots, seeds begin to push up towards the light, the chrysalis is transformed into a butterfly.
No fanfares accompany these transitions.
They happen because there is a sacred principle at work: considerable growth takes place in silence.

For most of us, however, silence is rare. We struggle to find a space free from the external noises of our culture – things whizzing and buzzing and throbbing and beeping all around us. For many of us, conditioned as we are to have the television or radio on, our phones streaming music, our tablets keeping us informed of 'breaking news', if conversation dries up we automatically fill the void with words or activity. Some of us hate silence because it reeks of loneliness. Others resist silence because it was used as a punishment in childhood, a sign of withdrawal of parental approval.

What was your experience of *silence* as you were growing up? What is your attitude to *silence* now?

Nor is it easy to still the interior noise of our own 'monkey mind', the thoughts that swirl in our psyche demanding attention, destroying our peace. Focused reflection is hard to come by as distractions draw us out to the chaotic periphery of our rational life, away from the still centre where God's Spirit waits.

Silence is rare, too, in most liturgical settings. Even though the rubrics hopefully signal a space, this is often ignored or kept to a bare few seconds. Congregations are denied the experience of sinking into a corporate stillness, of connecting with the deeper silence inhabited by God. Without such silence our liturgies risk being 'words piled upon words' until meaning has been wrung out of them entirely.

When in your day do *you* have time to be silent? *Where* does this happen? What is your experience of silence in liturgy?

Fasting from speaking is a spiritual discipline in its own right and one that is valued in the Christian contemplative tradition. Leaving the luxury of liturgy behind, no longer protected by pages and paragraphs of words, in silence we come to God as we came into this world – naked and needy. In that silence, God's Spirit can meet and minister to our spirit, our innermost being, and bring us the gifts of clarity, peace, relief, comfort … whatever God knows we need of grace for that moment.

The value of silence in aged-care ministry is immeasurable. Why is it so important? Because silence:

- enhances our ministry of presence
- quietens our ego
- provides space for us to listen – to God and to ourselves
- allows time for us to pray inwardly for the person and the situation, asking God for wisdom and the right words when we do speak
- signals that we do not expect a lot of conversation when people are very unwell
- indicates a willingness just to 'sit with' the other person, to keep them company
- gives space for people to formulate their answers
- soothes our discomfort and stops us saying things that are patently unhelpful
- enables us to be alongside people in moments of deep grief
- allows us to acknowledge that we do not have to have all the answers.

If we were fortunate enough to have a parent/caregiver who sat with us when we were little and sick in bed, we will know the blessing of companionable silence, of being able to open our eyes and see someone familiar there with us, of being able to hold a hand, of not having to talk or think.

That is what you can do for someone in a care home or A&E department or their own home: you can sit and be with them, hold their hand and keep them company. We can offer them the gift of silence: 'There's no need to talk unless you want to.' The freedom to be silent can be a relief.

Praying

When you think of *praying* with the elderly, what comes to mind? Spend a few minutes recalling your own 'prayer history' and current 'prayer practice'.

In the Catechism in the New Zealand Prayer Book there is a simple question and a concise reply:

> *What is prayer?* Prayer is our response to God's love.
> We pray in the name of Christ and by the power of the Holy Spirit (p. 934).

Just as we try our best to keep in contact with loved ones using any means at our disposal, our God is constantly reaching out to us through the Spirit, seeking a response, sending love letters to us by carrier pigeon and creation, by music and scripture, sunsets, upsets, life events, pain and joy. God's nature is Love, and to be true to that nature, God seeks the beloved – seeks you, seeks me. We may have heard stories of love letters being intercepted by protective parents and kept from the intended recipient until eventually, with no response, the saddened sender turns away. Well, God never turns away.

Prayer is our response to that outpouring of determined, dedicated love and affection, kindness and hopefulness sent our way each moment of each day by the Spirit. Prayer grows as we grow in our relationship with God; it emerges out of Love, is informed by Love. Even those who say they are 'not religious' will often tell you that yes, they do pray – for their families, for friends. So in your pastoral conversation, *don't hesitate to ask about prayer*:

- 'Are there times in your life when you have prayed?' and 'What about now?'
- 'What sort of prayer works best for you – in the past – now?'
- 'Have you ever prayed and been disappointed?' (May open up a pastoral need, so ask this only if you have time to help the person reflect on what happened and their image of God.)

A few of the elderly people we meet will have strong prayer lives, but even if they are experienced in praying for others, we may find that they are not used to praying for their own needs, even though the prayer of petition (asking) makes up much of the Lord's Prayer. They may have been taught that it's okay to pray for others, and to praise God in their prayer, but 'less worthy' to ask for God's provision for themselves. They may have thought that 'God already knows what we need, so why pray?' God does know, of course, but just as wise and loving parents cannot help their adult child until he or she invites them into the troublesome situation, so it is with God. God will not impose but waits to be included, to be asked.

So, why don't people ask? Some of us may have had a lifetime of struggling to ask those around us for what we need, so it's not surprising if we have the same struggle when it comes to asking God. We are used to being stubbornly independent; we are *not* used to noticing our feelings, or naming our longings, nor are we necessarily as honest as we might be about confessing our failures and foibles to ourselves, let alone to God. But God longs for the real you and the real me to come and meet the real God who is full of compassion and who understands our frailty ... and we do that when we bring ourselves as fully as we can to God in prayer. It doesn't matter whether we sing or walk our prayers or sit in attentive silence, whether we hold a cross or meditate on a painting, whether we use set prayers or allow prayer to bubble up from within – prayer is about turning towards the waiting God and letting God be God in and through us.

How do we encourage those we meet in a care facility or a private home who want to grow in their prayer life? We can:

- value and practise prayer in our own lives and speak of it naturally with those we meet
- go over a copy of the brochure on *Simple Prayer* (Appendix 2; colour pictures in Photo Appendix)
- encourage people to do a life review
- encourage them to talk to God in the morning, asking for what they need for the day
- encourage a time of reflection and thanksgiving in the evening
- explore the possibility of saying Grace at their main meal each day – this can be said quietly to themselves or, by agreement, aloud with others at their table
- introduce them to *lectio divina* or praying with scripture using the imagination
- invite them to meditate on a picture of Jesus interacting with people (Jean Keaton's drawings are especially evocative as they picture Jesus with children as well as adults. They are available on http://picturesofjesus4you.com/gallery1drawings. html, accessed 17.1.14). Or you could look for old paintings or drawings which show qualities of compassion, encouragement and acceptance, for example the pen and ink drawing by Rembrandt van Rijn of a child learning to walk (see, for example, http://www.mamo.org.uk/?p=150, accessed 17.1.14) or other suitable but publicly accessible images, e.g. 'Christ with Martha and Mary', Johannes Vermeer, 1655

- consider starting a weekly prayer group – mainly intercession for the institution, residents etc.
- if people are mentally able and want to go deeper, then offer Sheila Pritchard's *The Lost Art of Meditation* (Scripture Union, 2003), Philip Yancey's *Prayer* (Hodder & Stoughton, 2008) or Joan Bel Geddes, *Are You Listening God?* (Ave Maria Press, 1994).

Praying with another person is a practice that distinguishes pastoral ministry from other 'helping professions' with whom a resident or older person may have contact. We might use prayers from a prayer book if we have one to hand, or prayers from a person's own tradition if they prefer, but in practice what we really need to do is to rely on the guidance of the Holy Spirit. 'Likewise the Spirit helps us in our weakness; for we do not know how to pray as we ought, but that very Spirit intercedes with sighs too deep for words' (Romans 8.26).

As chaplains or ministers, we have the chance to offer prayer in a surprisingly wide range of situations and occasions with older people and with staff, some private and some public, for example:

- when a resident is new to the care home and feeling overwhelmed by multiple losses
- on the anniversary of a loved one's death
- in hospital wards or emergency rooms
- when we are at a deathbed
- when the institution's staff are under stress, e.g. dealing with an outbreak of sickness
- blessing an item of jewellery for a staff member to give to her partner
- when someone is anxious about being given a shower by a particular caregiver
- commending to God the issues discussed during pastoral conversation or counselling
- when the home's pet turtle went missing (surfaced months later after coming out of hibernation in the courtyard garden!)
- at the beginning of a meeting ... and sometimes at the end as well
- thanksgiving for pets when the care home had its own 'Dog Show'
- opening a new part of the care home
- blessing a chalet, apartment or villa before a new resident takes possession
- with a community group, part of the aged-care village, when one of their group has died
- Grace at a shared meal, e.g. a volunteer lunch
- as part of the care of a resident with Alzheimer's
- blessing a room following a death
- blessing of a new van for the community outreach programme
- blessing the entire retirement village
- when a staff member leaves.

Like the Celtic Church, which believed that the whole of life was worthy of being held in prayer, we can model a similar commitment to inviting God into all aspects of life in the aged-care institution and in our own church setting where we minister. Gradually people get used to the fact that we pray – they seek us out for prayer and they come to know that they can bring anything to God because they have seen us pray in all sorts of situations.

Some elders will talk about someone praying for them long ago – a parent or god-parent perhaps – and the feeling of love and security, that sense of connection with God which that time of prayer evoked. Even without that foundational experience, *people welcome prayer* – if it fits the situation or emerges naturally out of the pastoral conversation and is not used as a formulaic way of ending a visit! It is a privilege for us to be able to pray *with* people, aided by the Comforter and Peace-bringer.

Prayers of confession

There is one particular form of prayer which may emerge in our ministry with the aged: the prayer of confession and the giving of absolution. For many, confession is associated with Catholicism and a practice that, at its best, relieves guilt and reconnects the penitent with God and the community, but at its worst is a formu-laic process with little power to make lasting change in the penitent's life. In some Christian contexts corporate confession and assurance of forgiveness is absent from services; in others such as Anglicanism, corporate confession is part of most services and provision is made for individual confession in, for example, the rite 'Reconciliation of a Penitent' included in current prayer books such as the Church of England,[11] and the New Zealand prayer book.[12]

What is your own experience of personal confession and absolution – as penitent or priest? What is your attitude to the concept of someone being reconciled to God in this way?

Many of those we meet in aged-care contexts will have little experience of corpor-ate confession and may not have heard about individual confession or absolution, unless they have encountered a 'confession/forgiveness' process elsewhere, for ex-ample in Alcoholics Anonymous. So, if we can personally offer this form of prayer with integrity, it is up to us to raise the possibility and to assure people that being able to confess sin to God with the support of a compassionate witness, and being able to hear pronounced the timeless words of absolution, can prove life-changing.

---

11 See http://www.churchofengland.org/prayer-worship/worship/texts/christian-initiation/reconciliation-and-restoration-recovering-baptism/the-reconciliation-of-a-penitent-form-one.aspx.

12 New Zealand Prayer Book service, available on http://anglicanprayerbook.org.nz/750.htm.

Years ago, 'Betty' came to talk to me at a quiet day, held near a beautiful lake. She had 'something on her mind', she said. It transpired that she, like so many women of her generation, had found herself pregnant and had made the difficult decision to have an abortion. I listened to her as she told her story and then showed her the rite of reconciliation of a penitent. I invited her to take it away to read and to come back if she thought that making a formal confession was what she wanted to do. An hour later she was back. Together we went down to the lake's edge. The water lapped the lake edge gently as she made her confession to the God who had been waiting for her to bring her distress and guilt into the light of God's healing and forgiving love. Prayer and cool, pure lake-water washed away her burden.

A week later she wrote to tell me that she felt 'lighter', relieved of the weight she had carried for so many years.

Those of us whose tradition includes formal confession and absolution will already have access to forms of prayer which can be adapted for use in an aged-care home or as part of a pastoral visit. If your tradition and that of the person with whom you are praying does not use these forms of prayer, suitable scripture can be used as a vehicle for an individual who wishes to 'come home to God'.

The Luke 15.11–32 story of the return of the prodigal son remains widely known among older people and can be used imaginatively to enable them to begin to return to God, the forgiving father. In this story, the carefully rehearsed words of the penitent son are swept up in the joy of the father's welcome. All that matters is that the wandering soul has turned to make the journey home.

Other suitable scripture includes:

Psalm 32	speaks of turning back to God, making a confession and feeling God's mercy
Psalm 51	David's plea to God after he 'had gone in to Bathsheba' – crying out for forgiveness
Psalm 86.4–5	'Gladden the soul of your servant, for to you, O Lord, I lift up my soul. For you, O Lord, are good and forgiving, abounding in steadfast love to all who call upon you.'
1 John 1.9	'If we confess our sins, he who is faithful and just will forgive us our sins and cleanse us from all unrighteousness.'

Witnessing a confession is a profound privilege. If you would like to read more about this ministry, see 'Further Reading'.

Touching

Spooning

then we lay
as lovers do
curled into each other
warm and safe
until we stirred
and love built fire
and I opened my
heart and womb
to the sweet
and gentle
sharing of his
potent life
with mine ...

with love

now I lie
as patients do
alone and wary
until he comes
and says my name
and I open my
old, dry mouth
to the sweet
and gentle
spooning of
apple onto
my tongue ...

with love

What does this poem say to you about ageing and about 'touching'?

Jesus touched and was touched by people all the time as he walked the paths of Palestine and people sought his healing. Even touching the hem of his garment was enough to bring a cure (Mark 5.25–34) as his powerful touch brought divine energy to human need. Being touched was a blessing and a gift.

Being touched can still be a blessing, but many of us have been told that we have to be careful about touching anyone when we are engaged in pastoral ministry. For years this injunction was part of my spiritual direction, pastoral and supervision ministry, but in coming to work in aged-care, I was confronted by a realization that older people are often starved of touch – not intentionally, but as a consequence of their situation. With family far afield or visiting infrequently, no-one of their own to care for or cuddle, no companion animal to stroke, no neighbours dropping by or friends sharing a meal and a hug on home-going, older people in residential settings, or even living independently, can be deprived of healthy touch as perhaps no other group of people.

Think about two or three elderly people you know professionally or even in your own family – living independently or in care. Consider their need for touch and how that need might – or might not – be addressed.

It would be understandable if we wanted to fill this void by offering touch indiscriminately. However, touch remains a delicate issue for those who have encountered physical or sexual violence; ageing does not automatically diminish sexual interest or arousal; and dementia can affect people's self-control and lead to their making overtures to other residents or to staff. No matter how much we'd like to reduce older people's 'touch hunger', we do have to exercise some discretion in our pastoral practice of touching, so here are some pointers to consider:

- Some healthy touching can happen incidentally as people are assisted with their mobility, or receive personal cares.
- Learn from staff how to support or guide people, and never lift someone without staff input.
- The least problematic place to touch anyone in any context is the upper arm.
- Don't touch anyone until you are sure they know you are there, who you are and what you are asking of them. Not all visually-impaired people look blind, so you risk frightening them if you suddenly touch them without warning.
- In a one-to-one pastoral situation, *always* ask permission before touching *anyone*.
- Old people's skin is thin and subject to tearing even with the gentlest of touches. Unintentional though such injuries will be, they can lead to infection, so we do need to be careful.
- If seeing someone from a different culture, check if there are cultural factors affecting touch, e.g. to Maori the head is sacred and should not be touched.
- Refrain from hugging residents of the opposite gender unless in a public place with someone whom you know very well and trust.
- Some medical conditions can change touch sensitivity, e.g. diabetes can affect circulation and damage nerve endings, leading to reduced awareness of sensation or pain.

- If you experience inappropriate touch from a resident, talk to the clinical care manager and document the incident according to the institution's reporting system. You might think it an isolated instance but it could in fact be part of a pattern; by reporting you may be preventing harm to vulnerable residents.

When you look at a care-home context, there are a surprising number of opportunities for non-threatening touch with the residents: you – or some of your congregation/ network – may want to be part of some of the following literal 'touch-points':

- walking alongside someone, putting your arm lightly around waist or shoulder
- linking arms as you help someone find the way
- placing a hand on the shoulder as you push someone in a wheelchair
- in the privacy of a resident's room, holding a person's hand/s *very* gently
- giving a hug (with permission) – see *Little Book of Hugs* by Kathleen Keating, 1986 (various editions) for a lovely treatment of this practice, and if you sense that the institution would co-operate, perhaps liaising with the diversional therapist, arrange a Hug Day to lift the spirits of residents and staff
- gently massaging hands – use a moisturizing cream (check tolerance to fragrance/ allergies)
- combing or brushing a resident's hair (seek their permission first, of course)
- cleaning their fingernails
- providing a basic toenail cutting and foot massage service!

If you – or someone in your network – wants to explore other avenues for providing healthy physical touch, you may like to find out if the care home allows pet therapy (enlist the support of the diversional therapists). Check if there is such an organization in your area by searching online: http://www.petsastherapy. org/ (UK), http://caninefriends.org.nz/ (NZ), http:// www.deltasociety.com.au/ (AUS), http://www.therapy dogs.com/ (USA) (all sites accessed 13.1.14).

Touching and scripture

The Gospels are full of stories where Jesus touches people – to heal, to bless and to reassure. Part of your pastoral visiting may include the sharing of one of these stories and an invitation for a resident to use her imagination to be part of the scene – even perhaps to allow Jesus to touch her just as he touched the marginalized and the sick:

- touching the hem of Jesus' garment, Mark 5.25–34 (connecting with Jesus)
- the raising of Jairus' daughter, Mark 5.35–43 (resurrecting what is dead in us)

- the healing of a deaf, mute man, Mark 7.32–35 (releasing what is bound, giving freedom)
- becoming as a little child, Mark 9.36–37 (being close to Jesus frees us to trust).

If you prefer, use the context which is most familiar to the person you are with – gently suggest imagining Jesus coming to visit the old person in his own room, or sitting with him in the dining-room, or staying beside him at night-time in sleeping or wakefulness.

N.B. The section on Anointing focuses on a special pastoral practice of sacramental touch. The sections on Praying and Praying around the time of death will also include references to touch.

Anointing

You may or may not be familiar with the practice of anointing the sick with holy oil, but it has been part of the Church since very early times:

> Are any among you suffering? They should pray. Are any cheerful? They should sing songs of praise. Are any among you sick? They should call for the elders of the church and have them pray over them, anointing them with oil in the name of the Lord. (James 5.13–15)

In some traditions, any 'elder' may be part of this pastorally powerful action; in Catholic circles anointing is offered only by those in ordained ministry because it is considered a sacrament; in others, in addition to clergy, some lay pastoral ministers may be licensed to anoint with holy oil. Whether lay or ordained, those administering the sacrament may use approved services: e.g. visit the NZ Anglican Church website: http://anglicanprayerbook.org.nz/738.htm or the Church of England website: http://www.churchofengland.org/prayer-worship/worship/texts/pastoral/healing/layingonofhands.aspx or look in the Book of Common Prayer or your particular country's current prayer book for details.

However, the practical reality is that often the context and condition of the person you are praying with will dictate the need for a much shorter, informal type of encounter which provides explanations and involvement for family or friends if present, and does not rely on having copies of a service handy for everyone, nor need it take very long. Such a time of prayer looks something like this:

SHORT SERVICE OF ANOINTING

In the Church's tradition, anointing oil has been used as part of the prayers made for those who are unwell. Anointing is considered by many to be a sacrament – that is an outward sign of the work of God's Spirit within the heart, mind and body of … *(name)* this dear one, whom you love so much.

Special fragrant oil is used – this particular oil comes from … and has been blessed, set aside for this purpose. *(Make the oil available for each person to smell before continuing.)*

Let us pray:
We recognize and welcome your presence here, O God;
you travel with us throughout our life, you accompany us in our suffering,
through the valley of the shadow of death, and into the light of your rest and peace. As we keep silence for a moment, let us be open to your love reaching into our struggles and uncertainty, as you take upon yourself all our shortcomings and regrets … *(silence)*

May we each know the release which God's mercy and faithfulness brings. *(A brief pause)*

Now it is time to anoint … *(name)* making the sign of the cross on her/his forehead and hands.

… *(name)* I anoint you in the name of the Father, and of the Son, and of the Holy Spirit.

(When you have finished the anointing, invite those present to lay their hands on the person, if they wish, before you continue, saying:)

(name) May the love of the Father take away all fear and bring you hope. May you know the healing touch of Jesus, your brother, Saviour and friend.
May the Spirit bring you inner strength, comfort and peace of mind. AMEN.

(Take your time at this point, as sometimes people are very moved by this experience and can, understandably, be reluctant to disengage.)

Please feel free to join me in the old version of the Lord's Prayer if you'd like to …

May the peace of God which is beyond our understanding be with you all in the time ahead, and may the blessing of God who is Creator, Redeemer and Giver of Life, be with you and … (name) now and for evermore. AMEN.

In the context of aged-care ministry in a care home or in a parish, I believe there is a case for broadening the practice of anointing beyond its use with the sick, to include a range of situations in which the elderly might benefit from this outward sign of God's care for them, this reminder that the Spirit is at work within the person *and* the circumstances which are so challenging. I do not believe that this would in any way diminish the sacrament, so long as we seek the leading of the Spirit and don't offer anointing 'automatically' as part of every pastoral encounter.

Imagine for a moment that you are the minister in the situations below. Consider how anointing might quite naturally emerge out of the individual's conversation with you and the prayer you both make:

- when claiming the power of Jesus to act if someone is feeling spiritually overwhelmed or is affected by forces not of God, including 'things that go bump in the night'
- when affirming a person's choice to follow the way of Christ
- to mark a decision to stop something which has exercised power over the elder for a long time, such as a gambling habit
- as part of confession and reconciliation
- to mark a coming back to faith
- before any challenging medical test such as colonoscopy, stress ECG test for heart function
- before surgery
- after a major health event such as a bout of pneumonia, a nasty fall, a frightening diagnosis
- when unwell – not at death's door but in need of encouragement and spiritual comfort (many people know about the Catholic practice of giving the Last Rites in cases of imminent death, so they need reassurance that we offer this ministry as a way of helping them connect with the love of God at work within them at *any* time when spiritual support is required)
- to acknowledge the Spirit at work within the elder *and* the wider family when seeking reconciliation
- to pray for an absent family member facing illness, separation, redundancy etc.
- when coping with a bereavement at a distance, e.g. losing a sibling in another part of the country or overseas
- when close family are going to be away for an extended period and there is fear and pain in parting, not knowing if or when they may see each other again in the flesh
- to give thanks for and bless a new family member, for example great-grandchild.

When I think about anointing in the context of the care home, I think of those whom I have anointed in all sorts of situations similar to those listed above, and the way God works to bring peace. But I also think of the time I looked into a room and saw one of our senior nurses with 'Betty' in her last days:

'Connie' took a little moisturizer and, with kindness in her voice told 'Betty' what she was about to do. Then, with infinite gentleness, she dabbed the cream on each cheek, forehead, nose and chin, in a subconscious gesture of blessing. Connie stroked the furrowed face until the cream was absorbed, and stayed with Betty for another couple of minutes before she had to leave.

To me, Connie's action was another expression of anointing: it was a moment of sacred encounter, with no need of special words or oil. Connie took the commonplace, and, by her manner and the grace of God, ministered love and peace to Betty.

Take some time to reflect on an instance when you have received the sacrament of anointing. If that has not been part of your experience, then pray with John 9.5–7 in which Jesus 'anoints' the blind man not with oil, but with clay made from his own saliva and the dust of the earth.
Allow yourself to enter the scene and imagine Jesus reaching out to touch you ...

Singing

Humans naturally sing to comfort those who are restless, to soothe babies into sleep and to serenade loved ones with voices and loving. Opportunities to sing and be sung to are dwindling. Singing *together* is still a visible part of some cultures, but in the West, singing has largely been captured by the commercially driven music industry and turned into a spectator sport with participation limited to texting in a vote. Only at events of national significance such as sporting fixtures, or special events, at gatherings of particular ethnic or regional groups at special festivals such as the Eisteddfod in Wales or in worshipping Christian communities, do people get the chance to sing together. Singing *alone* is often relegated to the shower, yet *we are made for singing* – it is a part of our ability to communicate, and essential for our emotional and spiritual health. Now, you might be thinking, 'I'm no singer!' Even if that is true, it's not about quality of tone or accuracy of pitch, but about compassionate connection, so this material is to encourage you to think about including singing (even if it is more a case of saying the words in a range of tones) in your pastoral practice should a suitable occasion arise. In a care home we can sing in corridors as we walk arm in arm with a resident, we can sing in a one-to-one setting to offer comfort in times of stress or even in times of dying. We know that for those whose language is affected by stroke, words that are inaccessible when speaking may be recovered while singing. We know too that people often weep when music stirs their soul; singing releases pent-up or unrecognized emotion and brings our spirit comfort and strength.

☩ What is your experience of singing – alone or with others? What does singing mean to you?

As in so much of contemplative pastoral ministry, how this particular pastoral practice is played out with those you visit will depend on your capacity to be still enough to listen to the Spirit's wisdom and free enough from embarrassment to go ahead as best you can. So what might we sing, and when?

- The 23rd Psalm, 'The Lord's my shepherd' – is a 'go to' psalm in many situations but particularly when someone is literally walking through 'death's dark vale'. The tune 'Crimond' is well known; most people will have encountered this psalm through their own church attendance or when going to funerals.
- A hymn or song which you know means a lot to the person you are visiting.
- 'Amazing Grace'. This is another well-known hymn which seems to touch people deeply. Its message of redemption and grace is profound and poignant. It is appropriate in any pastoral situation, but especially if people are worried about what they have done in their lives, if they are anxious about dying and salvation, etc. The chorus sums up the Christian hope – 'I once was lost but now am found, was blind, but now I see.'
- 'Jesus loves me, this I know' – a children's chorus and something many may have known in their youth – in its childlike simplicity it reminds us all that we belong to God (for the three original verses and the song's history, see http://en.wikipedia. org/wiki/Jesus_Loves_Me, accessed 24.1.14).
- A favourite lullaby – perhaps one that your parents used with you, or you with your own children.
- Whatever the Spirit brings to mind from your own storehouse of hymns, choruses and spiritual songs from other sources such as movies or modern singers' compilations. We are not talking only about designated 'sacred' music but about anything that speaks of love:

Staff had told me 'R' was dying. She was given to 'challenging behaviour' but we'd formed a connection over the years. When I went in to see R, she was conscious, breathing laboured, colour grey. I sat with her, praying quietly, and what came to mind was the song, 'You are my sunshine'. So what I could remember of this very personal song of sweetness and affection, I sang to her, from my heart:

'You are my sunshine, my only sunshine, you make me happy when skies are grey. You'll never know dear, how much I love you, O don't take my sunshine away.'

I didn't know the relevance of it, if any, to her; I don't know if there was a blessing for her in those words or in my singing to her. I do know that she opened her eyes and looked at me for a moment, with her characteristic wry glance. I squeezed her hand, whispered 'God be with you' in her good ear, and went to see if the nurses had been able to contact her family yet. When I returned, her breathing had stopped.

'And flights of angels *sing* thee to thy rest!' (Shakespeare, *Hamlet*, Act 5, scene 2, emphasis added)

Laughing

How often do you laugh with those you meet when ministering in a care or private home?

The shortest verse of scripture occurs in John 11.35: 'Jesus wept', moved by the grief over the death of Lazarus. But nowhere is it recorded that 'Jesus laughed' ... I don't know what you think, but I believe he must have laughed because he *was* fully human, experienced a full range of human emotion, and besides, as many of you reading this already suspect, God has a sense of humour!

Humour plays an important part in our pastoral ministry and in care-home life generally:

For several years our staff put on a pantomime for the residents and their families near Christmas. Each year we would dress up, put on lots of make-up and make fools of ourselves in the big recreation room. Everyone laughed as we tried to remember our lines and what we were supposed to be doing, bumping into each other and hamming it up.
It was a lot of effort, but worth it because of the pleasure it brought.

It's important for us to help 'lightness' surface in what can seem a dark context; after all, everyone knows that the undertaker's hearse is never far away. There are countless times when situations *are* serious and we need to be sombre and respect-ful. However, all of us, residents, staff and chaplain/minister, cope better with the residents' pain and frustration, with the tiring physicality of ageing, with the immi-nence of dying which shadows any day, if we take whatever opportunities present themselves to temper the sadness with healthy doses of comedy, playfulness and gentle silliness.

How might we as ministers help bring laughter and humour to the care-home environment?

- If we are naturally quiet and shy, then we will need to get closer to God, asking the Spirit to let the joy of Jesus fill us up until it overflows.
- We can ask the Spirit to help us bring *holy* humour into our workplace – humour that is not sarcastic or contrived but emerges naturally out of the situation and who we are in Christ.

- We can pray for the grace we need not to take ourselves too seriously – helping an old person put in their false teeth or hearing aid works best with shared laughter!
- We can bring a light touch to conversations with staff, families, management – be alert for the funny but not at others' expense.
- As part of our pastoral conversation with an individual we can specifically ask the question – 'What has brought you joy?' or 'What makes you laugh?'
- We can join in with some of the residents' activities even for a few minutes, e.g. playing Boccia (a form of bowls), doing exercises, putting jigsaws together, playing housie, etc.
- We can share with others some funny events from our own lives, e.g. my account of dropping the Christmas apple crumble between bench and oven was guaranteed to raise a laugh.
- We can explore (if possible with the support of the diversional therapist) the visit of someone trained in therapeutic clowning. There are increasing numbers of clowns active in hospitals, hospices, and with the elderly, working wisely to bring a smile and lift the spirits.[13]
- We can take part in any staff production such as a pantomime, variety show, etc. If we can make the time, our participation will broaden people's perspective on Christian living, offer a glimpse of a 'person of the cloth'/church person having a bit of fun (usually at our own expense), and will bring us closer to the other nursing and management staff who take part.
- We can top up our own humour quotient by being around people who share our sense of humour, and by watching comedy shows, YouTube clips or movies that make us laugh.
- If not already happening, we can suggest setting up a monthly comedy movie event. There are many to choose from – around 90 minutes long and with text on the screen to aid comprehension. For example: *Patch Adams* (USA, 1998); *Mrs Caldicot's Cabbage War* (UK, 2002); *Calendar Girls* (UK, 2003) etc.

In terms of more organized 'laughter and humour' input, here are a couple of suggestions:

1 Opportunities for laughter can occur in the context of special services which you may be called upon to conduct, for example the celebration for a special anniversary in the institution's or church's history. In the middle of prayers, speeches and singing, we might introduce an activity like this:

---

13 To learn more about humour and healing with clowns, visit UK site: http://www.playful-clown.co.uk (provides Sacred Clowning workshops); NZ site: http://www.clowndoctors.org.nz (new training; value in the hospital setting); Israeli site: http://www.dreamdoctors.org.il/ (an international conference held in Jerusalem for medical clowns) or an article on http://en.wikipedia.org/wiki/Clown_Care (all accessed 14.1.14).

Preparation: before the service, inflate enough balloons to have two for each row of seats and a few spare. Make sure each balloon has enough ribbon tied to it, to allow you to retrieve it from the ceiling if it gets away.

FRONT OF ROOM

Seats   Aisle   Seats

BACK OF ROOM

Tie a balloon to the outer end of each row of seats. Give a bubble-blowing kit to each person sitting on the aisle on both sides – see above – and then say: 'It's a very special celebration today as we give thanks for so many people who have been part of this institution's story over the years. Celebrations often include balloons and bubbles – I am sorry that today we can't have bubbles in the form of champagne but we *can* have bubbles to blow and balloons to enjoy! So here's the invitation: those of you with a balloon tied to your chair, untie the balloon and pass it towards the aisle – see if you can get the balloons along to the central aisle without letting them sail up to the roof! Those of you sitting on the aisle – start to blow some bubbles and then pass the bubble-blowing kit to your neighbour to have a go and so on all the way to the end of the row.'
(This proved to be hilarious, with plenty of laughter, balloons popping and others ceiling-bound and lots and lots of bubbles. Family and available staff pitched in to help and we all enjoyed the fun of it.)

2   Set up a half-hour *funny-story sharing circle*. Once you get to know people at the care home, you will sense who might enjoy taking part in something like this. Six to eight people are enough so you can sit close enough to be heard. Enlist the help of staff to gather those who might enjoy this but forget it's on! Rather than stressing the need for confidentiality, ask folk to share only what they are happy for others to know. Begin with a story of your own that tells of a family event that evoked laughter and see where the conversation leads. One I use is of a time when my cousin was wallpapering his lounge and my 18-month-old son toddled over to his large ginger cat and as we watched, disempowered by disbelief, carried the cat to the bucket of glue and dropped her in! As you can imagine, it's not easy trying to catch a cross cat covered in glue!

      Towards the end of the session, bring the group to stillness and give thanks for the memories shared. Encourage them to continue to share such stories with their table-mates, family and staff.

Humour and grieving

Surprisingly, humour and laughter can be found in the midst of grieving even the hardest of losses. It is as if we need to take time to surface from the heavy swell of grief and take a big breath of fun. By gathering with others, eating together, perhaps making music together, laughing at something silly, just for a little while, we gather energy before diving back into the surging sea of loss and adjustment and irretrievable change.

Those 'outside' the grief may wonder how we can smile, let alone laugh; but we know that it is for our survival that we take this respite from the intensity of grieving. Without such a respite, the work of grief may not come to its healing completion and we may never truly laugh again.

Part of our role is to enable this 'surfacing from sorrow' to take place, without judgement or criticism from those not directly involved. Instead we can affirm the need for moments of lightness to help people along the journey of grieving.

Using a holding cross

Known to have a Christian background, 'Irene' was given a holding cross when she first came into residential care because she was disoriented and unhappy. Months later, she held her holding cross in her dying ... when she was beyond words, 'holding on' became her prayer, and connected her with the person of Jesus who had travelled through the valley of the shadow of death, and whom she knew and trusted to guide her 'home'.

A holding cross like the one pictured is a valuable aid to prayer. Not a talisman, or a lucky charm, it is a way of being linked to Jesus: a person can symbolically hold on to him, to God and know that she is safe, no matter what she faces. This particular holding cross is a small (4″ long) slightly irregular shape, designed to settle into your hand, but it can also be slipped under the pillow at night or popped into a shirt pocket. The ones I use are made with love from ancient kauri, with a small piece of paua shell to focus the finger and eye on the centre – the heart of the matter – the power of God to overcome fear and death

itself. The woodworker 'Ian' is a Christian who prayerfully makes each cross by hand, sanding it and oiling it until it is smooth to the touch. It is no surprise then that when I am prompted by the Spirit to give a holding cross to a resident, there is often a beautiful reaction, a sort of homecoming accompanied sometimes with smiles, sometimes with tears, sometimes a clasping of the cross to the heart or a strong holding on that lets me know that something is happening between the person and God, a connection between them that needs no words.

Residents may have other forms of Christian spiritual aids, for example Catholic rosary beads, or Anglican prayer beads. These are often associated with quite complex patterns of vocal prayer, e.g. there are six different prayers used with the Catholic rosary as people remember the 20 holy mysteries (see http://www.catholicity.com/prayer/rosary.html, accessed 16.1.14). There are many prayers to choose from for Anglican use (see http://www.myrosarybeads.com/anglicanrosary, also accessed 16.1.14).

While these may – and do – bring comfort, one of the most helpful things about using a holding cross is that no words are necessary: the person holds on and allows herself to rest in the peace and love of God. At a time when questions pile up on one another and answers evaporate, as memory fails and concentration dwindles, there is a joyous freedom in the simplicity of holding on.

I normally carry a spare holding cross with me and have found that even for people whose God connection has become very rusty, a sensitively worded offer of a holding cross to connect them with the great love of God in Jesus is rarely refused. Situations in which holding crosses have brought comfort include:

- when someone has a stroke or other rapid onset illness and is transferred to A&E
- when in ICU or the high dependency unit amid tension and uncertainty
- waiting for tests
- when undergoing treatment such as chemotherapy or dialysis
- pre- and post-surgery – nurses who value spiritual care will ensure this can be done
- when awake in the night
- when anxious or distressed
- when new to an institution and feeling disconnected from all that has been familiar
- when facing death
- when mourning the loss of someone they love
- when leaving a rehabilitation facility to attempt living on their own again.

As I write, I am thinking of one of the first things a little newborn child does – he wraps his tiny hand around Mum's or Dad's offered finger and holds on. His parents are claimed as for ever his with this timeless gesture of connection. And we can claim we are for ever Christ's as we hold on to his cross in our time of uncertainty, crisis and pain, or as death approaches.

May the Holy Spirit help you to find someone like 'Ian' who has the desire, equipment and time to make holding crosses with love, and, by doing so, turn his – or her – woodworking skills into a ministry that will be a blessing to many.

Sharing 'home' or pastoral Communion

'Sophie' was hospitalized following a fall. She was extremely deaf but was used to having Communion brought to her after a lifetime of regular church attendance. She had some memory loss and was at times very disoriented and forgetful, so

when I visited her in hospital neither her son nor I were sure she would still know what was happening. I introduced myself and she made no response, so I raised my voice and tried again. Still no response.

So, disregarding privacy and my own embarrassment, I yelled, 'Sophie, it's chaplain Sue here … Sue!' 'Soup?' she yelled back, 'I don't want any soup!'

When her son and I had composed ourselves, I went ahead and unfolded the white cloth and laid out the elements for Communion on the tiny space cleared on her bed-side table. She watched me intently as I consecrated the bread and wine. There was a moment of clear awareness when she put her hands out to receive first the bread and then the wine. She joined us in the Lord's Prayer, and her words were clear and firm.

I had used the barest framework of the traditional Eucharist but 'Sophie' had, somewhere in her psyche, connected with what she could see – the blessing of the elements, the offering and the receiving. Her memory provided the familiar prayer, and I had no doubt that she had indeed 'made her Communion' in spite of her limited physical faculties.

What is your experience of a one-to-one pastoral communion as priest, parish visitor or, in a time of illness, as the recipient of the sacrament in a hospital or home context?

Being able to share home Communion with an individual who is no longer able to attend church services is a privilege and a joy. For those in care homes who have little experience of being part of a faith community and only a tentative connection with 'someone up there' whom they turn to when their backs are up against the wall, the whole idea of sharing in Holy Communion may be foreign. For these latter folk, as we faithfully visit and listen to their stories, a time may come when they want to be part of the 'family meal' of God. We do well not to put obstacles in their way, not to insist on 'confirmation' or man-made rules about who is 'in' and who is 'out'. Instead we hold wide the welcome door and make a space for them at the table of the Lord. Many will value our bringing them Communion initially in the privacy of their rooms, when we can open up a scripture encounter between Christ and another person, so they can engage more deeply with the story:

'Wally' had been in a care home for only a few months. We had established a good rapport and he had been open to prayer in recent visits, so I mentioned to him the possibility of sharing Communion in his room. He was intrigued. Partway through the short service, I read 'Wally' the story of Zacchaeus (Luke 19.1–10).

Something about the way Wally was listening told me this story was touching him deeply. So I invited him to imagine that, like Zacchaeus, he was keen to see Jesus but, being 'short in stature', he needed to climb a tree to get a good view. 'Put yourself in the picture and imagine Jesus looking at you with warmth in his eyes, inviting himself to have a meal at your place.' It wasn't long before I could see Wally's eyes fill with tears. Something significant was going on.

I did not ask him to tell me or talk about it. We just waited for a few moments, and when he was ready we went on with the Communion. He received the bread and wine with reverence and joy.

Other relevant stories of Jesus which lend themselves to imaginative treatment in the context of pastoral Communions include:

- the woman who touched the hem of Jesus' garment: Mark 5.25–34
- Jesus calming the storm: Mark 4.35–41
- the father with the sick son who says, 'Lord, I believe, help my unbelief!': Mark 9.17–24ff
- the restoration of Peter: John 21.1–19 following his betrayal of Jesus prior to his crucifixion.

In a care-home context, we will also find people who want to stay connected to their spiritual heritage but are too weak or forgetful to attend the services offered. For such people a service of one-to-one Communion may well follow a shortened version of a traditional liturgy with which you and the recipient are both familiar, e.g. NZPB, pp. 732ff. However, you may need to use the shorter, simplified format if a person is very hard of hearing, very unwell or unable to concentrate for very long.

You will need:

- time to commit your visit to prayer – for the person you are visiting and for yourself, that you may be a vehicle of grace and keep out of God's way!
- bread or wafer, wine or grape juice – choose whichever suits the person you are visiting
- a portable communion set if you can get one. If not, make up your own, including something that can serve as a chalice and paten, something to carry the elements, a small good white cloth, a purificator (cloth to wipe the edge of the chalice clean) and anointing oil
- time: 30 minutes gives you adequate time to move gently through the service, to speak slowly, to wait in silence, to offer particular prayers and to take a leisurely leave-taking
- if you want to include some music, you will need to have laptop etc. with you
- focus: no matter what else is on your agenda before or after your meeting with this particular person, paying good attention to the person in front of you is a great gift. Through this gift of presence and the sacrament you share, God ministers to the individual in ways we cannot know
- a Bible so that, in your time with the resident, if a relevant passage of scripture comes to mind, particularly a passage that describes a direct encounter with Christ which can be used for imaginative prayer – you can have it at hand if you need to prompt your memory.

A simple pastoral Communion service follows.

PASTORAL COMMUNION SERVICE

We give thanks to God for bringing us to this moment when we will share the family meal of Christians throughout the ages. In sickness and in health, in peace and in war, in despair and in delight, the supper of our Lord Jesus Christ has nourished countless people, and feeds us now, strengthening us for whatever lies ahead, and assuring us of God's grace and ongoing, loving presence.

CONFESSION
And so we begin by bringing to God in confidence and in silence anything which we regret, any sins committed or good left undone, hurt inflicted on others or failures to live and to love like you, O Jesus.

Silence follows.

ASSURANCE OF GOD'S MERCY AND FORGIVENESS
May you know that you are forgiven and be at peace.
God strengthen you in all goodness and keep you in life eternal.
AMEN. (NZPB, p. 408)

PRAYERS FOR OTHERS AND FOR OURSELVES,
ENDING WITH THE LORD'S PRAYER (old version)
Our Father, which art in heaven,
hallowed be thy name.
Thy kingdom come; thy will be done
on earth as it is in heaven.
Give us this day our daily bread
and forgive us our trespasses,
as we forgive those who trespass against us.
And lead us not into temptation,
but deliver us from evil.
For thine is the kingdom, the power and the glory.
For ever and ever. AMEN.

GOSPEL READING (may be read a second time imaginatively)

HOLY COMMUNION

Jesus gathered with his friends in an upper room, knowing that he would soon be going to his death. He wanted to pray his goodbyes to them, and in doing so, he gave us a way of connecting with him and with all Christians through the ages, for all time. So now we come to share in this blessed sacrament, in which we are spiritually united with our Lord and Saviour, with our Lover and Friend. As we eat this bread and drink this wine, we are once again brought close to God and given inner strength and peace.

The Lord is here.	**God's spirit is with us.**
Lift up your hearts.	**We lift them up to the Lord.**
Let us give thanks to the Lord our God.	**It is right to offer thanks and praise.**

The night before he died, our Lord Jesus Christ took bread;
when he had given thanks to you, O God, he broke it,
gave it to his disciples, and said:
'Take, eat, this is my body which is given for you; do this to remember me.'
After supper, he took the cup;
when he had given you thanks, he gave it to them, and said:
'Drink this, all of you, for this is my blood of the new covenant,
which is shed for you, and for many, for the forgiveness of sins;
do this as often as you drink it, to remember me.' (NZPB, p. 733, slightly adapted)

The bread of life and the cup of salvation are shared.

THANKSGIVING AND BLESSING

Remembering Maria

She is sitting in her chair
legs propped up
snugly rug over her
breakfasted and toileted
wound dressed and pump primed
she is waiting

what am I doing, dear?
   waiting
what am I waiting for?
   until it's time to go home to God
what's it all about?
   it's about love

brief words meet her
   profound questions

that's what it all boils down to
now

her work is the work of waiting
of being
small moments of mystery
as life winds down
slowly
   slowing
      s-l-o-w-i-n-g
         s--t--o--p--p--i--n--g

        stopped.

Spend some time recalling an experience of accompanying someone you love in their dying. Reflect on the effectiveness or otherwise of any spiritual support you – or they – received.

Note anything which you would want to do differently in your own ministry of walking with someone through 'the valley of the shadow of death' (Psalm 23).

Accompanying the dying

When we provide spiritual support to the dying and their families, we often find ourselves acting as a kind of interpreter, helping families understand care-home protocols and staff briefings about what to expect,[14] answering questions, listening to concerns, offering support and a non-anxious presence in an emotionally charged situation. We need to have access to competent pastoral supervision because this ministry is costly, sometimes extremely sad, even if the deaths of older people can be considered 'natural' and in many cases are a welcome relief from the ravages of extreme age.

So that you are not hijacked by unexpected unresolved issues from your own background, take some time with this question:

What is your own experience of death and dying?
Is there any 'unfinished business' following the death/s of your own parent/s or close family?
How might this impact on your ability to be present for those who are dying or their families?

The work is demanding because we are brought face to face with our own mortality – one day this will happen to you, to me. We may have our own grief for the person who is dying, especially if we have known them well or if they have been like a 'father' or 'mother' to us. And we will be affected by the family interactions, staff standards of care, other people's grief. It is to God that we turn at the end of the day to 'unload', to 'refuel', to rest and recover.

In the death-denying culture of the West, the post-war generations' experience of this inevitable aspect of being human has been shaped by media depictions and by health professionals, many of whom still see death as an enemy to be fought at all costs. Elderly people and their families can easily 'buy into' this attitude and respond to approaching death by putting on a brave face and avoiding the emotions which are likely to emerge as the end of life nears: anger, fear, helplessness, confusion, or regret. Euphemisms about suffering and dying are common – we hear medical staff talking about someone 'experiencing discomfort' or 'passing', rather than 'suffering' and 'dying'. Families too struggle to use those words and may not want their loved one to be told they are dying, as if somehow if the word isn't spoken it won't happen.

---

14 Check to see if the Liverpool Care Pathway is still operational in the institution you are visiting. The LCP was introduced in the late 1990s to ensure that co-ordinated palliative care was offered by clinical and spiritual professionals in the final 48–72 hours of a person's life. However, the protocol proved to be unworkable in the public health system and is in the process of being replaced by an 'End-of-life care plan'. I would hope that spiritual support will be included in that plan as, with the LCP documentation, ministers and chaplains could contribute to the multi-disciplinary team's care of the dying person.

As ministers or pastoral carers, however, we can model and encourage a *different* approach to dying and death, first by helping people talk about death. This may be awkward – for them and initially for us – because as a society we don't talk about death easily or often. We may start by using metaphors such as 'reaching the end of the road' or 'approaching the finishing line' to ease the dying and their families towards honest, open and caring conversation about death and end-of-life care.

The second key aspect of our approach to ministry with the dying and their families is centred on the theology of the cross. Consider this passage:

> … the primary healing task is to enable suffering, dying people to know that God has not abandoned them … The presence of Jesus with us in suffering is not simply a passive solidarity in the midst of trials and tribulations … the theology of the cross is comfortable with acknowledging the situation as it is: death is death, and suffering is suffering. The comfort and consolation of the theology of the cross comes not from naïve optimism or malignant stoicism, but from the knowledge that where there is suffering, there is God. And where God is, there is hope of redemption.[15]

Take a few minutes to reflect on the above quotation.
What resonates with you? With what do you struggle?

The Jesus story, particularly the journey to the cross with all its suffering, rings true to those who are facing the end of their lives. It is our privilege to share that story with them as opportunity arises, speaking of a God who stands alongside them, of Jesus who experienced what it is like for a human being to anticipate death, suffer terrible pain, lose all he values, and finally to die. Speaking too of the Christian hope that death is not the end but the beginning of a whole new existence we cannot begin to imagine, lived in the light and peace of that immeasurable Love we call God.

No doubt you will have read theories about grief in the dying or attended workshops regarding the dying process from various perspectives, but what becomes clear in reality is that people do tend to die as they have lived:

- facing reality or avoiding it
- approaching death with courage or fear, with humour or despair
- needy and ego-centric, or other-centred, concerned more for family and friends
- manipulating those around them, or full of gratitude for the gifts of people and loving
- talking a lot about what is happening, or processing thoughts inwardly
- sharing their journey with others, or keeping their feelings to themselves
- with – or without – a working faith in God honed through a lifetime of prayer and worship.

---

15 John Swinton and Richard Payne, eds, *Living Well and Dying Faithfully: Christian Practices for End-of-Life Care*, Eerdmans, 2009, pp. 126–7.

'Nothing is impossible with God' and there is always the hope that positive change might occur even when relationships seem broken beyond repair. We can hope and pray for reconciliation, for healing of fears, even for a revitalized relationship with God, if the person wants to turn 'Godwards'. For none of us knows what happens between another person and God, even with that last breath.

So, how do we walk alongside someone whose earthly life is coming to a close? What challenges or opportunities can we expect to encounter along the way? How best can we bring all of our pastoral practices together to serve the individual and his or her family?

In the interests of brevity I am going to start with a series of key points beginning when we find out that someone from care home or parish has had a terminal diagnosis, and/or has suddenly deteriorated or been taken to hospital. Starting to accompany a dying person can mean some or all of the following:

- building a relationship with her[16] preferably *before* she becomes too unwell to talk
- asking her what her understanding of her medical situation is (check with staff if possible)
- through spiritual conversation establishing the nature of her God connection
- popping in regularly to see how she is doing
- asking her if it is okay to pray *with* her and asking what and who she would like prayer for
- discerning what might be helpful to her in terms of sacraments, holding cross, or other 'religious' items and actions
- finding out about her family – local, overseas, etc.
- ensuring she has what she needs around her to soothe her soul, for example music, favourite radio channel, photos, flowers, perhaps even visits from her dog or a Skype talk to family overseas
- asking her if she has thought any more about her final wishes (funeral, burial or cremation, etc. – these preferences may have been recorded on admission, so check her file first)
- if she wishes, facilitating reconciliation with family who have been out of touch
- if it's right for her and her family, anointing her and sharing a portion of the 'prayers around the time of death' service, even if death is not imminent.

In times when Christianity shaped the path of dying for the majority of the population in the West, it was normal for a priest to be called to help ensure the person was in right relationship with God prior to death, offering confession and absolution and calming fear. Nowadays, when fewer attend church or keep religious observance, this practice is less common, and it remains for us to raise these sensitive areas once we have established a good rapport with the person who is dying.

---

16 I am using the female pronoun for clarity here; statistically we may encounter more elderly women than men!

While she is still conscious we can begin by gently asking, 'Is there anything that you regret?' or 'If you could have your time over, what might you have done differently?' or 'Is there anything you'd like to get off your chest?' This line of questioning may uncover a need for a formal 'reconciliation of a penitent'/'confession and absolution' (see 'Pastoral Practices: Praying' section) or a straightforward owning up to something done long ago that has never before been shared, and, if she is open to it, an assurance of God's grace and mercy (e.g. 1 John 1.9).

Although in my experience the majority of the very old are not afraid to die, occasionally we may come across someone who is terrified or anxious.

> 'Terry's' mother had died in front of his eyes when he was five. It was a traumatic parting. Her death still brought him to tears in later life and he struggled with parting from his family as his death approached, no matter what we did to comfort him, no matter how faithful the family in keeping vigil. I trust that Jesus met Terry at his point of vulnerability and healed the deeply anxious little boy as he came into Love's care.

A second person, 'Y', was also frightened of dying but his situation was different:

> 'Y' was showing signs of deep anxiety as death approached, calling out as if terrified of what he was 'seeing'. His son who was a Christian told me that his dad had had some past involvement with the occult. Another priest whom I knew 'happened' to be visiting the care home that very day, so we prayed together for Y, in Jesus' name, releasing him from any evil influences, inviting the love and light of Christ into his being, praying for a peaceful dying. A day later that prayer was answered.

'Sally', a devoted Christian, had a different concern as she became increasingly unwell:

> 'Sally' was worried because she didn't feel like eating or drinking. 'Am I committing suicide in God's eyes because I just don't want to eat any more?' she asked, and went on to say that she did not want to be outside God's mercy. I assured her that she remained connected to God in love, and her body's diminishing desire for food was normal and part of the dying process. She was simply on the journey 'home' and her body knew it was time to stop eating.
>
> (I wish I'd thought to remind her about the heavenly banquet she would one day enjoy!)

If the dying person lapses into unconsciousness, it is really important that we – and the family – carry on as if she can still hear us. Nurses will tell you that hearing is the last of the senses to 'switch off'. I also believe that a person's innermost being, their spirit, remains accessible until commended to God at death. So we can:

- tell her what we are doing and who is with us, e.g. if someone is going to massage her feet
- sing to her whatever comes to mind – it doesn't have to be a hymn
- sit with her and pray aloud for her and her family
- hold her hand or stroke her forehead (she will pull away if she doesn't want this touch)
- read a portion of scripture or a psalm aloud to her or some other reading that is appropriate.

As death gets closer, accompanying might mean being on our own with the person if no family member is available. So, for as long as we are able, we sit by a bedside and watch as breathing changes, stops, starts, slows, stops, starts. We might pray. We might sing. We count the seconds between breaths, wondering how the heart keeps beating, waiting to see if there is another breath. It is an intense and privileged time, and we have no idea how long it may last.

I used to agonize over how long to stay, anxious about the person dying alone if I wasn't there because staff were busy. But one night that changed.

I had been sitting with a dying woman whose adult children were all overseas. I'd been called in by staff at 8pm, and by 11pm I had very reluctantly decided to go home because I knew that if I didn't get some sleep I would be little use to anyone the following day. As I got up to go, the thought came, 'She won't be alone, you know. I am here.'

The Holy Spirit's gentle assurance of what I knew in my heart but had overlaid with worry, allowed me to go home in peace that night and has helped me since then. We cannot be someone's family, there is only so much we can do, and we do that and leave the rest in God's hands.

As death gets closer and family begin to gather, they might appreciate being given some information on 'Keeping vigil' (a sample leaflet can be found in the Appendix and on the CD-Rom). Keeping vigil is a lost art which merits reclamation. It provides a way of engaging with the open-ended period before a person dies, recognizing that this waiting fulfils a special function in the life of the dying person and those who are present. The vigil-keepers may be family, or friends, or even a little team from a person's network of church or community contacts who are ready to 'keep watch' with the dying person until the end.

Sometimes we are present as a noisy family conversation goes on around a dying person. We may even have to draw the family's attention to a change of condition because they may be too tied up with their talking or cell-phones to notice. Sometimes family members fight in front of us, voices are raised, hurtful things are said. It'd be easy to judge them inwardly for their 'lack of respect' but all we can do is gently help them to be present to what is happening, present to their loved one as she takes her leave. We may also find that some family members find practices from another faith tradition helpful. I think of two situations when residents were dying, and adult grandchildren, with great reverence and love, offered chanted prayers, one from a Buddhist, the other from a Chinese spiritual perspective read from an iPad. Interestingly, when death came, they were happy to stay when I prayed traditional Christian prayers of commendation for their respective grandmothers.

Inevitably someone will ask, 'How long is this going to take?' Nursing staff are the best ones to respond to this common question. Experienced staff will say that there are some pointers to approaching death such as a change in breathing, the skin becoming mottled, extremities becoming colder, but they will also say that it is difficult to predict for sure. Families want to know, of course. Part of that desire to know is practical – should they alert a family member to catch a plane now or wait and see, should they make sure everyone comes in to say goodbye if they can, and so on. But part of that desire stems from our cultural aversion to not being in control. Natural dying, like natural childbirth, follows a rhythm and timing of its own and we cannot predict either. People struggle with that, and that is, I believe, a significant, if largely unacknowledged, part of the argument put forward in favour of voluntary euthanasia – it's about taking back control. However, significant things happen when we surrender control and allow 'nature to take its course'.

An old lady suffered a massive stroke 12 days before Christmas. Her children gathered and initially struggled with the not knowing of the dying process. They struggled with 'We can't do anything', just as many of us would struggle when faced with something we can't fix or make happen. They felt powerless, angry, sad, conflicted – a huge and exhausting range of emotions, until they came to a decision – they would just **be** *with their mum, they would sit with her for as long as it took, taking turns so she wasn't left alone; they would talk to her and to each other – so they did. They told stories, they looked at photographs, they reminisced. Their mum died four days before Christmas surrounded by love and laughter, tears and thanksgiving for the life she had given them and their lives together.*

Sometimes families cannot stay until their loved one dies. People lead complicated lives and there are all sorts of pressures. If we come across a family member who is overseas and cannot come right away, or someone who is here but has to leave because of other commitments, it can be helpful if we ask, 'What would it be like for you if your mum died and you weren't here?' By asking the question we are giving them an opportunity to consider the implications of their choices. If the answer is, 'I'd kick myself if I wasn't here and she died … I would always feel guilty', then that awareness helps inform their decision; if the answer is, 'I'm at peace with Mum, I've said my goodbyes. I know she understands what I have to do …' then they are free to leave, no matter what follows.

By reclaiming the sacred practice of keeping vigil, we are drawing attention to the value of simply *being* with loved ones when they are dying. For people shaped by a society which so values activity and productivity, this initially seems not only pointless but unmanageable. However, with support, families and friends can give

KEEPING VIGIL

How long is this going to take?

A vigil is a period characterized by intentional, focused, loving presence as family or close friends keep a dying person company in his or her final days.

Keeping vigil is counter-cultural and families can find this difficult – so can we if we are more attuned to *chronos* time (measured and orderly) rather than *kairos* time (open-ended, the 'right' time, God's time of fulfilment).

I can't hear what Mum is trying to say ... What if I miss something important?

Should I get my sister to fly home?

It is intensely demanding, yet privileged and memorable, to help a family make the most of keeping vigil. Part of this means deep listening, hearing questions, providing information, liaising with other health professionals or funeral directors, offering reassurance, praying or talking with family members together or individually, modelling respect and dignity in the face of the mystery of death.

Can he still hear us?
Is he in pain?

I can't stay here all the time! What if I have to go and get my kids and Dad dies while I am gone?

Keeping vigil offers family and the dying person space to be together. In this sacred 'time outside time', the dying person is kept company and supported by those closest to him. There may be gentle music, singing, reading aloud, sharing stories and memories; laughter and tears; hand-holding, foot massage, soothing of dry lips, wiping of brow or face.

Should we get someone to do the last rites or something?

The TV is turned off, visiting restrictions may be put in place, the wider world draws its blinds quietly as the person moves closer to the doorway to the next life.

What happens once Mum has died? What do we have to do? What about the funeral arrangements?

I don't know what to expect ... I've never seen someone die before ...

181

themselves permission to slow right down to the pace of the dying heart, and give their loved one a graced farewell.

Praying around the time of death

We may have walked with the resident in his or her dying, and with family who have been present when we visit, or we may have been called to the home after a sudden death and seen the person, and met family and friends for the first time. Whatever the situation, it is our privilege to be with people in pivotal moments of transition. What we do and how we do it can be profoundly helpful if we are alert to their situation and responsive to their unique needs – *or* it can be a hindrance if we are insensitive or hurried, bound by a set of rigid practices disconnected from their experience, or 'hiding' behind our role because we are anxious, or, still raw from our own grief, unable to be present to theirs.

Although it may be hard to do, so that we can be present to others who are facing the loss of someone they love, it is important that we have faced and done some inner work on our own losses, particularly the deaths of elderly parents or those occurring in similar circumstances.

Take some time now to reflect again on your experience of loving and losing and where you are up to in your grieving. Bring before God whatever remains tender, asking for the grace you need to enable you to be present to others in their times of loss.

When we come to offer prayer around the time of death, we come into an environment charged with emotion, grief and often exhaustion. Before we get round to praying, we need to consider:

- whether the resident who has died had a faith and would have wanted prayer
- what we know about the family dynamics
- the emotional state of the family members already present
- whether some of those present want prayer and others don't
- whether there are family who are absent but will come soon (i.e. within the hour)
- any family from another culture who may have their own particular way of being with someone who has died – perhaps saying special prayers or conducting a particular ritual
- the circumstances of the death – i.e. whether the body is able to be left as it is while family take time to face the reality of the death, or wait for other family to arrive before prayers are said, or whether it is better for the body to be washed and the bed-linen changed before offering prayer – depending on the family's wishes, this may be done by family or by the staff
- whether the body needs to be removed promptly because of its condition, in which case prayers may need to be said before any family are able to attend

- how much time we can give to the situation – expect to be with the family for up to two hours when called to a death and leave them only when they are clear about what their next step is and the immediate high emotion around the death is beginning to settle.

It also helps to be aware of the care-home protocols following a death. There will usually be a clear plan to cover what needs to be done, e.g. notifying the resident's GP and funeral director and arrangement of a time for the body to be collected. Some homes may allow family to stay overnight so the body can be collected in the morning. Often we can act as a liaison person with the family, supporting them through the unfamiliar territory that comes with the question, 'What do we do now?'

It is easier if the family already have a relationship with us, but if that is not the case, it need not take long for them to begin to trust us and talk with us if we are respectful, take time to listen to their preferences and do not insist on a particular way of doing things. In such a situation I would normally take copies of any prayers I might use and say something like:

> One of the ways we care for families at a time like this, is to offer prayer for the person who has died – for *(name of the deceased)* and prayer for you all in your grief.
> *(If the deceased has a faith, then mention this and the appropriateness of commending him/her to God's care.)*
> The prayers take only a few minutes; if you are happy for prayers to be said, you can join in if you like, or simply be present as the prayers are said.
> This is the sort of thing I mean *(hand copies around)*; have a look and I'll come back in a few minutes and you can tell me what you think …

A simple form of 'Prayers at the time of death' which seems acceptable to a wide range of people can be found in Appendix 2. I would usually preface it with a short thanksgiving for the life of the person who has died and proceed slowly from there, inviting those family members who wish to, to join in the prayers marked in bold print. After the Lord's Prayer, I would say a prayer relevant to those present, emphasizing the ongoing love of God and God's care for those who mourn, for example:

> May God, who holds us all close, especially when we are sad or afraid, be very close to each one of you as you mourn … and the blessing of God, Father, Son and Holy Spirit, be with you and remain with you as you grieve and as you celebrate *(name)*'s unique life. AMEN.

If someone is from a church background, then it would be appropriate to include the *Nunc dimittis* reading from Luke 2.29–32, in which the old priest Simeon expresses both his joy at seeing the infant Jesus, and his readiness to die.

What are the benefits of offering prayer around the time of death?

Shortly after 'Dorothy' had died, her family wanted prayers of farewell because they all knew that Dorothy believed in God. They had got used to a chaplain popping in, spending time with them to see how they were doing, and saying a prayer with their mum over the days of her dying, so it was natural to invite me to join them. To begin our prayer we stood around Dorothy's bedside, and held hands. Slowly we settled in to a sweet silence ... it was a profound moment of peacefulness, love and relief. The aroha[17] was tangible and no-one was in a hurry to be the first to speak or let go. We stayed in that holy space until there was a gentle lightening of the intensity of that moment. I squeezed the hands I was holding, and prayed aloud for Dorothy, giving thanks to God for her peaceful passing and her family's faithful companionship in her dying. A couple of the others made a prayer of their own. Then I invited them all to lay hands on their mother and we commended her to God. A quiet saying together of the old Lord's Prayer by those who wanted to join in, brought our prayers to a close. Hugs followed, tears too ... this chapter of the family story had come to an end.

In offering prayer after Dorothy's death, we honoured her faith without being dogmatic or wordy, we worked as a team linked by love for her, touch connected us with each other, and the ritual of laying hands on her in commendation gave tangible expression to our farewell. The benefits? A sense of dignity, appropriateness, gentleness, respect and deep spiritual connection with the divine, with God.

We may find that staff are grieving too when someone in a care home dies. Staff may have been caring for someone for many years, and have formed a relationship of mutual affection. It is only natural for them to miss the person who has died.

If the care home does not provide some way of acknowledging these losses, over time staff may become worn down and either leave or become 'toughened' so they are not hurt over and over again. We can offer a listening ear, time to talk about what the deceased resident has meant to them, and, if they are able, participation in a short service to bless the room before a new person arrives to fill the space. Details of such a service follow.

The scope of this book does not extend to funeral liturgies, but I have included a 'Prayer as the coffin lid is closed', in case you are asked for prayer in a private home or funeral home after family have spent time with the person's body, just before travelling to the funeral service itself.

Cultures differ in their funeral customs. In New Zealand, the Maori custom when someone dies is to hold a *tangi*, several days of mourning during which time the coffin is open so people can pay their respects to the deceased. This custom is being embraced by more New Zealanders, not just those of Maori descent. It may be that the family you are caring for wants their loved one home with them, and may appreciate prayer before the closing of the coffin lid prior to leaving for the funeral service.

The prayer below will need to be adapted where indicated * according to the gender and particular situation of the person who has died and their families:

17　*Aroha* – Maori for 'deep compassion, love'.

A Prayer as the Coffin Lid is Closed for the Last Time

The family gathers around the coffin.

We now come to that hardest of times when we see for the last
time the face of someone we have loved for so long.

The priest/minister invites any comments from those present before saying:

We give you thanks, O God, for this body which has carried
*name for * number years ...
(adapt next section according to the person's life focus)
through infancy and toddlerhood,
through the energetic days of school and sport,
then as wife and lover and mother, gardener and home-maker – years full of energy
and creativity.
...
And, though it has been hard, we are thankful too for the last season of
*name's life as this body has borne *her/him
through illness and ageing and dying.

This body's work is done.

The priest/minister anoints the body on the forehead with holy oil and then says:

*Name may the holy angels guard and guide you
as you take leave of this body and make your way to heaven where, in God's good
time, a new body awaits you – a spiritual body which can never die

*The coffin lid is closed by those present and after a moment's silence the priest/
minister continues ...*

The time has come – the lid has been closed,
you have moved from our sight
but not from our hearts.
You remain who you have always been to us:
much loved wife/husband, Mum/Dad
and friend *(adapt according to the person's key relationships).*
Your love for us and our love for you remains
what it has always been.
Death cannot take that love away or undo the good that has shone through you.

May God welcome you with love this day, console all those who grieve,
and help us celebrate your life. AMEN.

*Those present hold hands around the closed coffin as the priest/minister concludes
with a blessing or the Grace.*

Blessing of a room after death

A short gathering to bless a room after someone has died can be helpful to staff, and, if they wish to be present, to families and any residents who were especially close to the deceased. It is standard practice in New Zealand care homes and hospitals for rooms or operating theatres where people have died to be blessed.[18] Through culturally appropriate rituals, we give recognition to the value of each human life, we acknowledge the pain or struggle, the sadness, anger or regret expressed in that place of dying, and we cleanse and refresh the room for its next occupant.

The benefits of such a gathering are many:

- Staff who were close to the deceased resident but who cannot attend the funeral have a chance to pause and remember before the room is re-occupied, thereby enhancing their mental health.
- Family who have perhaps spent hours sharing memories or stories while keeping vigil or, after death, sorting loved one's personal effects, can find that this room blessing brings a natural conclusion to their association with the care home and some solace in sharing such a moment with friends or those who have cared for their relative closely at the end.
- If anger or disputes have occurred in this room, this service lightens the atmosphere.
- You have an opportunity – however briefly – to pray with and for the caregivers and any family or residents present.
- Room blessings start to build a community of prayer within the care home, as this little service models God's care for the individual and also for the nursing/caring team.
- A room blessing clearly brings to a close one chapter in the life of the care home and clears the space for a new chapter to begin.

If the care home is new to this practice then it might take quite some time before any of the caregivers will attend. Again we are faced with the value of building relationships with significant staff such as the care manager or experienced nurses or caregivers, so that they are more likely to listen when you talk about the benefits of blessing a room before a new person comes in. Depending on the particular practices of the care home, you may even have the chance to write a staff memo for circulation. There are also likely to be staff who would welcome this practice because, for their own cultural and/or religious reasons, it would enable them to feel spiritually more at peace in their working context.

What follows is a flexible service which takes about three to five minutes, and should not therefore interfere with busy staff routines. You can adapt the words and

---

18 See for example, http://www.whct.org.nz/news-chaplains/room-blessings (accessed 10.2.13).

actions for different contexts if need be, such as for use in a family bedroom if the person has died at home.

In preparation, ask the care manager or senior nurse for a convenient time and ask for that time to be made known to staff or, if possible, write the information in the communication book yourself a day or two ahead, so staff are aware of the room blessing. Then gather the following items:

- a small bowl of good quality and some water
- fern fronds or little leafy twigs with which to scatter the water
- a scripture reading or poem which suits the person who has died, perhaps used at the funeral service if it has already been held
- something that connects with the deceased person, such as a photograph if available, the name tag from the person's walker, the name sign from the door, or the hospital identification bracelet.

Once you are in the room, open the window as a symbol of your intention to refresh the space through the room blessing – and in some cultures this will also be a reminder that the soul of the deceased has left this room. Fill the little bowl with the water and set it aside somewhere you can easily access it. Place the photo or other symbol of the person at the head of the bed. It is important to try to start the room blessing at the time that has been set, but be ready to include any staff who arrive late.

A Simple Form of Room Blessing

Let's begin by taking a few moments of silence to set aside our busyness, and become still and fully present to this place, this moment and our purpose.
(Allow 15 to 20 seconds so people have time to settle – don't be tempted to skip this part.)

God of love,
companion on our journey in this life
and into the life hereafter,
be with us now as we gather
to remember our time here with *(name the person)*
to bless this room,
and to prepare this space for its next occupant.
AMEN.

There's an opportunity now for any of you who'd like to, to share a memory or a story about your time with *(name the person)* while he/she was a resident with us.
(This time may start slowly, but even if only one person shares some memory, it has value in creating an opportunity for staff or family if present, to tell others about their unique way of seeing the deceased – there is often laughter, sometimes tears, as the resident is remembered. This is done with respect and honesty, even if there have been difficult times.)

This reading *(give details)* seems to fit *(name the person)*/was read at the funeral.

Now we come to our time of blessing. *(Take the water and, making the sign of the cross over the water, say ...)*
In the name of our Lord Jesus Christ,
we set this water aside for the sacred purpose of cleansing and refreshing this room.
(Pause.)

Holy God, we acknowledge that the earthly life of *(name ...)* ended here.
We commend her/his spirit into your eternal Love. *(Silence.)*

Jesus, may the Power of your Spirit
expel any lingering influences or spirits that are not of God.
May your Light shine in any dark places,
may your Peace transform any sadness,
may your Compassion comfort those who are grieving *(give names if appropriate)*.
AMEN.

(Remove the photo/personal symbol from the pillow and then give out the leafy twigs and invite those present to sprinkle water around the room/en suite saying simple words such as 'Let there be light' or 'May there be peace in this place' – once they have done this, place the leafy ferns or sprigs on the pillow as a sign to other staff that the room has been blessed.)

(Invite those present to form a circle, holding hands and, if appropriate, lead them in the old version of the Lord's Prayer, before closing with …)

Loving God,
be with *(name any family members who are present)*; help them build a new pattern of life without *(name …)*.
May this room be a sanctuary for the person who becomes its next occupant.
Be with each one of these staff members *(name them if time permits, i.e. be with Kathy, with Alfred, with …)*
as they return to work and routines.
Strengthen them, hold them in your love,
and bless them, for they are a blessing to many.
In Jesus' name, we pray.
AMEN.

3

Spiritual Conversation and Activities Around Relevant Themes

Earlier in this book we explored spiritual conversation, with a focus on our time with *individuals*, listening to their story with heartfelt attention, alert for signs of their spiritual needs, alert too for the presence of Love in the midst of loss and gain, in their prayer and in their pain.

Now we turn to spiritual conversation in *group* settings and consider how we might enable people to engage with some major themes of life and notice God's grace along the way. What follows is a range of options for group work which will suit parish, community or aged-care contexts:

- Spiritual reminiscence for those with dementia – a small group (six to eight).
- A four-session study to use with or without a PowerPoint presentation (on CD), suitable for groups of up to 20 for Lent or Advent but relevant any time. These studies can also be used as stand-alone sessions or for individual spiritual conversation.
- Four single-session discussions with a group up to 20, e.g. a community 'day-care for the elderly' setting whom you see once or twice a year, or a church group, whom you see more regularly.
- Four single-session discussions with a small group (up to 12) whom you know well.

Working in groups with those who are elderly in any setting requires skilled facilitation as we will be faced with a number of impediments to the type of group process we are familiar with, for example in vestry, parish council or school meetings. Some things that make this group context challenging include:

- hearing and vision impairment
- people needing increased time to think before being able to answer a question or comment
- words not always coming out the way people intend, sometimes making little sense at all
- reduced concentration
- dominant personalities (although they can be found everywhere!)

- sleepiness – it's almost inevitable that someone will doze off, but don't take it personally!
- interruptions
- participants arriving late or leaving part-way through.

If we are not well prepared for this context, there is the very real risk that it will elicit from us 'elder speak' – patronizing, simplistic and ultimately disrespectful communication as a way of dealing with our own discomfort. If this happens, take it to supervision.

Introduction to spiritual reminiscence

One helpful approach to spiritual conversation in a small-group setting is 'spiritual reminiscence', an intentional looking back over one's life with specific questions for discussion. One of the foremost proponents of this process is Revd Dr Elizabeth MacKinlay,[1] who has written extensively on spiritual care and the elderly and has developed a straightforward programme of spiritual reminiscence for those with dementia.

Based on her spiritual tasks of ageing model[2] her six-week programme covers:

Week 1: Life – meaning.
Week 2: Relationships – isolation, connecting.
Week 3: Hopes, fears, worries.
Week 4: Growing older and transcendence.
Week 5: Spiritual and religious beliefs.
Week 6: Spiritual and religious practices.[3]

MacKinlay has demonstrated that, in a well-facilitated small-group context, people with dementia can participate, show insight, enjoy humour, interact with others, reflect on their lives, share wisdom, remember things long ago, feel connected to others, and laugh together. Over the course of the sessions, difficult topics such as illness and death can be talked about in a safe context, friendships are deepened and spiritual needs are met by this regular interaction and chance to talk about things that matter.

---

1 Elizabeth MacKinlay and Corinne Trevitt, *Spiritual Reminiscence for Older People with Dementia: A Learning Package*, Centre for Ageing and Pastoral Studies, ACT 2600, Australia, 2006. Please note an expanded, updated version of this learning package will be published through Jessica Kingsley Publishers in 2015.

2 Elizabeth MacKinlay, 'The Spiritual Dimension of Caring: Applying a Model for Spiritual Tasks of Ageing', *Journal of Religious Gerontology*, 12, 3/4, 2001, pp. 151–66.

3 MacKinlay and Trevitt, *Spiritual Reminiscence*, pp. 48–9.

A set of four studies with workbooks/PowerPoint presentations

These four studies are ideal for use in Lent but may be used at other times of the year. They cover the themes of: Journeying, Struggle and Suffering, Dying, and Resurrection, and can be used to help open up a range of issues people often have around these topics.

As you work through these with people, you will be addressing many of the spiritual needs identified earlier in this book. Giving people the chance to explore these themes in the relative anonymity of a group will go a long way towards making them more willing to talk about these issues in individual spiritual conversation as well, when you have time to visit them on their own.

Each workbook is four pages long (four × A4 which, if printed double-sided on A3 paper, makes a booklet). This, together with the PowerPoint presentation, provides enough material to resource you for your input as well as giving participants something to take away for reflection between the sessions. The material works best if you have had time to think through these questions yourself beforehand.

The illustrations in these workbooks are given in black and white here but on the PowerPoint presentation on the CD-Rom will be in colour. Some of the key pictures will also be in the Photo Appendix at the end of the book – again in black and white but in colour on the CD-Rom.

WORKBOOK Session 1: JOURNEYING

Page 1   Reflecting on one's life and where God has or has not been in it.
Pages 2–3 Choice of tools for reflection on one's life journey: timeline or metaphor of river.
Page 4   Reflecting on who has helped me grow and my spiritual/religious experience.

WORKBOOK Session 2: STRUGGLE AND SUFFERING

Page 1   The poem 'Uphill' by Christina Rossetti and a look at the struggles and suffering of Jesus.
Page 2   Struggles with ourselves and with other people.
Page 3   Struggles with injustice and ageing.
Page 4   Struggles with God and words from scripture.

WORKBOOK *Session 3: DYING*

Page 1   Death and Jesus; preparing for a 'good death': facing our mortality.
Page 2   Dealing with emotion; connecting with loved ones: friends or family.
Page 3   Putting things right; placing ourselves in the care of God.
Page 4   The promises of our God to us.

WORKBOOK *Session 4: RESURRECTION*

Page 1   Resurrection and Jesus: John 21.1–18.
Page 2   Reflection on a resurrection picture from creation.
Page 3   Consideration of the 'resurrection principle' – new life emerging from what has seemed a death; reflection of how 'resurrection' might be experienced in your own life.
Page 4   What do we hope[4] for in the life to come? Scriptures for reflection and prayer.

---

4 See Tom Wright's *Surprised by Hope*, SPCK, London, 2007, for a provocative but orthodox exploration of the Christian hope.

Workbook Topic 1: Journeying

- What has my life been like so far?
- Where have I been on my pilgrimage of faith, so far?
- Where am I at this moment?
- Where might God be leading me?

These are big questions which invite you to think about where God has been in your life, when and why you and God might have parted company, and where you are now or would like to be in your God-connection.

On the next three pages there are some diagrams and ideas to help you work with these questions. Ask for the guidance of the Holy Spirit so you can be as honest as you can with yourself and with God. Then choose which page you want to work with.

- Draw a simple timeline and mark the highs and lows in your life, especially periods of crisis, spiritual challenge or moments of discovery or spiritual growth – ask God to reveal any situations which need healing. Talk to God about what you discover.

OR

- Sketch a river as a symbol of your life's journey so far.
  (You don't have to be able to draw, and no-one is going to see this but you!) Then answer as many of these questions as you want to:
  Where did my river flow from? Where is my river flowing to?
  What special places/moments/rocks and rapids has my river encountered?
  How am I travelling on my river?
  Who is travelling with me?
  Where is Jesus? Where would I like him to be?
  What do I need from God at this stage of the journey?

  Finish by offering your sketch to God, along with any questions you have.

- Think back over your life and let the names or faces of people who have influenced your spiritual journey come to mind. They might have shown the kindness of God, or taught you to pray or mentored you through an important decision or simply lived a godly life which 'spoke volumes' but without words.

  Give thanks for each one and then imagine what each person might say to you now about where you are, at this time in your spiritual life.

  Spend some time thinking about your spiritual or religious experience/where you may have glimpsed something of God.

MY SPIRITUAL AND LIFE JOURNEY SO FAR

Birth

Death and beyond

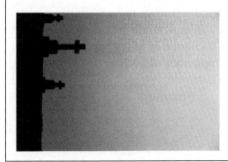

THE RIVER OF MY LIFE

Draw a river to represent your life so far – you can add rapids and rocks, or places of calm deep flowing, to help illustrate the various parts of your experience. Place a star wherever you have encountered something of God, of grace or goodness, or companioning love in the midst of sorrow or suffering.

Then explore the questions from page 1:

Where did my river flow from? Where is my river flowing to?
What special places/moments has my river encountered along the way?
How am I travelling on my river? What companion/s do I have on my journey?
Where is Jesus? Where would I like him to be?
What do you need from God at this stage of the journey?

WHO HAS HELPED ME GROW?

Spend some time thinking back over your life – then ask the Holy Spirit to help you remember the people who have influenced/shaped your spiritual life or who have helped you move towards God, towards the Holy.

When you are ready, spend some time in prayer, giving thanks for these people and what they have meant to you.

WHERE HAVE I GLIMPSED/FELT GOD?

Look through this list and see if you can recall any experience which made you feel closer to God, or more aware of there being 'something other'/a 'higher power'.

- A pattern of events – synchronicity.
- Answered prayer.
- Things/arrangements falling into place.
- An awareness of a presence/the divine.
- An experience, whether you call it God or not, that is different from our everyday life and experience – something 'other'/'higher power'.
- A direct experience of God, for example through the prompting of the Holy Spirit, etc.

Make a few notes about your experience, and if you would like to, talk to someone about it, for example a trusted friend, the chaplain, or a sensitive family member:

Workbook Topic 2: Struggling and Suffering

Uphill

Does the road wind uphill all the way?
    Yes, to the very end.
Will the day's journey take the whole long day?
    From morn to night, my friend.

But is there for the night a resting-place?
    A roof for when the slow, dark hours begin.
May not the darkness hide it from my face?
    You cannot miss that inn.

Shall I meet other wayfarers at night?
    Those who have gone before.
Then must I knock, or call when just in sight?
    They will not keep you waiting at that door.

Shall I find comfort, travel-sore and weak?
    Of labour you shall find the sum.
Will there be beds for me and all who seek?
    Yea, beds for all who come.

Christina Georgina Rossetti

Struggles and Jesus

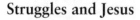

- Inner struggle or temptation – Matthew 4.1–11 – the story of Jesus in the desert, being tempted by physical need, psychological stress and offers of power/prestige.

- Struggling with people – the 'religious system' – Matthew 23.

- Struggling with injustice – calling us to love our neighbour *and* our enemies.

- Listening to the call of God on his life – in the temple as a 12-year-old – Luke 2.41–51; the Syro-Phoenician woman and the awareness of the broadening of his call to include the Gentiles – Mark 7.25–30.

- Choosing the way of the cross – Luke 22.39–44; Matthew 26.36–46, Gethsemane.

- Struggling with suffering – Matthew 27.45–50.

Our own struggles

1 Struggles with ourselves

What would I like to bring to prayer? To share with Jesus?

2 Struggles with other people

How have I suffered because of other people's choices and behaviour?

Has anyone suffered because of choices I've made?

What would I like to bring to prayer? To share with Jesus?

Who do I need to forgive? To whom do I need to say 'Sorry'?

3 Struggles with injustice

How have I experienced injustice?

Have I ever been blamed for something I didn't do?

How have I been an agent for justice in my lifetime so far?
For example, trying to reconcile family members or friends/sticking up for someone.

4 Struggles with ageing

What do I want to say to God or Jesus about ageing from my own experience?

In old age they still produce fruit; they are always green and full of sap, showing
that the Lord is upright; he is my rock and there is no unrighteousness in him.
(Psalm 92.14–15)

5 Struggles with God

E.g. the story of Jacob at Peniel from Genesis 32.24–30.
Many people struggle with God over the suffering of their loved ones or the innocent.
What have I struggled with God over? What has been resolved for me in that struggle?

What do I struggle with God over now?

THE WORD OF GOD

- 'Cast all your anxieties on me, because I care for you' (1 Peter 5.7).
- 'I will not leave you or forsake you' (Hebrews 13.5–6).
- 'I will not leave you comfortless …' (John 14.18).
- 'Come to me, all you who are weary and carrying heavy burdens, and I will give you rest' (Matthew 11.28).
- 'Peace I leave with you; my peace I give you' (John 14.27a).

Workbook Topic 3: Death

Camellias in full bloom (left). Fallen and decaying (right).

Death and Jesus

- Facing his own mortality (Matthew 20.17–19).
- Dealing with his emotions (Matthew 26.36–46; 27.46).
- Connecting with those he loved (John 13, 17), and (Matthew 26.17–30).
- Making provision for those left behind (John 19.26–27).
- Committing himself to God (Luke 23.46).

Preparing for a good death

1 Facing our own mortality

Where are you on the 'race' of life?

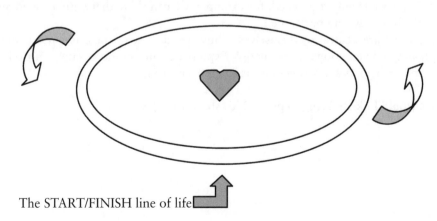

The START/FINISH line of life

What is it like for you to be at this point on your life's journey?

What do you want to say to God/Jesus about this time of your life?

What might God/Jesus want to say to you about this stage?

2 Dealing with our emotions

Different people will experience different emotions when they are faced with their own death. Things like panic, relief, fear, regret, anticipation, sadness and anger are not uncommon. Although it takes energy, it is worthwhile noticing how you are feeling in your body, naming or identifying the feeling, and owning the feeling by saying aloud, 'I feel …'. Then we are ready to acknowledge the feeling and make a response to it. If we are feeling frightened, for example, we can share that with a friend and/ or with God so we are not alone …

Emotions are neutral in themselves – how we deal with them is what matters. Repressing our emotions takes energy. Expressing our emotions safely can relieve tension and help us show others what is important to us.

What would I like to bring to prayer? To share with Jesus?

3 Connecting with loved ones: friends or family

In your imagination, invite those you love to a special meal – enjoy imagining all the fun and laughter and tears and memories you will share. As you prepare your guest list, be aware also of anyone you *don't* want to invite. This might signal some unfinished business – see *Putting things right* below.

4 Putting things right

We know that it is wise to put our affairs in order if we find that our time is short. But we also know that, ideally, long before we near the end of our lives, we can take steps to 'put things right'. This 'putting right' may be expressed in different ways, for example:

- apologizing to someone for something we have done that hurt him or her

- setting the record straight if we know that factual information is inaccurate

- getting in touch with long-lost family members or friends

- telling someone we love them

- making sure we act justly in the distribution of our material goods

- forgiving someone for a wrong we have suffered

- making our wishes known regarding our funeral and estate.

What do you need to 'put right' now so that you can be free of regret and live the rest of your life in peace?

5 *Placing ourselves in the care of God*

You were at my beginning, O God,
and you will be at my end.
You are Love.
From you I came,
and to you I shall return.
Grant me peace of mind, so that I may not fret or worry, but trust that your hand will hold and help me on the journey home to you. AMEN.

The promises of our God to us

- Psalm 23 reminds us that whatever we go through, we are accompanied: 'Even though I walk through the valley of the shadow of death, I will fear no evil, for you are with me; your rod and staff they comfort me' (Psalm 23.4).
- 'There is nothing in death or life, in the world as it is, or the world as it shall be, nothing in the whole of creation that can separate us from the love of God, in Jesus Christ our Lord' (Romans 8.38–39).

Jesus says:
- 'Do not let your hearts be troubled. Believe in God, believe also in me. In my Father's house there are many dwelling places … and I will come again and will take you to myself, so that where I am you may be also' (John 14.1–2a, 3b).
- 'Come to me, all you that are weary and carrying heavy burdens, and I will give you rest. Take my yoke upon you, and learn from me; for I am gentle and humble in heart, and you will find rest for your souls. For my yoke is easy and my burden is light' (Matthew 11.28–30).

Workbook Topic 4: Resurrection

Resurrection and Jesus

John 20.1–18:

- Mary Magdalene sees that the stone has been removed and runs to tell the other disciples.

- Simon Peter and John see the grave-clothes set aside and believe.

- Mary waits, and sees two angels.

- Mary sees someone whom she thinks is 'the gardener'.

- Jesus addresses Mary by name.

🕯 What would it be like to hear Jesus call *your name?* Put yourself in the picture.

- Jesus wanted his disciples – and us – to know that we can be a son or daughter of God – we are loved by the most patient, loving, wise and warm parent a person could ever have.

- Jesus, having been limited in time and place by the human body, is now released into the mystery and wonder of ongoing relationship with his disciples, and agency in the world.

- Through the Holy Spirit promised at Pentecost, relationship with God in Jesus Christ is possible for *any one* of us, anywhere in the world. The Holy Spirit will help us grow in our faith and in our relationships with each other and with God.

Portion of a window in St Paul's (Without the Walls) Canterbury, England.

209

1 A new tree grows sheltered by the broken trunk of an old tree ...

What might this picture have to say to you?

When you have had some time to think, make a few notes if you would like to, and then, in the privacy of your own room, talk to God about what you have discovered.

2 How have you seen the 'resurrection principle' at work in your life?

Here are some ideas of what 'resurrection' life might look like in *your* life. Tick the ones that you relate to. Feel free to add some more of your own.

- Being free to live without regret or anxiety. ☺

- Enjoying restored relationships. ☺☺☺

- Trusting that God holds us now and for all eternity. ∞

- Making the most of each day. **24/7**

- Caring for those around us. ♥

- Being open to the 'sacrament of the present moment' ... *right now*.

- Risking new things.

- Hoping and praying for those we love.

- Drawing on the guidance and strength of the Holy Spirit.

Add some more of your own ...

211

3 *What do you hope for in the life to come?*

The word of God

1 Corinthians 13.12
For now we see in a mirror, dimly, but then we will see face to face.
Now I know only in part, then I will know fully, even as I have been fully known …

John 11.25–26
Jesus said to her, 'I am the resurrection and the life. Those who believe in me, even though they die, will live, and everyone who lives and believes in me will never die.'

1 Corinthians 2.9–10
But as it is written, 'What no eye has seen, nor ear heard, nor the human heart conceived, what God has prepared for those who love him' – these things God has revealed to us through the Holy Spirit.

Revelation 21.1–4
Then I saw a new heaven and a new earth, for the first heaven and the first earth had passed away, and there was no longer any sea. I saw the Holy City, the new Jerusalem, coming down out of heaven from God, prepared as a bride beautifully dressed for her husband. And I heard a loud voice saying, 'Now the dwelling of God is with human beings, and he will live with them and be their God. He will wipe every tear from their eyes. There will be no more death or mourning or crying or pain, for the old order of things has passed away.'

Single studies for large groups

(Up to 20 people whom you may see occasionally.)

1 Using a familiar prayer for reflection

For use with a church-based group exploring the old prayer attributed to Richard of Chichester (prayers from other sources include scripture, Donne, Ignatius, St Teresa of Avila, etc.). This group spiritual conversation centres on drawing nearer to Jesus and gradually becoming free to live without fear and be more fully who we were created to be. A PowerPoint presentation for this discussion is available on the CD-Rom to help the group focus on one thing at a time. Distribute the handout nearer the end, when you want to reinforce what people can do to develop a little 'daily rule' of prayer and grow closer to Jesus.

2 'What's your good news?'

This topic is designed to open up the practice of talking naturally about our God-walk in the course of everyday conversation. I remember sitting in Ben Gurion airport on my way to New Zealand after a life-changing stay in Jerusalem. That morning's scripture (Luke 8.38) lit up for me: 'Return to your home and declare how much God has done for you' and I've tried to do that ever since. Sharing our story about what God has done for us (what is called our 'testimony' in evangelical circles) is the natural way to 'gossip the gospel', to let others see what God gets up to in an ordinary life. Beginning with sharing our experience of the goodness and kindness of other people, or the perfect timing of something in our lives, we can move on to talking about God's loving presence being revealed in countless ways if we have the eyes to see! 'What's your good news?' provides a simple way into that process, whether people are familiar with the concept of testimony or not.

Key question 1: 'What do you think of when you hear the term "good news"?'

Responses may include – 'Haven't got cancer', 'Safe arrival of a new baby', etc.

Decide which Gospel passage you are going to summarize: the Gerasene demoniac (Luke 8.26–37) or the woman at the well (John 4.7–27). Read aloud the key verses from your chosen passage as printed on the handout. Provide time for any questions of clarification but, for the purpose of this discussion, don't get sidetracked into things like the deaths of the pigs or the effects on the employment of the swineherds!

Key question 2: 'How often do we talk to other people about our "good news"?'

Responses may include – 'Not enough', 'Taught not to show off/brag', 'Nothing good to share', 'No-one wants to listen any more', etc. Help people unpack the need to notice what God is up to before we can share it with anyone, as per handout. See if people have any stories about the different sorts of ways God has been a loving presence or a bringer of hope or peace, etc.

Key question 3: 'Thinking back over the last week or two, has anything happened that might have God's fingerprints on it?'

To get the ball rolling, you may need to have some examples of simple things to share with those present – the sort of thing that anyone might experience, not some major God-encounter that happens only once in a lifetime; be as encouraging as you can about what is shared so people will feel they are making progress on *noticing* what God is up to in their lives.

Examples to share might include:

- answered prayer
- a sense of being upheld during the surgery or illness of someone close to you
- a feared medical procedure going smoothly
- courage and calm in the face of a difficult meeting
- a special conversation with a family member or friend
- a visit from the care-home cat just when you needed to touch a warm, soft creature.

3 Accepting help

I hadn't realized until I started working in a care home, how many falls older people had. Many of these happen because people either forget to ring their bells when they need help, for example to go to the toilet in the night, or they choose to try to manage on their own because they 'don't want to be a bother'. Fundamentally we like to be independent, but the drive to 'go it alone' persists long after we have lost the ability to manage by ourselves. Western individualism has played down the importance of community and the reality of our being **inter-dependent**. Coping on our own is actually a misconception as we depend on others to grow and produce our food, to manufacture everything we use; we need governments, law enforcement agencies and emergency services. Older people are in a position to allow others to serve them, to help them. It takes humility and grace to receive care from another, qualities which we see in Jesus when he allows a woman to pour costly ointment on his head during a meal, in spite of outrage expressed by those who witness her devotion.

To begin this group spiritual conversation, write **'Childhood achievements?'** on a large whiteboard and elicit from those present some of the milestones: rolling over/ sitting up/tying our shoelaces, potty training, riding a bike, learning to read and write, etc.

Key question 1: 'Who helped you achieve these things?'

Comments will probably focus on mum or dad, older siblings, teachers, etc.

214

Key question 2: 'How did it feel to be able to do those things?'

This will likely elicit comments such as 'Feeling competent', 'Gave me confidence', 'Able to keep up with older kids', 'Felt good about myself', etc. and the key response: 'Enjoyed being independent'. Open up the topic of independence and how Western society seems to put a high value on being able to 'stand on our own two feet' and manage on our own. Depending on the make-up of the group, it may be worth asking if other cultures also value independence to the same extent. At some point ask:

Key question 3: 'Do you believe that we are meant to "go it alone", to manage by ourselves?'

Use the rest of the handout to open up the concept of inter-dependence and the grace needed to receive, instead of being determinedly independent or finding our meaning by always *giving* to others. The concept of balance might surface – not physical balance but the fine line between allowing someone to help us and the importance of doing what we can for as long as we are able. For example, do we struggle to walk with our walker all the way to the dining-room three times a day, or do we walk halfway, accept the support of a carer and a wheelchair ride for the remainder?

Even though we might need more help as we age, we can still give to others – a word of appreciation, a smile and a thank-you to God in the evening for the kindness we have received.

4 Honouring our life

This topic begins with exploring how people are remembered, so, if you can, obtain a few obituaries (e.g. *The Times*, *The Week*) or epitaphs of various types including the humorous, pictures of statues of famous people, and buildings named after someone, etc. Use these to warm up for the first question.

Key question 1: 'How do you view your life?'

One of the main reasons for including this topic is to encourage people to consider leaving behind something of their story as a legacy for future generations, so there is a list of ways of doing this – you can add to this, of course.

Key question 2: 'How might you leave something of your story for those left behind?'

See if anyone present has already started this process and whether they will share something of what they did and how it worked, etc. Emphasize that the simplest thing can be a blessing, for example the sharing of Nana's 'secret' cake recipes or the story of how Nana and Poppa met, their first house and so on.

Key question 3: 'What did you do in your younger days which you regret?'

The concept of 'reframing' an earlier life event is introduced here in a very gentle way, by a suggested imaginary dialogue between our 'younger' self and who we are now. Offering the chance to revisit old events can be very healing if it is done in the light of a mature perspective and with the company of Jesus if that is appropriate to the group we are working with.

It is certainly *not* about berating oneself for being foolish or wicked, but about accepting that the decisions we made when we were young may well have been the only ones we could make at the time, given the circumstances, our abilities and the people we had around us. In this way we can begin to integrate parts of ourselves that we have been keeping at arm's length out of shame or fear. (As an additional resource for this section, if you have the time, you may like to read or play part of the lyrics of Leonard Cohen's 'Anthem', on *The Essential Leonard Cohen*, Sony/ Columbia, 2002, 497995 2, disc 2, track 9. The key phrase is 'Ring the bell that still can ring. Forget your perfect offering'.)

Key question 4: 'How do you measure "success"/"failure"?'

Use the quote 'Success', often incorrectly attributed to Ralph Waldo Emerson or Robert Louis Stevenson, to talk about a 'successful' life. Bessie Anderson Stanley wrote 'What is Success?' in 1904 for a competition. Mrs Stanley won the first prize of $250 and her poem was included in *Bartlett's Familiar Quotations* in the 1930s. See http://en.wikipedia.org/wiki/Bessie_Anderson_Stanley (accessed 27.2.14). You may need to preface the discussion by acknowledging that the poem was written at a time when it was common usage to use 'man' and 'he' when writing about people irrespective of gender.

Key question 5: 'As you look back, what has mattered most to you in your life?'

> ... and what does the Lord God require of you, but to do justice, and to love kindness, and to walk humbly with your God. (Micah 6.8b)

This quote brings to a close this topic – mainly to emphasize that God's way of seeing our lives is not in terms of pinnacles of achievement or the gathering of material wealth, status or power, but in the beauty and witness of a life that expressed justice, kindness and devoted companionship with God.

> There is a crack, a crack, in everything.
> That's how *the light* gets in. (Cohen, 'Anthem', emphasis mine)

We all have cracks in our 'perfect self-image' – that's how the light of Christ reaches our heart!

Using a Familiar Prayer for Reflection

The Prayer of Richard of Chichester

Who was Richard of Chichester?

- Faithful follower of Jesus.
- Thirteenth-century Bishop of Chichester.
- Caring priest.
- Scholar.
- Great administrator.
- Strong reformer.
- Loved by his people.

Richard gave us this prayer:

> Thanks be to thee, my Lord Jesus Christ,
> for all the benefits thou hast given me,
> for all the pains and insults thou hast borne for me.
> O most merciful redeemer, friend and brother,
> may I know thee more clearly,
> love thee more dearly,
> and follow thee more nearly,
> day by day.

The Hebrew people celebrate the exodus – the time when God rescued them from slavery in Egypt – which still forms part of each Shabat – focusing on freedom.

As Christians we thank Jesus for all the benefits won for us by his life, death and resurrection so we may know 'the glorious freedom of the children of God.' (Romans 8.21)

What does freedom in Christ mean?

'For I am convinced that neither death, nor life, nor angels, nor rulers, nor things present, nor things to come, nor powers, nor height, nor depth, nor anything else in all creation, will be able to separate us from the love of God in Christ Jesus our Lord.' (Romans 8.38–39)

What do you need to be freed from?

Freedom in Christ means freedom:

- from fear, especially fear of death
- from worries about the future
- from guilt about past wrongdoing
- from having to pretend we are okay all the time
- from having to fix things or make people happy
- from loneliness and self-criticism.

How do we learn to know Jesus more clearly, love him more dearly and follow him more nearly day by day?

We wake and thank Jesus for life –
we ask God for what we need for today,
we commend those we love into God's care.
We can pray the Lord's Prayer and the prayer gifted to us by Richard of Chichester.
If we are able, we read or listen to a portion of the Bible.

During the day we can remember that each of us bears the image of Christ – we are Jesus' hands and voice to and for each other. So we try to be kind and helpful and not take offence or gossip.

At bedtime we give thanks for the gifts of the day,
we bring to Jesus any pain or sadness or difficulties,
we commend those we love into his care, and
we ask that we may sleep, held safe in the arms
of our redeemer, friend and brother, Jesus.

Freedom in Christ also means:

- knowing Christ's friendship and acceptance

- knowing we are forgiven and forgiving others

- trusting God no matter what is to come

- approaching death knowing we go to God who is Love

- being honest about how we really are

- commending loved ones and problems to God; leaving God to do what is best

- being part of a loving community whom we serve in the perfect freedom of God.

'What's Your Good News?'

Talking to other people about your faith, or about God, can be a bit of a challenge. Most of us have been brought up with the old adage, 'When in company, never talk about politics or religion!' We might have heard of someone giving their testimony or even seen them standing up at the front in church, talking about their experience of God; we might have thought that it would take a lot of courage and a super-special God-moment to get us to stand up there! But I am talking about something far more organic, the bubbling up *into our ordinary conversation* of words that tell of the joy and peace and hope and courage and strength of encountering God *in the midst of everyday life*.

Story

On a recent visit from overseas to see family in London, Nana and Poppa were a bit taken aback when, at their first family dinner, their three-year-old grand-daughter Ruby, whom they were meeting for the very first time, suddenly said, 'And what's your good news?' A bit embarrassed, Ruby's mum hastened to explain that this question was part of her daughter's pre-school routine, but she needn't have worried. Nana and Poppa appreciated it anyway and told Ruby how good it was to be there with her and her baby brother and Mummy and Daddy! For the remainder of their visit, and now when they see each other on Skype, 'What's your good news?' regularly pops into the conversation.

Key question 1: 'What do you think of when you hear the term "good news"?'

Gospel

The man from whom the demons had gone begged that he might be with Jesus; but Jesus sent him away saying, 'Return to your home and declare how much God has done for you.' So he went on his way, proclaiming throughout the city how much Jesus had done for him. (Luke 8.38–39)

OR

Then the woman left her water jar and went back to the city. She said to the people, 'Come and see a man who told me everything I have ever done! He cannot be the Messiah can he?' … They said to the woman, 'It is no longer because of what you said that we believe, for we have heard for ourselves, and we know that this is truly the Saviour of the world'. (John 4.28–29, 42)

Key question 2: 'How often do we talk to other people about our "good news"?'

But what if our good news *also* included what God has done in our lives? Of course we'd have to recognize God at work *before* we could talk about it, and we might not be used to noticing. For example: we may be used to thinking of 'co-incidences' not 'God-incidences' or forget that people can be the bearers of God's love and provision for us. God comes to us through other human beings, pets, nature, creation, music, films and books, art and sculpture, loving care, unexpected kindnesses, something happening at exactly the right time, people turning up when we need them.

Key question 3: 'Thinking back over the last week or two, has anything happened that might have God's fingerprints on it?'

Action

Keep an eye open for God-moments, give thanks for them each night and share them with those around you next day.

Closing prayer

Thank you, dear God, for this chance to explore some of the ways you come to meet us in the midst of our ordinary days. Give us the words and the courage to begin to share our stories of your grace with those around us. Through Jesus Christ. AMEN.

Accepting Help

It is really hard for most people to accept that we can no longer do what we have always done. We find it hard to relinquish our independence: it starts when we need someone else to shop and drive and do the housework for us, and then we need someone to wash us, dress us, feed us like a mother bird, brush our hair, change our catheter bag, put cream in intimate places, lift us up and carry us to our place of dying. We put off accepting help by saying things like, 'I don't want to be a bother', or 'I thought I could manage on my own', or 'I've always done it in the past', or 'You're far too busy, I didn't want to trouble you'. But the truth is that in not accepting help when we do need it, we may upset those around us and put ourselves at risk of falls and fractures or worse.

Ice Breaker

The achievements of childhood.

Key question 1: 'Who helped you achieve these things?'

Key question 2: 'How did it feel to be able to do those things?'

Key question 3: 'Do you believe that we are meant to "go it alone", to manage by ourselves?'

You may like to refer to John Donne's 'No man is an island …'

> No man is an island,
> Entire of itself,
> Every man is a piece of the continent,
> A part of the main.
> If a clod be washed away by the sea,
> Europe is the less …
> Any man's death diminishes me,
> Because I am involved in mankind,
> And therefore never send to know for whom the bell tolls;
> It tolls for thee.

OR

Genesis 2.18:
Then the Lord God said, 'It is not good that the man should be alone. I will make him a helper as his partner.'

Scripture is the story of the people of God, the *community* as well as individuals. We are created for partnership – with each other and with God.

Key question 4: 'How is getting older affecting your independence?'

(Extra questions if needed)
'What's it like for you now to have people doing things for you?'
'What's the hardest thing about having people doing things for you?'

Scripture

Jesus *accepted* the care of a woman at Bethany when she poured oil on his head in the home of Simon the leper (Mark 14.3–8). What did she do that helped Jesus so much?

Action

Talk to God about something that is becoming a real struggle. If you sense it's the right time, then practise letting someone help. Your gift to them is a smile and a 'Thank you'!

Closing

Help us, dear Jesus, to accept that we can no longer do what we have always done. Following your example, may we accept the help offered by those who care for us now.
May they be blessed in their giving and we in our receiving. AMEN.

Honouring Our Life

Key question 1: 'How do you view your life?'

Many people think that their life is of little importance. We judge ourselves against public figures or relatives who have 'made it big'. But each person's story will never be replicated, nor will it ever be heard if we do not encourage each other to make a record of the highs and the lows of our 'extra-ordinary life' for those around us whom we love. How we do this will depend on our opportunities and how well we are when we start. 'Gertie', a superb cook, wrote out her 'secret' cake recipes with a story for each of her grand-daughters when they turned ten! Here are some other ideas:

- Writing a formal family history, perhaps with links back to earlier generations – a telling of the individual story within the larger family story.
- Putting together a dozen pieces of 'wise advice' or 'things I've learned in life'.
- Finding a special journal and filling it with the key points of our life.
- Making a digital memory book, using modern technology to record video clips, family photos, even music that has touched our heart.
- Gathering family members – or anyone willing to listen – and telling them stories: stories about life before 'modern technology' and transport, stories about hardship and struggle and finding and losing, stories about happy times.

Even if we leave this opportunity to the last minute, with the help of a volunteer biographer (a friend or family member or someone trained through the hospice movement) we can still piece together a patchwork of our lives as a parting gift to those who have loved us.

Key question 2: 'How might you leave something of your story for those left behind?'

Key question 3: 'What did you do in your younger days which you regret?'

If you did something in your younger days which you wish you hadn't, you can revisit this situation and 'reframe it'. Imagine a dialogue between your younger self and who you are now. With the wisdom of hindsight, with compassion for who you were at that time, and seeing more clearly the situation you found yourself in, offer this younger 'you' a few wise words of kindness and understanding, perhaps even of forgiveness. If you want to, you can invite Jesus to witness this conversation and then embrace you – the young and the old – in the bond of love.

Key question 4: 'How do you measure "success"/"failure"?'

He has achieved success who has lived well, laughed often, and loved much;

Who has enjoyed the trust of pure women, the respect of intelligent men and the
love of little children;

Who has filled his niche and accomplished his task;

Who has never lacked appreciation of Earth's beauty or failed to express it;

Who has left the world better than he found it,
Whether an improved poppy, a perfect poem, or a rescued soul;

Who has always looked for the best in others and given them the best he had;

Whose life was an inspiration; whose memory a benediction.

'Success' (Elizabeth-Anne 'Bessie' Anderson Stanley, 1904)

Key question 5: 'As you look back, what has mattered most to you in your life?'

> ... and what does the Lord God require of you, but to do justice, and to love kind-
> ness, and to walk humbly with your God. (Micah 6.8b)

God's way of seeing our lives is not in terms of pinnacles of achievement or the
gathering of material wealth and status, but in the beauty and witness of a life that
expresses justice, kindness and companionship with God.

Single studies for small groups

(Up to 12 people you know well and see regularly.)

These sessions work best if you can arrange three long tables to form a 'U' shape around which a dozen chairs can be placed so you are close to those who attend and the tables can be used for activities, etc. This is a more intimate setting, and with a group whom you see on a regular basis there is a chance for people to develop greater levels of trust and to share more, provided facilitation is skilled and sensitive.

1 Reconciliation and forgiveness

This topic has come up in earlier pages for individuals, but a group spiritual conversation can alert a wider number of people to the value of working through times of anger, bitterness, guilt or estrangement. This topic is approached using two pictures (coloured versions are on the CD-Rom), to spark discussion about inter-*national* reconciliation and inter-*personal* reconciliation.

- War-damaged statue of Christ (right arm severed) stands in the Kaiser Wilhelm Memorial Church in Berlin and bears in German the words: 'Father, forgive us our sins, as we forgive those who sin against us' (English translation mine).
- A section of Rembrandt's 'The Return of the Prodigal Son' showing the father's heart-welcome.

The first picture may provoke a difficult discussion as we cannot know how people have been affected by events connected with the Second World War in particular. However, if we approach this with prayer, the Spirit will guide our conversation and enable us to respond with sensitivity. Time for individual conversation afterwards may need to be arranged if anyone is clearly struggling with memories or strong emotions. The second picture aims to encourage people to have the confidence to 'come home' to God, no matter how long they have been away or what they have done. Individuals may want to talk to God directly themselves or share their story with us or a trusted friend. Reconciliation is available to anyone.

You may like to finish by playing something like 'Psalm 32', by Sons of Korah (*Redemption*, track 6), which emphasizes the toll of keeping silent about our sins/failures/anger and the willingness of God to redeem and restore. Again, it is important to let people know that you are available for one-to-one conversation if they want to discuss anything that has emerged from the group session today.

2 Grieving

Grief is triggered whenever someone suffers a loss.[1] Whether that loss be the death of a spouse, selling the family farm or business, adult children moving away, deteriorating health, redundancy, no longer being able to go to church, etc., *only the individual experiencing the loss* knows the significance of it.

When people were younger and experienced major losses, responsibilities often meant that they had no time to reflect or process their grief and had to pull themselves together and get on with life. But when they become ill, slow down, and particularly when they have to come into an aged-care home, these earlier losses are added to the constellation of losses for which they now need to grieve: loss of health, income, friends through distance or death, frequency of family connection, loss of roles and purpose, vision, hearing, mobility and other physical deterioration, loss of memory and/or clear mental functioning, loss of independence. We *cannot* know how they feel, but we *can* stand alongside them and listen as they try to find a way through what amounts to an avalanche of grief triggered by loss upon loss.

Instead of having their own home, being part of a community and having a reason to get up in the morning, they find themselves in a single room with unfamiliar faces all around, routines that don't fit their normal patterns of living, food that they might never choose to eat, and a degree of depersonalization that comes with institutional reality no matter how excellent the care, for example naming clothing, handing over their medication to someone else, a rigid routine of meals, shower rosters ... it seems as if the losses are never-ending. Probably at no other time in their lives do people experience such potentially overwhelming grief as when they come into a care-home setting. But there is one thing in their favour: they do have the time to grieve if given the right support. Group spiritual conversation can introduce people to tools which they can use for individual grief work in their own way or supported by you, another minister or chaplain or a caring staff member or trusted friend. These three tools are:

1 The Psalms, particularly psalms of lament, which trace the movement from orientation, through disorientation to reorientation as described by Brueggemann[2] (it helps to write these three words up on a whiteboard or draw people's attention to them on their handout).
2 'Praying our goodbyes' – a method of processing losses devised by Joyce Rupp[3] which has proved flexible and helpful for many people working through a range of losses.

---

1 If you are unfamiliar with the grief process, see 'Further Reading' section at the end of the book.

2 Walter Brueggemann, *The Message of the Psalms: A Theological Commentary*, Augsburg, Minneapolis, 1984.

3 Joyce Rupp, *Praying our Goodbyes*, Ave Maria Press, rev. edn, 2012 or www.joycerupp.com/PrayingGoodbyes.html.

3   As people begin to recover from their losses, *making a choice* to live fully the rest of their days, praying their own version of the prayer of Habakkuk, who wrote, with courage and determination, the 'Though … yet …' prayer:

> *Though* the fig tree does not blossom, and no fruit is on the vines;
> though the produce of the olive fails and the fields yield no food;
> though the flock is cut off from the fold and there is no herd in the stalls.
> *Yet* I will rejoice in the LORD; I will exult in the God of my salvation.
> God, the Lord, is my strength; he makes my feet like the feet of a deer,
> and makes me tread upon the heights. (Habakkuk 3.17–19)

Psalm 13 (briefly describe the context before playing the song): the song begins with the despair and disorientation of being in exile, to emerging anger and bitterness as they rage against their captors, before reorientating themselves as God's people by invoking God's justice on those who destroyed Jerusalem. *Redemption Songs*, Sons of Korah, Wordsong: Australia, 2000, WACD001, track 1.

Key question 1: 'Where do you think you currently are? In a reasonably settled place? Unsettled, dealing with a lot of uncertainty? Or are things settling down again after an upheaval?'

You may like to begin by talking briefly about the movement from orientation to disorientation to reorientation, perhaps using a simple example such as children leaving home for further education, travel or to make their own way in the world … Any example will do so long as the movement from relative stability through a challenging event which is experienced as loss and/or grief, to a place of adjustment and new patterns of life, is clear.

Key question 2: 'How might you rewrite these verses of Psalm 13 to make it your own?'

The text of Psalm 13 is provided in the handout sheet for participants. You may like to work out an example to share with them to help them think about options.

Key question 3: 'Who or what have I not yet properly farewelled?'

Again this needs sensitive handling as the question may evoke tears or discomfort in some present. Ensure that you have time at the end to check how people are if they have become upset … an additional visit may be appreciated if you can manage it. Part of the difficulty people sometimes face is that others do not take their grief seriously, e.g. the death of an old companion animal, the moving from the family home that is patently too large and requiring too much maintenance, etc., the parting with a grandchild who leaves to travel overseas.

Give an example of what a 'praying our goodbyes' ritual might look like, either from your own experience or using the example below:

A friend was moving to live overseas for a long time and he wanted to 'pray his goodbye' to the home he and his family had lived in for 20 years. The rest of the family had already flown out of the country, so he was alone. He decided to gather some symbols which represented the life they had lived in that place (e.g. baby photos, an old skateboard, a tin of paint, a toy digger, etc.) which carried rich meaning for him. He wrote a letter to God about his home and family's life there, how he felt about leaving and what he needed from God to help him support his family and stay positive in a totally new country. Then he put the letter and the memorabilia in an old suitcase and buried it deep in the back garden, praying as he did so, asking for the grace he needed in the time ahead. It took the whole afternoon, but the process was hugely helpful and enabled him to leave without having to look back – literally or metaphorically.

Write your own 'Though ... yet' prayer to get a sense of what the process is like before introducing the group to it.

3 *Letting go*

This is a sensitive topic and requires prayerful preparation and facilitation. We start off in a light-hearted manner by putting on the central table items to represent a lifetime of acquisition, things solid enough to hand around so people can touch them and get a sense of what they are, even if their sight is impaired, for example a baby's dummy, a rugby ball, toys – car, house, boat, Barbie and Ken dolls, paper money, aeroplane, shoes, a bone china cup and saucer etc., a tennis racquet, a gardening fork, an ornament – whatever comes to mind. Allow enough time for each item to be examined by those present. Discussion may emerge about other things that should be there! Once the group is warmed up to the topic, read the focus verse twice and begin the rest of the session.

As we continue to age, we are confronted by the need to let go ... and let go ... and let go. Many of you here will have 'down-sized' your home perhaps more than once – some of you might be in small villas or studio apartments in the village, others of you are residents and you've had to choose only a few special things to bring with you into the care home. But it's not just about letting go of *things* ...

Key question 1: 'What might have been "painted in God-colours" along the way?'

Think about – wherever there's been love and laughter, wholesome creativity, struggle or suffering, in special times of awareness of God or when giving service, forming friendships ...

Key question 2: 'What *else* have you had to let go of in the past few years?'

People may mention pets (care-home policy might prohibit animals), driving (independence), managing own finances (appointing Enduring Powers of Attorney, etc.), decision-making (control), freedom to go out (especially if limited in mobility), seeing friends (moving away from a familiar neighbourhood) ... the list will be quite sobering and the mood of the group may be sombre. Acknowledge that they have let go of a lot and it can't have been easy.

Key question 3: 'What/who helped you to let go?'

People may talk about having no choice, thinking of others such as family, and not wanting to be a burden, realizing that the time had come to make a move so they wanted to do it before it was forced upon them, a growing awareness that it was time to 'de-clutter' or to simplify. They may have been helped in their decision by a wise friend or family member, someone they trust. They may have drawn on their relationship with God and a strong belief that they could trust God with whatever lies ahead. Reinforce the sentiments expressed in St Teresa of Ávila's bookmark: **God alone is enough.**

4 Giving your blessing

You may like to re-read Genesis 27—35 so you can provide more detail than I have already included in the handout should people want to know more about the story.

However, the focus is on their experience of blessing and introducing the idea that it might be something which could form part of their leave-taking of loved ones.

The questions are straightforward, although it may help if you have some ideas or examples of your own to share. Participants may be slow to answer Key question 3, 'How does God bless you?', so a prompt from you might be necessary to get them started: through the beauty of creation, through people who care for us, through giving us Jesus, through the Spirit at work in our lives, etc.

A gentle offering of anointing can help bring this reflection to an appropriate close, if we are comfortable with this liturgical act and it is accepted by those with whom we are ministering.

Music: 'A blessing', Margaret Rizza, *Icons 1, Instrumental Music*, Kevin Mayhew: Suffolk, 2003, 1490109, track 10.

Reconciliation and Forgiveness

This war-damaged statue of Christ (his right arm severed) stands in the Kaiser Wilhelm Memorial Church in Berlin, Germany. The plaque, in German, bears the words: 'Father, forgive us our sins as we forgive those who sin against us'. This church is partnered with Coventry Cathedral, England, in an initiative for reconciliation called 'The Cross of Nails Community'.

Take some time to look closely at this statue and to get in touch with your own thoughts and feelings about forgiveness towards a nation or nations whose actions may have caused you personal loss or pain.

This picture is of the main section of Rembrandt's masterpiece, 'The Return of the Prodigal Son'. Based on Luke 15.11–32, the painting demonstrates the father's heart-welcome to his estranged child. No questions asked, no recrimination or blame, just a loving, accepting, gathering-in embrace.

All of us are the 'prodigal' to some degree; we often run away from God and may wonder if we can ever 'come home'. This painting gives us the answer to that question.

🕯 Take some time to look closely at this painting and to get in touch with the thoughts and feelings it evokes in you. It doesn't matter how long you have been away or how far you have wandered. You are welcomed home, and a banquet is prepared to celebrate your return. Isn't that something?

Grieving

Grief is a very personal experience, triggered when we suffer *any* loss which is significant to us. As we get to advanced age, our losses start to add up, and, unless we deliberately choose to work our way through our grief, the cumulative effect of historic and current losses can affect our ability to make the most of the time we do have. Here are three ways of easing the burden of grief, helping you to let go of old sadness or more recent losses which upset your peace:

1   using the Psalms as vehicles of lament
2   'praying our goodbyes'
3   writing our own 'though/yet' prayer inspired by a 'minor' prophet, Habakkuk, whom you may never have heard of!

The Psalms can help us lament

When we are in the middle of a lot of change we can feel as if the ground is unsteady beneath our feet. We can move from a place of stability (orientation) through times of struggle or questioning (disorientation) to a settled but different life, enriched by a reclaiming of God's promises of steadfast love and provision (reorientation).

Key question 1: 'Where do you think you currently are? In a reasonably settled place? Unsettled, dealing with a lot of uncertainty? Or are things settling down again after an upheaval?'

What the Psalms teach us is that we can talk or yell or sing to God *honestly* about what we are experiencing because wherever we are, God wants to be. It was natural for the Hebrew people to sing their sadness to God in psalms of lament, for example when they were taken into captivity in Babylon. They were grieving the loss of homes, livelihoods, people, rhythms of prayer, their own culture, everything familiar. In their state of disorientation, they cried out, 'How can we sing the Lord's song in a strange land?' They acknowledged the difficult situation they were in, expressing anger and bitterness towards their captors, before reorientating themselves as God's people by invoking God's justice on those who destroyed Jerusalem. (*This Psalm is played or read aloud for you now.*)

No matter what was happening, the Hebrew people kept the lines of communication with God open. We see Jesus doing this himself: when in the most extreme pain and anguish on the cross, he cried out to God the first line from Psalm 22: 'My God, my God, why have you forsaken me?' It was an honest, desperate cry, but Jesus knew that this psalm contained a full description of his suffering, called on God for deliverance and ended with a statement of trust in God who 'did not hide his face from me, but heard when I cried to him' (v. 24) and deserves worship and praise.

Lamenting helps us transition from deep inner desolation to crying out to God, and reconnecting with what we already know of God, trusting that God is there for us in whatever lies ahead.

Key question 2: 'How might you rewrite these verses of Psalm 13 to make it your own?'

How long, O LORD? Will you forget me for ever?
How long will you hide your face from me?
How long must I bear pain in my soul and have sorrow in my heart all day long?

Consider and answer me, O LORD my God …

But I trusted in your steadfast love;
my heart shall rejoice in your salvation.
I will sing to the LORD because he has
dealt bountifully with me. (Psalm 13.1–2, 3a, 5–6)

Praying our goodbyes

Joyce Rupp talks about 'praying our goodbyes' (*Praying our Goodbyes*, Ave Maria Press, 2012). She offers a fourfold process which we can follow to help us find a pathway through grief and loss to new life. This path begins with:

- *Recognition.* I name what I am feeling and thinking about the loss of someone or something significant in my life. It does not matter how other people perceive the loss; until I acknowledge how the loss affects *me*, I will be stuck and inwardly unsettled.

- *Reflection.* I go against cultural norms of busyness and deliberately take time to slow down, make space to be on my own for a while so I have time to think, and allow myself to feel the loss and grief, however difficult this might be. It is the time too, Rupp says, when we can tell God how things really are for us, being as real as we can. Sometimes we need to take time out from reflection, but we are encouraged to come back to it, to invite God into it, and to trust that God will be there with us, even if we cannot 'feel' God's presence. In time that will change if we are faithful to the process of reflection.

- *Making a ritual.* We are used to the formal rituals of funerals and memorial services, but what do we do when our loss doesn't involve the death of a loved one? We make up our own ritual and include the use of symbols/images, prayer and movement – we don't have to involve anyone else unless we want to.

- *Reorientation.* Through the use of reflection and ritual we are helped to reorient ourselves, to turn in a new direction towards healing, towards new patterns of life. This does not mean that we are going to forget who or what we are fare-welling; it means that, having given our feelings and thoughts quality attention, and expression, we can now begin to turn to face this life again with some energy to devote to living it.

Key question 3: 'Who or what have I not yet properly fare-welled?'

You don't need to answer this question out loud, just give it some space in your mind for a few minutes and see what comes up for you. An indicator of an unresolved grief is finding tears welling up in your eyes or a feeling of deep sadness or other emotion. Just notice what happens for you and then you can work with it later yourself or ask for some support.

The 'though/yet' prayer

A 'minor' prophet, Habakkuk expressed what many of us still feel today: how do wrongdoers appear to prosper and God appears not to act? He addresses God vigorously and comes to accept that God is working things out, perhaps through unusual means and in God's own time. Habakkuk finishes his writing with a profound statement of faith and trust in God:

> *Though* the fig tree does not blossom, and no fruit is on the vines;
> though the produce of the olive fails and the fields yield no food;
> though the flock is cut off from the fold and there is no herd in the stalls.
> *Yet* I will rejoice in the LORD; I will exult in the God of my salvation.
> God, the Lord, is my strength; he makes my feet like the feet of a deer,
> and makes me tread upon the heights. (Habakkuk 3.17–19)

When you have some quiet moments, reflect on Habakkuk's words and rewrite them for yourself, for example: '*Though* my hearing is failing and my family is far away … though … *Yet* I will …'

Letting Go

For we brought nothing into the world, and we can take nothing out of it.
(1 Timothy 6.7, NIV)

Somehow we forget the truth of this scripture verse. By the time we reach our three-score years and ten, most of us in the developed world will have acquired a range of relationships (family, friends, work colleagues), a large number of material assets (home, car, wealth), identity, membership of various interest or service or faith groups, a sense of belonging or status in the community, a job or vocation, something that gives our life meaning and purpose. Some of this may have been painted with God-colours along the way, colours that never fade but become part of you and light your way to eternity.

Key question 1: 'What might have been "painted in God-colours along the way"?'

Think about – wherever there's been love and laughter, wholesome creativity, struggle or suffering, in special times of awareness of God or when giving service, forming friendships …

As we continue to age, we are confronted by the need to let go … and let go … and let go. Many of us here will have 'down-sized' our home, perhaps more than once – but it's not just about letting go of things …

Key question 2: 'What *else* have you had to let go of in the past few years?'

Key question 3: 'What/who helped you to let go?'

An elderly nurse said a couple of days before her death, 'I am ready to jump off the edge into the arms of God.' She meant it and with that statement of faith came a peaceful dying. She had a clear sense of God's trustworthiness, just like a little child who joyfully lets go of the branch and jumps into her father's waiting arms.

The eternal God is your refuge, and underneath are the everlasting arms. (Deuteronomy 33.27a)

The Bookmark of
St Teresa of Avila

Let nothing disturb you.
Let nothing frighten you.
All things pass away;
God never changes.
Patience obtains
all things.
The person who has God
lacks nothing;
God alone suffices.

Giving your Blessing

In the later chapters of Genesis, through the complex story of twin brothers Esau and Jacob, we discover the power of being blessed. In chapter 27, younger son Jacob tricked his father Isaac into blessing him before he died. Once given, the blessing could not be undone, however distraught Esau's pleas. Isaac's blessing gave voice to all that he wanted for his son, all that he could offer him; it was considered binding and Esau had no choice but to make his own way as best he could, unblessed.

Much later in the story of the brothers, Jacob, understandably afraid of meeting Esau who is heading in his direction, sends gifts ahead of him to appease his wronged brother. Anxious and alone, Jacob then has a mysterious night-time encounter, wrestling with an unnamed man until dawn. Though injured, Jacob will not let go until he is given a blessing. The man asks his name and then says: 'You shall no longer be called Jacob, but Israel, for you have striven with God and with humans and have prevailed' (Genesis 32.28). To Jacob's relief, when he does finally meet Esau there is an emotional reconciliation and Esau accepts Jacob's generosity, past pain is washed away by the grace of forgiveness.

As Israel, Jacob is blessed by God to 'be fruitful and multiply; a nation and a company of nations shall come from you … the land I gave to Abraham and Isaac I will give to you … and to your offspring after you' (Genesis 35.11–12).

Key question 1: 'What do you make of this story? Have *you* ever received or given a blessing to someone?'

In our culture the concept of seeking a parent's blessing still floats around in our collective psyche, surfacing sometimes when people are about to be married or setting off on a big adventure. It is as if we know that somehow a blessing puts a seal of approval on something or someone important. But intentionally giving our children a blessing is not common practice. We might give them a hug and tell them in passing that we love them. We might think that it's enough to draw up a will to distribute our assets, such as they might be. But a will can be a cold document, contested if not considered equitable, the preserve of lawyers and arguments over interpretation and intent.

A minister was visiting an old lady who was actively putting her affairs in order as she didn't think she had long to live. They talked about her family and she said that she needed to find a way to let her children know that she loved them. An idea came to the minister's mind. He knew that she still wrote letters, so he asked her if she might like to write them something. She seemed drawn to the idea, but the minister had no way of knowing if she would act on it. He just knew inwardly that it was not up to him to write them for her, even at her dictation. While the minister was out of town, the old lady died. When he came back he rang her son to offer his condolences. 'Something lovely Mum did – she wrote us each a letter ... it was in her own writing ...'

A blessing can come through a letter, a digital recording, a loving conversation or a special touch. However it is conveyed it is priceless, because, while a part of us might like a blessing that included a sizeable portion of assets, what most of us really want, and need, is to know that we are loved, accepted and precious.

Key question 2: 'What do you think of the idea of blessing those you love? How might you do it? What/who might you need to help you?'

Key question 3: 'How does God bless you?'

Minister: As we listen to a piece of quiet music, I am going to come to each one of you. If you would like to receive a blessing, then I will anoint you with holy oil as an outward sign of God's life flowing through your spirit with fresh energy and love. If you feel a bit shy or awkward about this and prefer not to take part, that's fine, just shake your head and we can bless each other with a smile.

Bibliography

Brueggemann, Walter, *Spirituality of the Psalms*, Augsburg, Minneapolis, 2002.

The Church of the Province of New Zealand, *A New Zealand Prayer Book*, Collins, London, 1989.

Florence Susan Squellati, *When You Lose Someone You Love*, Helen Exley, 2002.

Geddes, Joan Bel, *Are You Listening God?* Ave Maria Press, 1994.

Goldsmith, M., *In a Strange Land: People with Dementia and the Local Church*, 4M Publications, Nottingham, 2004.

Greenblat, Cathy, *Love, Loss and Laughter: Seeing Alzheimer's Differently*, Lyons Press, Guilford, CT, 2011.

Janata, Peter, *Study Finds Brain Hub That Links Music, Memory and Emotion*, http://www.news.ucdavis.edu/search/news_detail.lasso?id=9008 (accessed 6.3.14).

Koenig, Harold G., *Spirituality in Patient Care*, 2nd edn, Templeton Foundation Press, Philadelphia, 2007.

Lentz, Robert and Gately, Edwina, *Christ in the Margins*, Orbis Books, Maryknoll, 2003.

MacKinlay, E., 'The Spiritual Dimension of Caring: Applying a Model for Spiritual Tasks of Ageing', *Journal of Religious Gerontology*, 12, 3/4, 2001, pp. 151–66.

MacKinlay, Elizabeth and Trevitt, Corinne, *Spiritual Reminiscence for Older People with Dementia: A Learning Package*, Centre for Ageing and Pastoral Studies, ACT 2600, Australia, 2006. An expanded, updated version of this learning package will be published by Jessica Kingsley Publishers in 2015.

MacKinlay, Elizabeth, *Spiritual Growth and Care in the Fourth Age of Life*, Jessica Kingsley Publishers, London, 2006.

May, Gerald, *Care of Mind, Care of Spirit*, Harper Collins, New York, 1982.

McLaren, Brian, *Naked Spirituality*, Hodder & Stoughton, London, 2011.

Pickering, Sue, *Spiritual Direction – A Practical Introduction*, Canterbury Press, Norwich, 2008.

Pritchard, Sheila, *The Lost Art of Meditation: Deepening your Prayer Life*, Scripture Union, London, 2002.

Puchalski, C. and Ferrell, B. R., *Making Health Care Whole: Integrating Spirituality into Patient Care*, Templeton Press, West Conshohocken, PA, 2010.

Rupp, Joyce, *Praying our Goodbyes*, rev. edn, Ave Maria Press, 2012 (also in Kindle edition).

Sachs, Oliver, http://www.ted.com/talks/oliver_sacks_what_hallucination_reveals_about_our_minds.html.

Shakespeare, William, *Hamlet,* Act 5, Scene 2.

Shelly, Judith and Fish, Sharon, *Spiritual Care: The Nurse's Role*, 3rd edn, IVP, Downers Grove, Illinois, 1988.

Swinton, John and Payne, Richard, eds, *Living Well and Dying Faithfully: Christian Practices for End-of-Life Care*, Eerdmans, 2009.

Thomas, Ruth, http://www.midlandmentalhealthnetwork.co.nz/page/160-midland-regional-dementia-advisor+dementia-dementia-care-information-leaflets.

—— *Behavioural Staging: Leaflet 3, The Different Helping Strategies for Each Stage*, 2012, see website above.

Wright, Tom, *Surprised by Hope*, SPCK, London, 2007.

Yancey, Philip, *Prayer*, Hodder & Stoughton, London, 2008.

Further Reading

Anderson, Megory, *Attending the Dying: A Handbook of Practical Guidelines*, Morehouse, London, 2005.

Bradbury, Paul, *Sowing in Tears: How to Lament in a Church of Praise*, Grove Books, Cambridge, 2007.

Cassidy, Shirley, *Sharing the Darkness: The Spirituality of Caring*, DLT, London, 1988.

—— *Light from the Dark Valley*, DLT, London, 1994.

Cowley, Joy, *Aotearoa Psalms*, 13th edn, Pleroma Christian Supplies, Otane, NZ, 2008.

—— *Psalms Downunder*, Catholic Supplies, Wellington, 1997.

—— *Psalms for the Road*, Catholic Supplies, Wellington, 2003.

—— *Notes to a Friend*, Pleroma Christian Supplies, Otane, New Zealand, 2013. Also available as an eBook.

Fischer, Kathleen, *Imaging Life After Death: Love that Moves the Sun and Stars*, SPCK, London, 2005.

Foster, Richard, *Prayer: Finding the Heart's True Home*, Hodder & Stoughton, New York, 1992.

Frielingsdorf, Karl, *Seek the Face of God: Understanding the Power of your Images of God*, Ave Maria Press, Notre Dame, IN, 2006.

Gatta, Julia and Smith, Martin L., *Go in Peace: The Art of Hearing Confessions*, Canterbury Press, Norwich, 2013.

Hawker, Paul, *Soul Survivor*, Wood Lake Publishing, 2007.

—— *Secret Affairs of the Soul*, Northstone Publishing, 2000.

Hay, David, *Religious Experience Today: Studying the Facts*, Mowbray, London, 1990.

—— and Hunt, K., *Understanding the Spirituality of People Who Don't Go to Church*, University of Nottingham: Centre for the Study of Human Relations, 2000.

Hoblitzelle, Olivia Ames, *The Majesty of your Loving: A Couple's Journey through Alzheimer's*, GMB, Cambridge, MA, 2008.

Hutchinson Joyce, and Rupp, Joyce, *May I Walk You Home?*, Ave Maria Press, Notre Dame, IN, 1999.

Jamieson, Christopher, *Finding Sanctuary: Monastic Steps for Everyday Life*, Phoenix (Orion Books), London, 2007.

—— *Finding Happiness: Monastic Steps for a Fulfilling Life*, Phoenix (Orion Books), London, 2009.

Jones, Gemma M. M., *The Alzheimer Café: Why it Works*, The Wide Spectrum Publications, Sunninghill, 2010, http://www.thewidespectrum.co.uk/About.htm.

Kübler-Ross, Elisabeth, *Death, the Final Stage of Growth: On Death and Dying*, Routledge, London, 1989.

Matthews, Melvyn, *God's Space in You*, John Hunt Publishing, Alresford, 2003.

Nouwen, Henri and Gaffney, Walter J., *Aging, the Fulfilment of Life*, Image (Doubleday), London, 1990.

Nouwen, Henri J. M., *Our Greatest Gift: A Meditation on Dying and Caring*, Hodder & Stoughton, London, 1994.

Savary, Louis M., Berne, Patricia H. and Kaplan-Williams, Strephon, *Dreams and Spiritual Growth: A Christian Approach to Dreamwork: With More Than 35 Dreamwork Techniques*, Paulist Press, 1984.

Saunders, James, *Dementia: Pastoral Theology and Pastoral Care*, Grove Books, Cambridge, 2002.

Snowdon, David, *Aging with Grace*, Fourth Estate, London, 2001 (the Nun Study). For further information visit https://www.healthstudies.umn.edu/nunstudy/ or http://en.wikipedia.org/wiki/Nun_Study.

Tacey, David, *The Spirituality Revolution: The Emergence of Contemporary Spirituality*, HarperCollins, Sydney, 2003.

Taylor, Barbara Brown, *When God is Silent*, Canterbury Press, Norwich, 2013.

Taylor, Jill Bolte, *My Stroke of Insight: A Brain Scientist's Personal Journey*, Plume, 2009, www.ted.com/talks/jill_bolte_taylor_s_powerful_stroke-of_insight?language=en.

Vanier, Jean, *Befriending the Stranger*, DLT, London, 2005.

Worden, J. W., *Grief Counselling and Grief Therapy*, Routledge, London, 1989.

Wuellner, Flora Slosson, *Beyond Death: What Jesus Revealed about Eternal Life*, Upper Room Books, Nashville, 2014.

Appendix 1: Sacred Space Service Sheets

These and the other short services of the Word
are in photocopiable form on the accompanying CD-Rom.

A SACRED SPACE

Spring and Hopefulness

I am about to do a new thing; now it springs forth …
I will make a way in the wilderness and rivers in the desert.
(Isaiah 43.19)

Leader World events can shock us, O God.
Civil wars and global strife, terrifying weather events,
the innocent abused, the poor made poorer,
such things can leave us wondering and wordless.

All We come to you the Comforter,
the One who knows our questions,
shares our anguish,
and fires our anger into prayerful action.
(*A newspaper is placed on the altar*)

Leader As we gather today in the fragrance of spring,
we see all around us new life awakening.

All Let us honour the signs of such hope in our midst,
and draw strength from your presence within us.
(*Spring buds and fragrant flowers are placed on the altar*)

Leader God of hand and heart,
Giver of new life every minute of every day:

All We come to be renewed by your resurrection hope,
inviting us to new life in your love.
(*A picture of a butterfly is placed on the altar*)

We share Psalm 1.1–3:

Leader Happy are those who do not follow
the advice of the wicked,
or take the path that sinners tread,
or sit in the seat of scoffers;

All but their delight is in
the law of the LORD,
and on his law they meditate
day and night.

Leader They are like trees
planted by streams of water,

All which yield their fruit in its season,
and their leaves do not wither.
In all that they do, they prosper.

We listen and join in the chant:
'Ubi caritas et amor, deus ibi est.' (Taizé)
'Where there is kindness and love, God is there.'

The Blessing

May God's creative energy, which is never exhausted,
bring us a new sense of hope and peace.
O great Lover of our souls, may your blessing
be upon us this night and all our nights. AMEN.

We listen to: 'Hymn to Hope' (Secret Garden)

Leader: In a time of silence we bring to God our regrets,
our failures to love and to live as Christ teaches us.
Silence
May we know that we are forgiven.
Let us approach our God in peace.

Reading: John 4.7–1: The Samaritan woman at the well.

We listen to: 'O Lord hear my prayer' (Taizé)

We move into a time of personal silent prayer and reflection.

As the music begins again, the leader will offer a time of corporate prayer, and then invite you to join in The Lord's Prayer:

Our Father, which art in heaven,
hallowed be thy name,
thy kingdom come; thy will be done
on earth as it is in heaven.
Give us this day our daily bread
and forgive us our trespasses,
as we forgive those who trespass against us.
And lead us not into temptation,
but deliver us from evil.
For thine is the kingdom, the power and the glory.
For ever and ever. AMEN.

A poem is read: 'Spring-maker'

The athletic stretch of leafy limb,
the fresh-clothed branches dancing,
the joy of bent seed straightening,
swelling through darkened soil
to break ground into light:
all are signs of hope for us.

The urge to live persists,
endures and *will* do so.
It will
though we seem to be moving slowly
in the opposite direction …
shrinking in strength and height,
at risk of falls and breaks
we are cautious with our movements
and could fall prey to grey
thoughts and sadness, but

Spring calls *us* back to life afresh:
noses full of fragrance,
glimpses filled with glory,
splashes of bright colours
through our day, say
'All is well. All *is* well.'
For you are with us, Spring-maker,
in all ways, for ever, *with us.*

A SACRED SPACE

Friendship

Thus the scripture was fulfilled that says,
'Abraham believed God, and it was reckoned to him as
righteousness', and he was called the friend of God.

(James 2.23)

Leader Can it be true? Can I be a friend of the high and holy One?
All Can it be true? Can we dare to believe
that you, O God, seek us out
and long for conversation
in the quiet of the evening,
in the garden of delight?

Leader Can it be true? Can I be a friend
of the One who came to earth
and took on flesh for us?
All Can it be true? Can we dare to believe
that you, O Jesus, are indeed our brother,
our Saviour *and* our friend?
That we can share with you our dreaming,
our songs and sighs and love?

Leader Can it be true? Ah, yes – dear friend,
help me receive your company, your joy.
All Can it be true? Ah, yes – dear friend,
for you have laid down your life for me.
That's what a friend does, doesn't he?
Now what can I do?
Lay down my life for you, too?

We share Psalm 18.1–3, 6, 19:

Leader I love you, O LORD, my strength
All The LORD is my rock, my fortress
and my deliverer,
my God, my rock in whom I take refuge,
my shield, and the horn of my salvation,
my stronghold.
Leader I call upon the LORD who is worthy to be praised,
so I shall be saved from my enemies …

All In my distress, I called upon the LORD;
to my God I cried for help.
Leader From his temple he heard my voice,
and my cry to him reached his ears …
All He brought me out into a broad place;
he delivered me because
he delighted in me.

Silence for reflection and a thought to 'take away'.

How might I be a friend to God and let God be a friend to me?

We sing THE GRACE together:

May the grace of our Lord Jesus Christ, and the love of God
our Father, and the fellowship, the fellowship of the Holy
Spirit, be with us, for evermore and evermore and evermore.
AMEN.

Holding the 'Friend of God' heart, we reflect on what we have just said: 'Now what can I do?'

Leader   In a time of silence we bring to God our regrets, our failures to love and to live as Christ teaches us, as well as our desire to live with and for God.
(Substantial silence – 2 minutes – then we symbolically give our friendship to God by offering our hearts on the altar.)
May we know that we are forgiven.
Let us approach our friend God in peace.

Reading: John 15.12–17: Jesus talks to his disciples.

We listen to: 'O Lord hear my prayer' (Taizé)

We move into a time of personal silent prayer and reflection.

As the music begins again, the leader will offer a time of corporate prayer, and then invite you to join in the Lord's Prayer:

Our Father, which art in heaven,
hallowed be thy name,
thy kingdom come; thy will be done
on earth as it is in heaven.
Give us this day our daily bread
and forgive us our trespasses,
as we forgive those who trespass against us.
And lead us not into temptation,
but deliver us from evil.
For thine is the kingdom, the power and the glory.
For ever and ever. AMEN.

We listen to: 'You've Got a Friend' (James Taylor)

For reflection: Imagine Jesus singing this song to you.

Perhaps you've had some experience of needing a friend during your long life?

Perhaps you've had the chance to be a friend to someone else over the years?

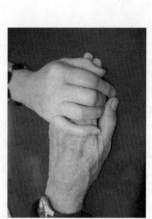

Perhaps you've been surprised to find friendship here?

Turn to your neighbour and share something of your 'friendship' history if you want to for a few minutes.

A SACRED SPACE

God knows …

Trust in the LORD with all your heart, and do not rely on your own insight. In all your ways acknowledge him, and he will make straight your paths.
(Proverbs 3.5–6)

Leader O God, you are Wisdom, beyond our understanding.
All **So many people seek wisdom elsewhere, searching Google or Wikipedia, finding only human knowledge, partial, tainted 'truth'.**
(A laptop or tablet computer is held up and placed on the altar)

Leader You, O God, are Truth, full of integrity.
All **In you there is no deceit. No hidden agendas or selfish schemes shadow your love for us.**
(A Bible is placed on the altar)

Leader You are Life-Giver and Lover of us all.
All **Your vision stretches to eternity beyond the farthest star. You alone can show us the Way.**
(A large eternity symbol ∞ is placed on the altar)

Leader Help us today to come closer to you to trust you with our deepest needs and our longing for love.
In the name of Jesus we pray. AMEN.

We share Psalm 19, selected verses

Leader The heavens are telling the glory of God; and the firmament proclaims his handiwork.
All **Day to day pours forth speech, and night to night declares knowledge.**
Leader There is no speech, nor are there words; their voice is not heard;
All **yet their voice goes out through all the earth, and their words to the end of the earth …**
Leader The law of the LORD is perfect, reviving the soul; the decrees of the LORD are sure, making wise the simple … (1–4, 7).

Leader Moreover, by them is your servant warned: in keeping them there is great reward.
All **But who can detect their errors? Clear me from hidden faults … (11–12).**

All **May the words of my mouth and the meditation of my heart be acceptable to you, O LORD, my rock and my redeemer. AMEN. (14)**

Blessing

The peace of God, which passes all understanding, keep your hearts and minds in the knowledge and love of God and of his Son, Jesus Christ our Lord; and the Blessing of God, Father, Son and Holy Spirit, be upon you/us and remain with you/us now and always. AMEN. (NZPB, p. 544)

We listen to: 'Come my way, my truth, my life' (Margaret Rizza)

Leader In a time of silence we bring to God our regrets, our failures to love and to live as Christ teaches us.
Silence.
May we know that we are forgiven.
Let us approach our God in peace.

Reading 1: 1 Corinthians 13.8–13 (*The Message*).

Love never dies. Inspired speech will be over some day; praying in tongues will end; understanding will reach its limit. We know only a portion of the truth, and what we say about God is always incomplete. But when the Complete arrives, our incompletes will be cancelled. When I was an infant at my mother's breast, I gurgled and cooed like any infant. When I grew up, I left those infant ways for good.

We don't yet see things clearly. We're squinting in a fog, peering through a mist. But it won't be long before the weather clears and the sun shines bright! We'll see it all then, see it all as clearly as God sees us, knowing him directly, just as he knows us!

But for right now, until that completeness, we have three things to do to lead us towards that consummation: Trust steadily in God, hope unswervingly, love extravagantly. And the best of the three is love.

We listen to: 'My soul is at rest in God alone, my salvation comes from God.' (Taizé)

We move into a time of personal silent prayer and reflection.

As the music begins again, the leader will offer a time of corporate prayer, and then invite you to join in the Lord's Prayer:

Our Father, which art in heaven,
hallowed be thy name,
thy kingdom come; thy will be done
on earth as it is in heaven.
Give us this day our daily bread
and forgive us our trespasses,
as we forgive those who trespass against us.
And lead us not into temptation,
but deliver us from evil.
For thine is the kingdom, the power and the glory.
For ever and ever. AMEN.

Reading 2: A portion of the poem 'God knows'.

And I said to the man who stood at the gate of the year:
'Give me a light that I may tread safely into the unknown.'
And he replied:
'Go out into the darkness and put your hand into the Hand of God.
That shall be to you better than light and safer than a known way.'

'God knows' was written by Minnie Louise Haskins. King George VI memorably used this segment in his Christmas Broadcast to the British Empire in 1939. The rest of the poem explores the partial knowledge of human understanding and the greater purposes of God.

We listen to: 'The Call of Wisdom' (Will Todd)

A SACRED SPACE

The Light of the World

Listen! I am standing at the door, knocking; if you hear my voice and open the door, I will come in to you and eat with you, and you with me.
(Revelation 3.20)

Leader There's a song, Lord, that says something like:
'I hear you knocking, but you can't come in.'
Too often that is what I sing to you.

All I hear you knocking, Lord, in the beauty
all around me and in the suffering too.
You want to be with me in my joy and grief.
Why can't I open the door and let you in?
(A NO ENTRY sign is propped up in front of the altar)

Leader I don't know if I dare have you enter my heart and see the
deepest secrets of my soul.
If you knew what I was really like
I am afraid you'd turn away.

All But you do know, don't you,
and you're still there, knocking, still.
So – why won't I open the door and let you in?
(A large ? sign is propped alongside the No Entry sign)

Leader Fear and shame are no match for your love, of that I'm sure.
All So help me, help me, my dear God, to open up that door.
(A door-knob is placed on the altar)

We say: George Herbert's poem, 'Love bade me welcome'.

Leader Love bade me welcome, yet my soul drew back, guilty of
dust and sin.

All But quick-eyed Love, observing me grow slack
from my first entrance in,
drew nearer to me, sweetly questioning,
if I lack'd anything.

Leader 'A guest', I answer'd, 'worthy to be here.'
All Love said, 'You shall be he.'
Leader 'I, the unkind, ungrateful? Ah, my dear,
I cannot look on Thee.'

All Love took my hand and smiling did reply,
'Who made the eyes but I?'

Leader 'Truth, Lord; but I have marr'd them: let my shame
go where it doth deserve.'

All 'And know you not,' says Love, 'who bore the blame?'
Leader 'My dear, then I will serve.'
All 'You must sit down,' says Love, 'and taste my meat.'
Leader So I did sit and eat.

We sing: 'The Lord is my light, my light and salvation, in him I trust,
in him I trust.' (3x) (Taizé)

Commentary

Hunt's painting reinforces the concept of God searching for us,
longing for us to respond. Our reluctance to 'open the door' stems
from many things, for example feelings of unworthiness, fear and
doubt. Jesus remains 'outside' waiting until we are willing to begin
the process of opening the door from within. In the painting, there is
no handle on the outside – God will not force his way into our hearts.
We have the choice to respond – or ignore his inviting presence.

Leader In a time of silence we bring to God our regrets, our failures to love and to live as Christ teaches us.
(*Silence*)
May we know that we are forgiven.
Let us approach our God in peace.

Reading: John 9.1–7: The healing of a man born blind.

We listen to: 'The Lord is my light, my light and salvation, in him I trust, in him I trust.' (Taizé)

We move into a time of personal silent prayer and reflection, meditating on the painting of 'The Light of the World'.

The chant leads us out of the silence and into a time of corporate prayer, ending with the Lord's Prayer.

**Our Father, which art in heaven,
hallowed be thy name,
thy kingdom come; thy will be done
on earth as it is in heaven.
Give us this day our daily bread
and forgive us our trespasses,
as we forgive those who trespass against us.
And lead us not into temptation,
but deliver us from evil.
For thine is the kingdom, the power and the glory.
For ever and ever. AMEN.**

A SACRED SPACE

Frailty and Fatigue

Do not cast me off in the time of old age;
do not forsake me when my strength is spent.
(Psalm 71.9)

We listen to: 'It was a Very Good Year' (Frank Sinatra)

Leader When I was young I never thought I'd live to be this old.
I never thought at all about what life one day might be.

All I'd watch the old folk round the town
and see them with a stick, or blind,
and now it seems I'm one of them
though I'm still young here in my mind.
(A walker is pushed up to the altar)

Leader My body hurts, it's worn and frail, it's past its
'use-by date' no doubt.

All Being sick and tired is now the truth,
no longer just a turn of phrase.
I've well and truly lost my youth
and can't look far ahead these days.
(A pile of pill-containers is put on the altar)

Leader But you, O God, are full of grace,
and understand this awkward place
in which we find ourselves right now.
You have been with us all the way.

All You *are* here with us as we pray *and*
light our lives – both work *and* play.
(A picture or sculpture of praying hands is put on the altar)

We listen to: 'My soul is at rest in God alone' (Taizé)

We share Psalm 71, selected verses

Leader: Rescue me, O my God, from the hand of the wicked,
from the grasp of the unjust and cruel.
All: For you, O Lord, are my hope,
my trust, O LORD, from my youth.
Leader: Upon you I have leaned from my birth;
it was you who took me from my mother's womb.
All: My praise is continually of you. (4–6)

Leader: O God, from my youth you have taught me,
and I still proclaim your wondrous deeds.
All: So even to old age and grey hairs,
O God, do not forsake me,
until I proclaim your might
to all generations to come. (18)

THE BLESSING

Leader: The LORD bless you and keep you;
the LORD make his face to shine upon you,
and be gracious to you;
the LORD lift up his countenance upon you,
and give you peace. (Numbers 6.24–26)

Leader In a time of silence we bring to God our regrets,
our failures to love and to live as Christ teaches us.
(Silence.)
May we know that we are forgiven.
Let us approach our God in peace.

Reading: Luke 2.25–38: Simeon and Anna.

We listen to: 'Lord, now lettest thou thy servant depart in peace'
(*Rachmaninoff Vespers*, Tenebrae)

We move into a time of personal silent prayer and reflection.

As the music begins again, the leader will offer a time of corporate prayer, and then invite you to join in the Lord's Prayer:

**Our Father, which art in heaven,
hallowed be thy name,
thy kingdom come; thy will be done
on earth as it is in heaven.
Give us this day our daily bread
and forgive us our trespasses,
as we forgive those who trespass against us.
And lead us not into temptation,
but deliver us from evil.
For thine is the kingdom, the power and the glory.
For ever and ever. AMEN.**

Poem for Reflection

'I am who I am'
said God to old Moses at the burning bush
and sent him off – stunned – to save God's people.

'I am who I am' too –
made in the image of God;
not just what I've been: a mix of roles that took my life
and work and energy and time;
not yet what I will be:
a body returning to the elements, patchy memories
in busy minds, a face in pictures fading,
a voice captured in some digital device, echoing
down the years, drifting into silence …
a spirit freed to go to God.

Help me to be fully who I am *now*, O God,
and to give you glory through my being,
through my essential, eternal self.
May I live with humour and with hope,
with your light sparkling in my eyes
as I look with love on those around me
and see your life in them,
as I meet each day believing you are with me now,
through to the ending, and to the new beginning.

A SACRED SPACE

Rocks and Stones

Be a rock of refuge for me, a strong fortress to save me.
(Psalm 31.2b)

Leader There's a delectable treat called 'Rocky road' –
it's a temptation, O God.
It's made of marshmallows and nuts and chocolate:
a sweet-toothed person's dream –
a diabetic's nightmare!

All Real rocky roads are anything but sweet, O God.
We've cut our feet, and stumbled
too often as we've travelled down life's highway.
(Rocky Road confectionery and some fist-sized rocks are put
on the altar)

Leader We've leaned on people, thinking them as solid as a rock,
only to find, when life turned turtle,
they've not always been there –
they'd other things to do.

All (A GONE FISHING sign is placed on the altar)

Leader But you, O God, are always there for us.
You are our sure foundation, our security.

All You pick us up when we fall,
you bind our wounds and set us on our feet.
You make sure we are standing on the solid ground
of your love and faithfulness.
You are with us each step of the journey,
making our path secure, for you are the Way.
(A 'footprints on the beach' picture is placed on the altar)

We share Psalm 71, selected verses:

Leader In you, O LORD, I take refuge;
let me never be put to shame.

All In your righteousness deliver me
and rescue me;
incline your ear to me and save me.

Leader Be to me a rock of refuge,
a strong fortress to save me,

All For you are my rock and my fortress. (1–3)

Commentary

Ephesians 2.19b–20 says that Christians are 'members of the
household of God built upon the foundation of the apostles and
prophets, with Christ Jesus himself as the cornerstone'. Faith
in Christ is a secure foundation for living and dying. When all
around us is changing, as bodies become weaker, as minds begins
to wander, as families become less accessible, as peers and friends
die, the security we can have in Christ is beyond price.

Blessing

May we find in Christ a sure footing,
the ground of our being that never quakes,
the eternal rock of refuge, and the blessing
of God, Earth-maker, Firm Foundation
and Guiding Spirit, be with us now and forever.
AMEN.

Leader In a time of silence we bring to God our regrets,
our failures to love and to live as Christ teaches us.
Silence.
May we know that we are forgiven.
Let us approach our God in peace.

Reading: Matthew 7.24–27: the wise and foolish builders.

We listen to: 'Rock of Ages'

We move into a time of personal silent prayer and reflection.

As the music begins again, the leader will offer a time of corporate prayer, and then invite you to join in the Lord's Prayer:

Our Father, which art in heaven,
hallowed be thy name,
thy kingdom come; thy will be done
on earth as it is in heaven.
Give us this day our daily bread
and forgive us our trespasses,
as we forgive those who trespass against us.
And lead us not into temptation,
but deliver us from evil.
For thine is the kingdom, the power and the glory.
For ever and ever. AMEN.

We listen to the text of the 'Footprints' poem.

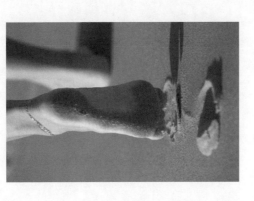

We listen to: 'You raise me up' (Secret Garden)

Appendix 2: Pastoral Practices

Resources on 'Simple prayer', 'Keeping vigil' and
'Prayers at the time of death' are also in
photocopiable form on the accompanying CD-Rom.

Simple prayer ...

Insert any more information you want to in this spot.

It is not selfish to pray in this way. It is a necessary part of deepening our relationship with God.

Gradually, as we see God working in the ordinary things of life, we begin to trust God with more of our self and with our loved ones.

We come to know that we are forgiven and free to be the person God created us to be, uniquely ourselves, using our gifts and talents to serve others as best we can.

We come to know that God is with us even in the most difficult times.

And we come to know from our own experience that God is worthy of worship and praise and glory.

Prayer – Finding the Heart's True Home
by Richard Foster
(Hodder & Stoughton 1992)

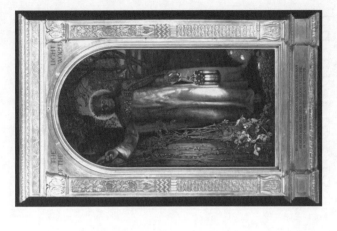

Simple prayer ...

Whether we are 'old hands' at praying or just beginners, we will always need to pray the prayer of simplicity, in which we bring our cares and concerns to God as honestly as we can.

Before we get round to asking God for what we think we might need, we simply start with where we are at – we talk to God about what is happening in our lives, with our families and friends, at work or at home, sharing with God our thoughts, and just as importantly, our feelings.

Feelings are important in the spiritual life, because they are valuable indicators of our soul's health or unease, and of our desires and hopes and dreams.

Once we begin to recognize what is going on in our innermost reality, we can bring that to God, trusting that God accepts us just as we are, right this moment, with all our ups and downs.

It can be hard to be open with God, especially if we find it difficult to share our truth with other people, or have not had anyone who loves us enough to listen.

But Jesus is always waiting at the door of our heart. God is always willing to listen to our pain and our longings and our struggles and our joy. The Holy Spirit is always present to help us pray and bring our truth to the One who created us and loves us beyond all imagining.

Take a few moments to quieten your mind and then imagine opening the door to Jesus and inviting him in. Talk to him about your life and what is really going on for you.

Keeping vigil ... sacred waiting

Keeping vigil

We will do our best to support you during this time of uncertainty and shifting emotions.

Feel free to ask for anything you need to help you as you keep your loved one company and wait for what you know must come – the end of a chapter in your family story and the passing of the torch to the next generation.

A space for your notes or questions:

Contact details of follow-up support:

A prayer you may like to use as you keep vigil …

Dear God,

Be with us as we wait and watch with …

Help us to remember the good times and forgive each other for the times of struggle or disappointment.

As … nears the end of this earthly life, may we trust that your arms are open wide in welcome, mercy and healing.

Help us to turn to you in our distress and receive your comfort and peace.

We make our prayer through Jesus, who has walked through the valley of the shadow of death and passed beyond to new life.

AMEN.

Some things that you may find helpful during this time …

o Even if you are not sure whether you can be heard, talk to your loved one and to each other as if your loved one can hear you.

o Keep voices quiet and the atmosphere peaceful if you can.

o Hold your relative's hand lightly, if you are both comfortable with touch.

o Play your relative's favourite music from time to time.

o If there is any family conflict, have your say away from your loved one's room.

o You may like to arrange a roster so someone can be with your loved one all the time.

Keeping vigil …

Keeping someone you love company in their dying may be a new experience for you and you may be wondering what to do or how to be.

Most of us lead busy lives, so it can take a while to slow down and allow ourselves to be still and present at a bedside. We are used to DOING things, but keeping a vigil is more about BEING … being with your loved one in his/her dying; being with your own mixed feelings of sadness, relief, regret, anxiety or loss …; being with other family members, some of whom you may not have seen for a long time.

Keeping vigil can be a precious time, and you will be well supported by the care-home team: nurses, carers and chaplain.

PRAYERS AT THE TIME OF DEATH

Though I walk through the valley of the shadow of death,
I will fear no evil:
for you are with me,
your rod and staff comfort me. (Psalm 23.4)

O compassionate God,
you are our companion in life;
you accompany us into the mystery of death,
and beyond to the hope of resurrection.

Be with us as we begin to farewell ....

As .... leaves this earthly life and our love,
may he/she be welcomed by your love
and rest in the place you have prepared,
where all pain is gone,
where all struggles cease,
where there is healing and peace. AMEN.

Gracious God, nothing in death or life,
in the world as it is or the world as it shall be,
nothing in all creation can separate us from your love
made visible in Jesus Christ. (Romans 8)

God of mercy and love,
we commend .... into your loving care.
Enfold *him/her* in the arms of your mercy.
Bless *him/her* in *his/her* dying and in *his/her* rising again in you.
Bless those whose hearts are filled with sadness,
that they too may know the hope of resurrection;
through our Saviour Jesus Christ. AMEN.
May you dwell this day in peace,
and rest in the presence of God. AMEN.
(NZPB, p. 815, adapted)

As Jesus teaches, we pray:

Our Father, which art in heaven,
hallowed be thy name,
thy kingdom come; thy will be done
on earth as it is in heaven.
Give us this day our daily bread
and forgive us our trespasses,
as we forgive those who trespass against us.
And lead us not into temptation,
but deliver us from evil.
For thine is the kingdom, the power and the glory.
For ever and ever. AMEN.

Photo Appendix

All the photos are available in colour on the CD-Rom.

General photos for use by readers

All photos are by Sue Pickering unless otherwise stated.

1. Sunrise or sunset?   2. Forest trail, near Turangi, New Zealand.

3. Boardwalk near Rotorua, New Zealand.   4. A mature tree.

Self-care for the minister or caregiver

1. Wood pigeon (Kereru), New Zealand.

2. Road sign.

Wednesday of Holy Week Eucharist

Anointing of Jesus, from Augustine's 'La Cité de Dieu', c. 1475–80, illustration attributed to Le Maitre François.

Easter resurrection talk and activity

The flowered cross, Easter morning.

Sacred Space

1. Monarch butterfly.

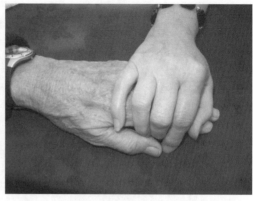

2. Comforting hand.

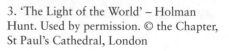

4. Footprint on the beach (clipart).

3. 'The Light of the World' – Holman Hunt. Used by permission. © the Chapter, St Paul's Cathedral, London

Honouring Special Days: Good Friday reflection

As the centrepiece, choose a picture/representation of the head of Christ that carries meaning for you – e.g. taken from a modern or traditional source. As you are only going to be using such an image during the service and not printing it at all, there should be no issue with copyright. One such image is 'Head of Christ Crucified' by Master of Liesborn, but you will find others on the internet or from your own resources.

Set-up for Good Friday service.

Memorial Service

1. Room set up for service.

2. Horizon (clipart).

All Souls Memorial Service

1. Pilgrim Path to Holy Island, Lindisfarne, England.

2. Baby (clipart).

Simple Prayer brochure

1. Clipart child praying

2. 'The Light of the World'
– Holman Hunt. Used by
permission. © The Chapter,
St Paul's Cathedral, London.

Pastoral Practices

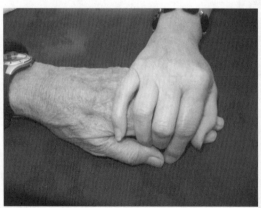

1. A comforting hand.

2. A holding cross.

Workbook topic 3: Death

1. and 2. – Camellias in full bloom and decaying.

Alternative pictures to use if required: 3. Lilies in bud, bloom and beyond. 4. Dead shark, Waikanae Beach, New Zealand.

Workbook topic 4: Resurrection

2. A new tree emerging from the old (source unknown).

3. Monarch butterfly, newly hatched, with its empty chrysalis.

1. Portion of a window in St Paul's (Without the Walls), Canterbury, England.

Single studies for smaller groups

1. Christ – Kaiser Wilhelm Memorial Church, Berlin.

2. 'The Return of the Prodigal Son', Rembrandt; original in The Hermitage, St Petersburg. Used by permission.